Dedicated to the victims of Hurricane Andrew,
including the humans

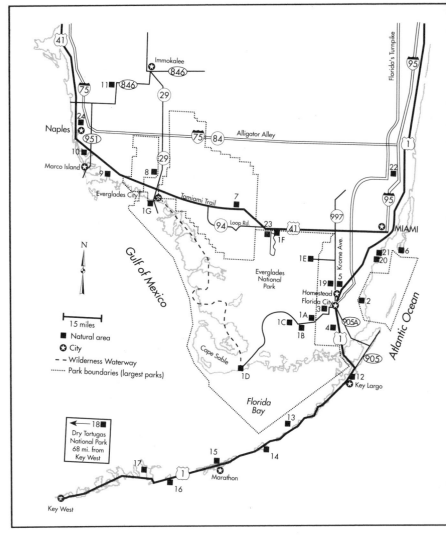

Key to Natural and Semi-Natural Areas on Map

1* Everglades National Park
    A Main Entrance and Visitor Center
    B Royal Palm
    C Long Pine Key
    D Flamingo
    E Chekika
    F Shark Valley
    G Everglades City (Gulf Coast)
2* Biscayne National Park
3 Navy Wells Pineland Preserve
4 Southern Glades Wildlife Area
5 Castellow Hammock Nature Center
6 Bill Baggs Cape Florida State Recreation Area
7* Big Cypress National Preserve
8* Fakahatchee Strand State Preserve
9 Collier-Seminole State Park

10 Briggs Nature Center
11 Corkscrew Swamp Sanctuary
12 John Pennekamp Coral Reef State Park
13 Lignumvitae Key State Botanical Site
14 Long Key State Recreation Area
15 Crane Point Hammock
16 Bahia Honda State Park
17 National Key Deer Refuge
18 Dry Tortugas National Park
19 Preston B. Bird & Mary Heinlein Fruit & Spice Park
20 Fairchild Tropical Garden
21 Matheson Hammock Park
22 Greynolds Park
23 Miccosukee Indian Village
24 Naples Nature Center
* Boundaries marked on map.

EXPLORING
WILD
SOUTH
FLORIDA

A Guide to Finding the Natural Areas
and Wildlife of the Everglades
and Florida Keys

SUSAN D. JEWELL
with drawings by Manabu Saito

Pineapple Press, Inc.
Sarasota, Florida

Pineapple Press, Inc.
P.O. Drawer 16008
Southside Station
Sarasota, Florida 34239

LIBRARY OF CONGRESS CATALOGING-IN-PUBLICATION DATA

Jewell, Susan Diane, 1955-
Exploring wild south Florida : a guide to finding the natural areas and wildlife of the Everglades and Florida Keys / by Susan Diane Jewell.
- - 1st ed.
    p. cm.
Includes bibliographical references (p.   ) and index.
ISBN 1-56164-023-9
1. Natural history --- Florida --- Everglades. 2. Natural history --- Florida --- Florida Keys. 3. Natural areas --- Florida --- Everglades --- Guidebooks. 4. Natural areas --- Florida --- Florida Keys --- Guidebooks. I. Title.
QH105.F6J49   1993
508.759'39 --- dc20   92-36561
                                        CIP

First Edition
10 9 8 7 6 5 4 3 2 1
Design and composition by Millicent Hampton-Shepherd
Printed and bound by Arcata Graphics in Kingsport, Tennessee

FOREWORD

South Florida is a very new land in every sense of the word. It emerged from the sea only recently as geologic time is reckoned. In the early years of the 19th century, most of its residents were still Native Americans. The movers and shakers of modern development were slow to discover the potentials of south Florida, and the pace of growth did not really pick up until the 1920s. But it has been accelerating ever since! In the rush to build south Florida, patches here and there were overlooked. It is these relatively untouched fragments of Florida that Ms. Jewell wants her readers to explore.

While south Florida offers a fascinating mix of things tropical and temperate, it is more akin to the Caribbean than to the North American continent and presents unique opportunities to visitors who are interested in the unusual habitats and species to be found here. The diversity of life approaches that of the true tropics — more species of trees and shrubs are found on North Key Largo than in all of the northeastern United States!

South Florida is an area of startling contrasts — from the quiet depths of Corkscrew Swamp and the tropical hardwood forests of the Keys to the thriving, bustling atmosphere of Miami. As Ms. Jewell states, appreciating the landscapes of south Florida takes some adjustment on the part of the observer. You won't find the grandeur of towering trees and spectacular mountains that draw visitors to our older, western parks. But south Florida is a land of great beauty — the quiet, subtle beauty of wide vistas of sky, grassy plains, and shallow colorful seas balanced with a counterpoint of shady hammocks of tropical vegetation.

Exploring Wild South Florida offers a great deal more than the usual guidebook. It presents the reader with a synopsis of the human and natural history of the area combined with "all the visitor needs to know" to learn about, interpret, and enjoy the complex natural systems of south Florida. It is hoped that this awareness will encourage a greater interest in preserving the unaltered bits and pieces of south Florida so that future generations may continue to enjoy them.

Alexander Sprunt IV
Tavernier, Florida

TABLE OF CONTENTS

AUTHOR'S PREFACE

Life in Homestead must not have been exciting enough. Too many boring days in paradise? I found myself implanted directly in the center of the biggest natural disaster to ever hit the U.S. — and I do mean the center. The middle of Hurricane Andrew's eye swept virtually down my street.

What a place for a scientist to be! It took several weeks after the initial trauma for me to appreciate that. But let's start from the beginning.

August 22, 1992: I went to work as usual collecting data at Flamingo in Everglades National Park. At 5 PM, with the hurricane still east of the Bahamas, the National Hurricane Center issued a hurricane watch for Florida's east coast. That compelled the park rangers to pull all patrol boats and forced the closing of the park the next day for preparations. When I returned to my office that evening, I backed up my computer, covered it with plastic, and generally did what I could to protect my office. Then I drove to town, filled my gas tank, got cash reserves from the automatic teller, and went to the supermarket to stock up. There were about 40 people in the checkout line at 11 PM and the canned food and bread shelves were almost bare.

August 23: I arose at 7 AM and, after hearing the current track of the storm and its upgraded strength, I began an intense 14 hours of preparation. Although the hurricane was estimated to be 24 hours away, with no guarantee that it would strike my town, it was already a Category 3 storm (winds 111-130 mph). That was far too strong to gamble with. I never realized how much there was to prepare, even for my small cottage. Something as easy as filling the bathtub with water becomes time-consuming because, if you're like me, first YOU HAVE TO CLEAN THE TUB. Ditto all the other "simple" things.

At mid-morning, the National Hurricane Center upgraded Andrew to Category 4 (winds 131-155 mph). A few hours later, Andrew whirled over the Atlantic at Category 5 speeds (over 155 mph). My heart tensed at the news. During the rest of the day, the hurricane oscillated between Category 4 and 5. It was located due east of us and was barreling due west. I spared no effort in my preparations.

At about 9 PM I went to my neighbors' house to take refuge before the storm's anticipated dawn arrival. They had a big, sturdy house. Mine had a flimsy tin roof. I brought with me a duffle bag of valuables and irreplaceables.

Also seeking refuge with the neighbors was a family with two children and two dogs that had evacuated from Key Largo ("from the frying pan into the fire," but that's hindsight; the storm missed the Keys). We drank rum and cokes and fell asleep by midnight. I slept on the couch in the living room. The storm was not expected to hit until about 7 AM.

August 24: At 3 AM I bolted awake when the ceiling fan stilled. With all the windows closed and shuttered, the air had instantly become oppressive. I realized the power had gone out. I heard the wind outside. I knew then that we were not going to be spared.

The others also awoke and we congregated downstairs. The radio said the storm had picked up tremendous forward speed and arrived hours earlier than expected. Although it was still night, we could see outside through a tiny unshuttered window because of the intense lightning. I saw the power lines to my house snap. When some *shuttered* windows shattered and branches began battering the big house, we backed away from the window to an interior room. The wind roared like an endless freight train. All manner of debris struck the house. The front door, which was bolted, blew open and one of the kids' dogs disappeared outside. My transistor radio was useless because of the atmospheric disturbance. The fury before the eye lasted a nerve-wracking 45 minutes.

When the eye arrived at about 5 AM, I ventured outside in the darkness long enough to see the silhouette of my house had changed — it had no roof. All the trees in the neighborhood were gone. I came back to the big house rather shaken.

We breathed a sigh of relief during the eye, thinking that the worst had past, because normally the first half *is* the worst. But, as we discovered, this was no normal hurricane. Nothing I can even imagine could match the fury of the second half. The noise was deafening. The whole 11-room house shook. The brick chimney fell into the house, crushing the upstairs bathroom and creating a void where the roof once was. We were underneath on the first floor when the ceiling started to collapse, so we scrambled into a tiny room where we seven people and the four remaining dogs huddled through the rest of the night. Someone had to continually keep his weight against the door between the rooms because of the air rushing down from the gaping roof. Something hit a gas line to the house and caused a gas leak inside. Fortunately, we were using flashlights, not candles. You could say the house was well ventilated by then anyway.

The sustained winds were approximately 150 mph, but the gusts were the undisputed killers. Hurricane strength categories are based on sustained winds, not peak winds. The highest gust officially reported was 217 mph, but all the anemometers in the strongest wind area flew

9

the coop well below that, so who knows? The storm's second half was also about 45 minutes at its worst, but the intense squalls lasted several more hours.

About 8 or 9 AM I first ventured outside. The destruction that met my eyes was indescribable. The world had turned to endless rubble. There was not a leaf on a tree, except a few native palmettos and pines. It's an image embedded in my mind forever. And, oh, how quiet! Not a single bird, not a car, not even a cricket. No leaves for the wind to rustle. Dead quiet. Except you could hear someone talking a block away, since there was nothing to block or absorb the sound (I believe that happens in the Arctic, too).

Happily, the dog was found unhurt cowering under a van. We seven humans emerged without a scratch. Sadly, a 12-year-old girl three blocks from my house was killed when a beam fell in her bedroom. A National Park Service acquaintance was fatally crushed under his collapsed roof.

The Aftermath: The days that followed the storm melted together for me. Clocks and calendars were vestigial. We worked day after day from sunrise to sunset in the blistering heat, putting temporary roofs on houses, hauling trees, and clearing debris. I rode my salvaged bicycle around to check on friends. I even hauled almost a half ton of chimney bricks out of the upstairs bathroom, bucket by bucket. There wasn't a shade tree left in southern Dade County, nor any ice, nor a cold drink. It was kind of like doing field work in the middle of the Everglades.

The quiet lasted only a day or so. After that, noises gradually picked up until there was a constant din 24 hours a day: hammers pounding nails on roofs, chainsaws carving uprooted trees into manageable chunks, generators as loud as hydro stations but emitting a trickle of power, huge double-rotored Navy helicopters (and news crews, of course) landing in any field they could find, giant military cargo planes, emergency sirens.... It sounded like a war zone.

In the space of a few hours early that Monday morning, a whole society collapsed. Rules evaporated. The rich were homeless. Everyone was equal. My saving grace was that I was accustomed to rough field conditions. Plus, I didn't own an electric can opener. You see, the day the storm hit, the plea went out, "Send canned food!" When the cans arrived, the plea became, "Send can openers!" The simple life proved its merits.

I am not anxious to experience another hurricane, yet I am not ready to flee from south Florida. There is still too much left for me to explore.

Homestead, Florida
September 1992

INTRODUCTION

Fantastic! If you're reading this book, you must be seriously considering a trip to explore the less beaten paths of south Florida. What an exciting place you've chosen to spend your free time. You will be rewarded with endless expanses of wilderness, lush tropical vegetation, and wild animals not found anywhere else in the United States.

But if you're anticipating the equivalent grandeur of the lofty Rocky Mountains, the towering redwoods, the bizarrely shaped pinnacles of southwestern rock formations, the colorful desert wildflowers in spring, or the crashing ocean waves on our northern coasts, you must redirect your expectations. South Florida has just as many natural wonders as other regions, *but they are subtle*. They don't shout at you. They whisper. They entice you to take a closer look, to listen a little harder, to wait just a little longer.

To many people, the subconscious definition of "scenic" is a break from monotony: more topographic relief for the eye, more colors, more shapes and objects to keep the eye and brain occupied. That's why many people don't think of the Everglades region as scenic. The vast flat expanses of mangroves or sawgrass afford little change and are often silent and monochrome. By this definition, the Keys seem slightly more scenic: the colorful exotic flowers, the bright blue and green waters, the rustling palm fronds in the breeze, and the islands dotting the bay all keep the mind busy interpreting them. Now take a closer look!

A flock of roseate spoonbills sifts through the water, straining for small shrimp or fish. A zebra butterfly dances vivaciously through the air, then alights on a leaf to rest. A rainbow tapes the sky together as a thunderstorm threatens to rip it open. Underwater, a bevy of dazzling parrotfish pokes around the purple sea fans, rasping the nourishing algae from a star coral. This is the south Florida you won't want to miss!

Wilderness is a concept conceived by the white man. The Native Americans did not have a word for wilderness — wilderness was the normal world. There aren't many truly wild places left in south Florida. Even places that appear to be untouched have been indirectly altered, such as Everglades National Park, whose upstream waters have been tampered with outside its boundaries. What are referred to as natural areas in the pages that follow have not escaped the human touch.

I.
AN OVERVIEW

HOW TO USE THIS BOOK

Geographically, this book concentrates on Collier, Dade, and Monroe counties, the three southernmost counties in Florida. Visitors who use Homestead as a central location will find that most of the places described below can be explored in a day trip. Not all parks and natural areas in the three counties were included.

If this is your first trip to south Florida, you'll probably want to stick to the "major" attractions, such as the Anhinga Trail at Everglades National Park, Corkscrew Swamp, and Pennekamp Coral Reef State Park. If you've already been to those places or have more time, you'll be looking for new sights. Included are a variety of places from tame (barely venturing from the road) to wild (canoeing 50 miles from civilization). Some will require less than a half day to explore and some will warrant several days. There should be something for everyone who wants to get outside and learn about the natural world of south Florida. This book will help the first-timer, the repeat adventurer, the high school or college ecology class, and the foreign visitor to find the most interesting natural areas to explore. And you folks who live here year-round, have you explored your own "backyard"? Whether you're a nature photographer, an amateur naturalist, or just tired of the city, you can discover a retreat with this book.

If you're traveling from the northern states or another country, hopefully you'll have access to "Exploring Wild South Florida" several weeks or months before departing on your trip. Then you can use it to plan your itinerary, saving you time (and possibly money) when you arrive. Use the time before your trip to write or call for information on hours of operation, entrance fees, and tour schedules.

No conscientious naturalist would divulge specific locations of rare plants and animals. While most readers would respect the regulations protecting our natural resources, an unscrupulous collector may not. Therefore, only general locations will be given.

This book is not intended as a field guide to plants and animals, and no attempt is made to be all-inclusive. Some species of special interest are discussed and illustrated. Examples would be poisonous plants and endangered wildlife.

Distances and measurements are given in miles, feet, and acres. Temperatures are given in degrees Fahrenheit (°F), and occasionally also in Centigrade (°C). Here are some conversions that foreign travelers may find helpful:

1 mile = 1.6 kilometers	1 kilometer = 0.62 miles
1 foot = 0.3 meters	1 meter = 3.3 feet
1 acre = 0.4 hectares	1 hectare = 2.47 acres
1 pound = 0.45 kilograms	1 kilogram = 2.2 pounds
(°F-32) 5/9 = °C	(9/5 °C) + 32 = °F

Each area has a suggested best time of year to visit it, in case you are able to choose the season. The criteria are sometimes sketchy, sometimes concrete, and often just a matter of personal preference.

Information on pet regulations in the parks is included for a very important reason: Florida can get very hot even in the winter. There is a Florida statute that prohibits leaving pets in unattended vehicles, because they can suffer greatly or even die from the heat. Since many parks don't allow pets (except guide dogs), and pets usually cannot be left unattended at a park or motel, your visit may be greatly restricted if you bring Fido with you. If possible, leave your pets at home with a friend or relative.

PLANNING YOUR TRIP

Getting to South Florida

Public transportation to Miami is very convenient. The arrival point by air is most frequently Miami International Airport, a 45-minute drive from Homestead. Occasionally people fly to Marathon or Key West if they plan to tour the Keys. However, this usually requires a connecting flight from Miami, which is costly and time-consuming. Buses and trains also serve Miami. Major highways connect greater Miami from all directions, allowing a person to drive easily from elsewhere in Florida. To visit Corkscrew Swamp Sanctuary, Everglades City, Faka-hatchee Strand State Preserve, Collier-Seminole State Park, Briggs Nature Center, and Big Cypress National Preserve, you can also fly to Fort Myers or Naples. They are, however, all only a few hours' drive from Miami.

Public transportation to and within the Keys is poor. There are no trains, and bus service is minimal. It is usually necessary to rent a car. The major car rental agencies can be found in the Miami area; smaller independent agencies are scattered throughout the Keys.

South Florida Weather

There is continual controversy over whether south Florida should be classified as tropical or subtropical. The problem is that there are several definitions for both. If only the latitudes between the Tropic of Cancer and the Tropic of Capricorn are considered tropical, then south Florida is not tropical. If the definition is an area that has historically remained frost-free, then the part of the Keys south of Key Largo would qualify. If the definition is an area where tropical plants grow, then many parts of south Florida would qualify. South Florida is at least subtropical.

Regardless of official definitions, south Florida *feels* tropical. Its southern latitude and maritime surroundings result in high year-round temperatures and humidities. Table 1 shows representative air temperatures for several locations in this area.

TABLE 1.
Thirty-year average air temperatures (°F) of selected locations in south Florida (1951-1980) (NOAA 1982).

Month	Everglades City	Homestead	Key West	Tamiami Trail	Tavernier
Jan	64.6	65.0	68.7	66.6	69.3
Feb	65.0	65.7	70.1	67.1	69.7
Mar	69.4	69.6	74.1	70.8	73.7
Apr	73.3	73.1	77.1	73.6	76.8
May	77.2	76.6	80.6	77.3	79.6
Jun	80.3	79.4	82.9	80.7	82.0
Jul	81.9	80.8	84.5	82.4	83.7
Aug	82.5	81.2	84.3	83.2	84.1
Sep	81.6	80.4	82.6	82.5	82.6
Oct	77.4	76.5	80.1	78.6	79.1
Nov	71.3	70.9	75.5	73.0	74.7
Dec	66.1	66.4	71.0	68.0	70.7
ANNUAL	74.2	73.8	77.7	75.3	77.2

The table shows that the warmest month is usually August and the coldest month is January. Notice how much warmer the average temperature is in the Keys (Tavernier and Key West) than on the mainland. The lowest temperature in the 1951-1980 period in Homestead was 27°F (-3°C) and the highest was 98°F (37°C) (NOAA 1984). The three-digit temperatures that wilt other parts of the country don't occur here. The moderating influences of the Atlantic Ocean, the Gulf of Mexico, and Florida Bay are responsible for that. It doesn't seem to matter — the relative humidity makes it feel just as hot! Hence, there is the southern equivalent of the wind-chill factor, called the "heat index." The National Weather Service defines the heat index as "the temperature that a human body would feel when humidity and air temperature are factored in" — and it's frequently above 100 in the summer, meaning the air *feels* like it's over 100°F.

While northern Florida has four relatively distinct seasons, southern Florida has only two. The latter's air temperature extremes range from the upper 20s to the upper 90s. A normal year would register from the lower 40s to the mid-90s. It is precipitation more than temperature, however, that gives south Florida its two seasons — wet and dry (some would claim the two seasons are "mosquito" and "nonmosquito"). The wet season extends from May to October, and the dry season is November to April. Table 2 shows the mean rainfalls for the 1951-1980 period.

TABLE 2.
30-year average rainfall (inches) of selected locations in south Florida (1951-1980) (NOAA 1982).

Month	Everglades City	Homestead	Key West	Tamiami Trail	Tavernier
Jan	1.51	1.71	1.74	1.73	1.94
Feb	1.82	2.07	1.92	1.63	2.03
Mar	1.87	2.11	1.31	1.91	1.33
Apr	2.01	3.03	1.49	2.45	2.17
May	4.97	6.99	3.22	5.97	4.96
Jun	9.77	10.35	5.04	9.51	7.23
Jul	8.40	7.55	3.68	7.53	4.33
Aug	7.14	8.09	4.80	7.10	4.54
Sep	9.31	8.94	6.50	8.26	6.92
Oct	4.08	6.88	4.76	4.88	7.01
Nov	1.33	2.03	3.23	1.60	2.05
Dec	1.34	1.38	1.73	1.28	1.88
ANNUAL	53.55	61.13	39.42	53.85	46.39

The chart reveals the increase in rainfall beginning in May or June and the decline in November, with peaks in June and September. The precipitation from May to August frequently falls in short, intense daily rainstorms. A visitor to south Florida during those months can expect rain (usually in the form of a thunderstorm) for 10-30 minutes almost every day. The clouds form from the sun's rays evaporating water in the Everglades and ocean. The precipitation in September and October tends to fall less frequently but in larger amounts per event. This is because tropical storms are more frequent then and often drop many inches of rain in one event.

The most reliably good weather (less chance of thunderstorms, tropical storms, cold fronts, intense heat, or mosquitoes) is in March and April. The weather is truly delightful. In fact, it's often so dry that some species of trees lose their leaves regularly every April, and great piles of crunchy leaves can be raked from beneath barren trees. A New England "fall" is in the autumn, while south Florida's "fall" is in the spring.

The months of November and December are also good times to visit for several reasons. The rainy season has ended, but the vegetation is still lush. The weather is cooler and less humid. There is only a small chance of a cold front strong enough to discourage you from exploring. As a bonus, the lodging rates are usually the lowest until mid-December.

WHEN YOU ARRIVE

Driving in Miami

Driving around the greater Miami area (which includes Homestead and Florida City) can be facilitated if you know a few simple tips about the layout of the roads. There are four quadrants, like Washington, D.C.: Northwest, Northeast, Southwest, and Southeast. Roads are numbered beginning with the lowest in downtown Miami and ascending outward. Thus, there is a NW 60th Street, a SW 60th Street, and so on. "Streets" are oriented east-west, and "Avenues" are oriented north-south. Many of these larger roads are blocked occasionally by the network of canals that laces the city. The "Avenues" ending in the number "2" (such as 72nd Avenue) or "7" (such as 107th Avenue) are most likely to have bridges over the canals and continue straight through. The smaller "Courts" (north-south) and "Terraces" (east-west) are rarely more than a few blocks long.

Homestead and Florida City have dual street numbering systems, just to confuse visitors! The numbering system from Miami continues as far south as Florida City: the "Street" numbers will be in the 200-300s and the "Avenue" numbers will be in the 100-200s. Interspersed are

Homestead's and Florida City's own numbering systems, which have the same pattern as Miami's. They originate in the centers of the respective towns and have smaller numbers.

If you're looking for a specific address, the building's street number will give you a clue. Most addresses have long numbers that indicate their block. For example, 24850 SW 187th Avenue would be between 248th Street and 249th Street in southwest Miami.

If you're the type that gets lost easily, head for the Keys. It's almost impossible to get lost — there's only one main road! That road is U.S. 1, also called the Overseas Highway. Beginning at the southern end of Florida City, the road's shoulder is marked with small green "Mile Marker" signs. Not coincidentally, they are placed at one-mile intervals. The numbers descend from about 126 in Florida City to 0 in Key West. Thus, you can always tell how far you are from Key West. Addresses in the Keys are given by Mile Marker numbers or fractions thereof, such as MM 102.5. Occasionally you'll hear the added qualifier of "bayside" (the place you're looking for is on the side of the road toward Florida Bay) or "oceanside" (it's on the side toward the Atlantic Ocean). From almost anywhere in the Keys, you can easily tell which side is which.

Two roads bisect the Everglades east-west. They are locally known as Tamiami Trail and Alligator Alley. Tamiami Trail is actually U.S. 41 and runs between Miami and Naples. It was completed in 1928 after 13 years of construction. Alligator Alley runs from just west of Fort Lauderdale to Naples. It is also known as State Road (SR) 84 and has recently become part of Interstate 75. Since most of the locals (and most maps) use the colloquial names of Tamiami Trail and Alligator Alley, and they sound more fun, they will be used hereafter.

What to Wear

The weather information above should give you an idea of the type of clothing you'll need. Most of the year, shorts or lightweight pants are comfortable. Any time you plan to go on a trail, it's better to wear lightweight long-sleeved shirts and long pants to prevent mosquito, chigger, poisonwood, and sunburn problems. Clothing should be loose so that it doesn't stick to you from the humidity.

It's amazing how cold it can feel during a winter cold front, when the temperature is in the 40s or 50s (°F), the wind is blowing, and it's damp. At these times (usually from late December to early March), it's good to have several lightweight layers of sweaters and jackets.

Sunglasses and a sun hat are necessary most of the year. Comfortable walking shoes or jogging shoes will be suitable for the trails, especially if you don't mind getting them wet.

Restaurants are very casual in south Florida, particularly in the Keys. Even in restaurants that serve gourmet food, most people wear casual clothing. Shorts are not uncommon in restaurants.

Fishing Licenses

State saltwater fishing licenses became required on January 1, 1990. A license is required for Florida residents and nonresidents, with the following exceptions: 1) an individual under 16 years of age, 2) an individual fishing from a charter boat that has a vessel saltwater fishing license, 3) any Florida resident 65 years of age or older, and 4) any Florida resident fishing in saltwater from land or from a structure fixed to the land. Residents may obtain a 10-day or 1-year license, and nonresidents may obtain 3-day, 7-day, or 1-year licenses. Freshwater fishing licenses are also required. Licenses may be obtained from county tax collectors' offices or from bait and tackle shops.

Conservation Tips

Good conservationists bring their creed with them wherever they go. Because of the tremendous volume of tourists coming to south Florida every year, the natural resources are being stressed to the limits. You can help to make sure that your visit here has a minimal environmental impact by observing a few suggestions:

1. *Conserve water.* Except during periods of heavy rainfall, south Florida often has a critical water shortage. This shortage usually occurs during the winter tourist season, which coincides with the dry season. During droughts, a county may impose water restrictions. Historically (and ridiculously) these have come when there was already a water shortage — not earlier, when it could have prevented one. Restrictions can include a requirement by restaurants that waiters serve water only on request. You should refuse water at restaurants unless you plan to drink it. Don't criticize the restaurant for poor service if water is not automatically provided.

Other restrictions, such as watering lawns and washing cars, probably won't affect tourists. But keep your showers short, and use your ingenuity to think of other ways you can save water. The lack of water is bad enough, but a compounding problem is that it drives engineers and city planners to find new ways to retrieve water (like drilling a new well), usually at a cost to the environment.

2. *Drive carefully to avoid hitting wildlife.* Watch for snakes warming themselves on roads in the winter as the air cools in late afternoon or escaping high water after heavy rains (especially on the main Everglades National Park road to Flamingo). Drive slower than the speed limit in Key deer areas (such as Big Pine Key), crocodile areas (such as the stretch of U.S. 1 from the mainland to the Key Largo), and panther areas (such as Alligator Alley and the Tamiami Trail). Headlights, particularly high beams, temporarily blind animals and cause them to freeze in their tracks; keep this in mind when driving in rural areas at night.

If you are motor boating, watch the water ahead of you for ripples that might indicate a manatee is surfacing. If you are near a manatee, cut your motor to neutral until the manatee has moved away. Observe posted signs warning of manatee areas.

3. *Be a responsible fisherman*. Fishermen should not leave monofilament line in the water or on land. A new state law commencing in March 1992 makes this illegal. Everyone should collect line they find littering the water — many animals have been slowly strangled by discarded fishing lines. Don't go fishing just for sport. Fishing just for human enjoyment is pure harassment of the fish. The fish do not play games for fun with fishermen — they fight for their lives. Fish that are to be released should be handled carefully with wet hands and placed promptly and gently underwater.

4. *Protect coral reefs*. If you snorkel or dive, don't touch the corals. Simply touching a live coral can cause the sensitive polyps to die. Don't stand on the bottom or kick up silt. Collecting of coral (even if it's dead) is illegal in Florida. Collecting of tropical fish for aquaria usually causes them to die prematurely. Do not feed the fish on the reef because it changes their natural diets and habits.

5. *Don't collect souvenirs from the wild.* All national and state parks prohibit the collection of plants, animals, rocks, and so on. This is a good policy to follow everywhere. Take photographs instead.

6. *Don't feed wild animals.* Key deer, alligators, raccoons, and other wildlife learn to associate food with humans. This has caused many deer to wander into busy roads and get killed. It has caused some attacks on humans by the gators looking for handouts. The gator usually gets shot as punishment.

7. *Recycle your containers*. Shamefully, there has never been a "bottle bill" in Florida. However, Everglades National Park has a new system to collect aluminum, glass, and plastic for recycling. Seventy-five bins (made from recycled plastic) are located in campgrounds, picnic areas, visitor centers, and at Flamingo and Shark Valley. The bins are raccoon-proof. The state parks have bins for aluminum and other recyclable materials. If you keep a lookout while you're driving outside of the parks (especially in the Florida Keys), you may see a shopping center parking lot with trucks or bins for recycling aluminum, glass, plastic, and newspaper.

Local Precautions

There are probably no more hazards in south Florida than anywhere else in the country...just some different ones. You have chosen an adventurous and occasionally risky hobby. Everyone should have a safe and enjoyable trip. However, every person is different and has varying reactions to adverse conditions. While park rangers and other staff are well-trained, they cannot predict the weather, wildlife-people interactions, and the experience level of each person they advise. You must rely on your own common sense and recognition of your experience level to have a safe trip.

Your trip to Florida should be perfectly delightful, without any of the misfortunes mentioned below. The chance of a safe trip is increased if you are aware of the following.

Weather

Thunderstorms

The thunderstorm season begins around May and lasts until October, the duration of the wet season. The heaviest months are June to September. Within these months, a thunderstorm is possible almost daily. In extreme southern Florida, daily thunderstorms occur on an average of 70–80 days per year. Thunderstorms may occur at any other time of the year. They are caused by heat rising from the warming land, creating unstable air above. A cumulonimbus cloud (or "thunderhead") indicates a potential thunderstorm.

The major hazard of these storms is the lightning they produce. In Florida, a single day of intense thunderstorms can cause 10,000 lightning strikes. Next to being under the center of a thunderstorm, the most dangerous place is near the leading edge. Don't assume you are safe if the storm hasn't quite hit. And don't underestimate lightning. It causes about 10 deaths and 25 injuries a year in Florida, or about 10 percent of lightning-caused deaths in the United States.

If you are out on the water when a thunderstorm approaches, try to get to land, where you are not as exposed. Do not get into the water; water conducts electricity. Never stand under the tallest object around. Drop anything metal you are carrying (sorry, that means binocs and cameras, too). If you find yourself in the midst of lightning strikes with no shelter, as on an open boat, kneel down on your hands and knees, away from the motor, antennas, and console. The hands and knees posture makes a "path of least resistance" for the electricity to follow and gives you a better chance of survival than by sitting or lying.

Other hazards from thunderstorms include high winds and hail. High winds are almost always associated with thunderstorms, while hail is infrequent. High winds can be a problem for canoeists, who should always be vigilant for thunderstorm development.

Hurricanes

Southern Florida has the highest probability of any region in the country of getting struck by a hurricane. The National Weather Service considers June 1 to November 30 as the official hurricane season. There have been hurricanes or tropical storms in the Atlantic Ocean during every month of the year except April. The height of the "tropical activity" (tropical waves, depressions, storms, and hurricanes) is late August to mid-October. Therefore, you can minimize the possibility of encountering a tropical storm or hurricane by avoiding these months for your trip.

Hurricanes play an important ecological role. During late summer, when the temperature of tropical waters can rise too high for marine organisms, hurricanes disperse the heat. That is why higher ocean temperatures increase the chance of a hurricane forming.

Don't count on the local municipal emergency shelters being able to accommodate tourists during a storm. Especially in the Keys, the shelters cannot even support all the residents. If you travel to south Florida during the hurricane season, it is possible you will be mandated to evacuate to higher ground. There is only one road off the Florida Keys that everyone must use, and there is little controversy that it is inadequate to handle a major evacuation. Campers in Flamingo are especially vulnerable and may be evacuated by rangers before anyone else is. Before heading south during hurricane season, check the National Weather Service (see "Other Sources of Information") for tropical weather activity.

Tornadoes and Waterspouts

Tornadoes are common in Florida. March, April, and May are the busy months for tornadic activity. Tornadoes are not as common in the southern tip of the peninsula as in the central and northern parts. South Florida also has the aquatic version of the tornado — the waterspout. A waterspout is a tornado that forms over a large body of water, such as the ocean. Most often, a waterspout is short-lived, relatively weak, and never reaches land. The funnel may never even touch the surface of the water. Such a waterspout is not hazardous, but if you see a funnel cloud of either type, seek shelter in a sturdy building.

Poisonous Plants

The initial panic an amateur botanist feels when seeing south Florida plants for the first time is that so many of them look alike. The generic morphology (form) of a tropical leaf is a shiny surface with smooth edges and a pointed tip. This facilitates water dripping off the leaf in such a humid, rainy environment. The myriad of look-alike plants presents a problem to the careful naturalist who won't touch any plant that he or she can't identify. Some plants in this region have parts that are toxic if ingested or if touched by a sensitive person. Only three are likely to give the average person a rash if merely touched, and those three are described below. Two of those (manchineel and poisonwood) fall into the category of having a tropical-looking leaf, and they are considered tropical trees.

The three described below are not the only poisonous plants in the area. To be safe from an irritating rash or worse, always identify a plant before touching it. If you find you have brushed against one of the three species mentioned, wash your skin with plenty of sudsy cold water as soon as possible.

Manchineel

The most infamous of our native poisonous plants is manchineel, in the family Euphorbiaceae. This small tree (up to 30 feet) has shiny alternate leaves 2-4 inches long, with faintly round-toothed margins and pointed tips. Manchineels are known for their sap, very irritating if it contacts human skin or internal tissues, and the fatally poisonous (if ingested) fruit, which looks like a small green apple (1-1.5 inches long). Manchineels can be found locally in the Keys, around Whitewater Bay, and on Cape Sable (particularly in the buttonwood hammocks along the coast), but it is unlikely that you will encounter one. Public pressure to remove these "undesirable" trees has caused most of them near houses, trails, or roads to be destroyed. The tree is also very sensitive to frost. It has been placed on the state's protected list and classified as "threatened."

Poisonwood

The second of the three poisonous plants is another tree, known as poisonwood or Florida poisontree. It is in the poison- ivy family and shares the characteristic caustic sap. Touching the leaves yields a blistering rash similar to poison-ivy. Poisonwood has alternate compound leaves with five shiny leaflets that are smooth-edged and pointy-tipped. Unlike manchineel, there is a good chance that you will encounter a poisonwood tree in south Florida. It grows in wet and dry habitats, near roadsides and in unspoiled wilderness, in hammocks, in pinelands, and in coastal regions — in other words, just about any-

Poisonwood

where. But it is becoming increasingly scarce, suffering the same fate as the manchineel. Because of its irritating sap, many homeowners obliterate this tree from their yards. This causes problems for wildlife, since the fruits are a valuable food. The threatened white-crowned pigeon, a tropical fruit-eating bird found in the Keys, is especially dependent on poisonwood fruits. Biologists from the National Audubon Society's Research Department in Tavernier, who recognized the value of poisonwood to the pigeons, have been trying to educate the public to save poisonwood trees.

Poison ivy

The third poisonous plant is the familiar three-leaved poison ivy. Since this plant is so common elsewhere in the country, it's not necessary to describe it here, but you should expect it just about anywhere around south Florida, including the Keys.

Vertebrate Animals

Snakes

There are four kinds of poisonous snakes in south Florida: the eastern diamondback rattler, the dusky pygmy rattler, the Florida cottonmouth (also known as the water moccasin), and the eastern coral snake. Encounters with these snakes are rare. The nonpoisonous Florida water snake is often mistaken for the less common cottonmouth, and the nonpoisonous scarlet snake and scarlet kingsnake can be confused with the coral snake. Coral snakes are primarily nocturnal and burrow under loose litter, so it is not likely you will encounter one by accident. If you see a brightly colored snake whose identity you are unsure of, recall the adage "Red touch yellow kills a fellow" to remind you that if the red and yellow bands are touching each other, you are looking at a poisonous snake.

Pygmy rattlesnakes are the most likely poisonous snakes you will see. They often warm themselves on paved roads. They are usually less than two feet long, with a dusty appearance and round, dark blotches. Their rattles are so tiny they often go unnoticed.

Sharks

Sharks are common in the warm Florida waters. The majority are small, nonaggressive, and nonthreatening to humans. In the very few attacks that have occurred, the sharks were not intentionally attacking humans. Swimmers in shallow murky water are at risk because the sharks can smell something swimming nearby, but they can't see what it is. Spear-fishermen have had fish they just caught snatched from their hands. One diver lost her hand this way. Some sharks eat lobsters, so sport lobsterers also should be cautious.

To decrease your chances of getting bitten by a shark, avoid standing or swimming in shallow, murky water and don't hold fish or lobsters in your hand underwater. This is also a good reason for divers and snorkelers to refrain from attracting reef fish by feeding them.

Alligators

Although they appear lethargic and slow-moving, these giant reptiles can react with blinding speed when provoked. Normally, alligators that have never seen a human are no threat to people. The problem arises when a gator that lives near houses or a park becomes accustomed to people feeding it. Thereafter, that gator recognizes humans as a source of food. Since an alligator has little intelligence, it can't distinguish that the food does not include the whole package! Everglades National Park and other parks have regulations that prohibit people from feeding gators. It is extremely important to observe this regulation for your safety.

In the wild, female gators are very protective of their young. Since they may guard them for over a year, no time of year is without defensive females. Therefore, if you are walking in an area where there are gators, look and listen carefully, and be ready to back off if you hear the babies' squeaky whimpering defense calls.

Insects

Most people deal with insects by applying repellents. While this works, repellents are not without hazards sometimes worse than the original problem. The active ingredient in most repellents, called DEET (N,N-diethyl-m-toluamide), has been linked to seizures and several deaths in the United States (MMWR 1989). It is absorbed through the skin and into the circulatory system. About 10-15 percent of the amount applied to the skin passes into the urine. Insect repellents with DEET can eat through vinyl and plastic. Watch bands and car seats can be damaged if your DEET-covered skin contacts them. Here is a summary of some precautions to take when using repellents (MMWR 1989):

- wear long sleeves and pants and apply repellent only to exposed skin or to clothing
- use low concentrations of DEET
- never apply repellent to wounds
- apply once every 4-8 hours; over-application will not improve effect
- wash skin after returning indoors

Certain people, such as children, are more sensitive to repellent than others. Be courteous by not spraying repellent near other people. Never spray it indoors — some people don't dare venture outside without first saturating their skin and clothes, leaving others inside to breathe the DEET.

Mosquitoes

From June to November, coinciding with the wet months, the mosquitoes can be unbelievable. It's been suggested (tongue in cheek?) that Everglades National Park be closed for the summer because of mosquitoes, analogous to other parks closing for the winter due to heavy snow. Too many foreigners have had miserable trips to the Everglades because they didn't know about our mosquitoes.

Now that you have been sufficiently warned of the worst, you'll be happy to know that many months of the year can be devoid of mosquitoes. The months of December to May usually are dry enough to prevent mosquitoes from hatching, and cold fronts kill the adults.

Mosquitoes need water to hatch their eggs. The eggs hatch 5-10 days after flooding by rains or high tides. Standing water, such as accumulates in old tires, flower pots, and gutters, is perfect for the proliferation of mosquitoes. Therefore, many people contribute to their own mosquito problems by allowing mosquito breeding places in their yards.

You are more likely to encounter mosquitoes in the coastal mangrove areas and hammocks than in the freshwater marshes. The common saltmarsh mosquito shuns strong sunlight, so you are better off in the open than in the shade and better off in the daytime than at night.

The female mosquito needs the protein from blood to form her eggs, thus it is only the female that bites. The males feed on nectar; they do for marsh flowers what bees do for meadow flowers — they pollinate them. We need mosquitoes.

County mosquito control commissions spray insecticides daily in developed areas during the peak of the mosquito season. The aerial spray (Dibrom) contains diesel to help it settle to the ground. Dibrom and the ground-sprayed Baytex and malathion are killers of butterflies and honeybees.

Scorpions

The scorpions in Florida are not the same as the ones found in the southwestern United States. Ours are not fatally poisonous, but their stings can make a person ill. Scorpions are found throughout south Florida, including the Keys, but you will not be likely to see one unless you are searching for it. Scorpions prefer to hide under wood (such as fallen trees or lumber) rather than rocks. If you turn over a piece of wood, be sure not to use your bare hands. A better idea would be to use a walking staff or tripod leg to flip the wood over. Always put the wood back exactly as you found it, so unseen creatures are not left homeless.

Fire ants

People can ignore swarms of mosquitoes, listlessly swat at horseflies, and calmly step around rattlesnakes. But have you ever seen a human do anything other than frantically explode at the attack of fire ants? The ants in question are the red imported fire ants (*Solenopsis invicta*), which were accidentally introduced into Alabama from Brazil in the 1920s. Since then, they have spread throughout the southeastern United States, eventually reaching south Florida in the early 1970s.

Fire ants are red and less than an eighth of an inch long. They are not often seen unless their mound is stepped on. Fire ants have one of the quickest reaction times to nest agitation of any ant, and it's usually too quick for the agitator. They leave itchy raised pustules that persist for weeks. The nest mounds are piles of dirt about 6-12 inches high and can most often be found in disturbed areas, like the side of a road.

Other insects

No-see-ums or "sand-gnats" (*Culicoides furens*) are minuscule insects which take painful bites that leave welts. No-see-ums are so small and quick that most people don't even see what bit them, hence the colloquial name. They appear at dawn and dusk, usually near mangroves and salt water, and stay for a brief but nasty hour. Because of these tiny insects, camping tents must have the fine-meshed no-see-um-proof netting, not just mosquito netting.

Deerflies (*Tabanus* spp.), which look like giant house flies, are large and slow enough so that it's hard to miss them even before they bite. This is lucky, because their bites take more than their fair share. They are active in open sunlight, usually in the summer.

Chiggers are almost microscopic orange larval mites (not true insects) that burrow under the skin, causing itchy welts that can last for weeks. The best prevention for chiggers is wearing long pants tucked into your socks, not sitting on rocks or logs, and showering immediately after hiking.

Miscellaneous

Humidity

Photographers beware! The south Florida humidity and salt spray can wreak havoc on your delicate equipment. Binoculars and spotting scopes are often victims, too. Wipe moisture and salt spray off the exterior surfaces frequently. Carry a heavy plastic bag with you in case of a sudden downpour. Additionally, there is the intense heat to contend with. Keep your equipment and film in the shade or in a cooler.

Sunburn

Locals can usually tell who the tourists are — they have the peeling sunburns or the dark tans. People who have lived a long time in Florida have learned how harmful the sun's rays can be. They protect their skin and consequently look pale compared to visitors. Skin cancer is prevalent in the South and getting more common every year as the protective ozone layer in the atmosphere is depleted. No time of the year is safe. In winter, although the Earth's axis is tilted away from the sun, the Earth is closer to the sun, so the rays are very strong. In summer, the Earth is farther from the sun but the rays are more direct. If you are swimming, boating, or just wading through water, you'll get a double whammy, because the rays will reflect off the water. Use sunblock, or wear a hat and long sleeves to keep the sun off your skin. Prolonged exposure to strong ultra-violet (UV) rays can damage the retinas of your eyes, so wear glasses that block UV rays.

Crime

Regrettably, the greater Miami area has attained a high crime rate, some of which is aimed at tourists. Thieves watch people for signs of vulnerability, such as being lost or in unfamiliar surroundings. Rental cars are popular targets, so don't leave valuables in them. Crime is not common in most of the places mentioned in this book, but disguising yourself as a local and using common sense will go a long way toward deterring it.

A BRIEF HUMAN HISTORY

The first Europeans to gaze upon the shores of Florida were the Spanish explorers, lead by Juan Ponce de León in 1513. Ponce de León, who was seeking riches and natives to capture as slaves, bestowed the name "Florida" and claimed the area for Spain.

The native Tequesta inhabited southeast Florida and the Calusa inhabited southwest Florida until they were eradicated by Europeans or fled to West Indian islands. Spain and Britain alternated ownership of the Florida peninsula until 1821, when Florida was ceded to the United States. John James Audubon, the famous artist and naturalist, first visited the Florida Keys in 1832 and lived in a house on Whitehead Street in Key West for a few months. The house has been preserved as a museum and is open to the public (see Florida Keys Audubon Society in "Other Sources of Information").

Until the late 1800s, few Americans lived in south Florida. Much of the area was marsh and swamp. Only a narrow strip of coastal ridge from Miami northward was dry enough for development. There were few roads — most people traveled by boat.

In the late 1800s, Miami became a boomtown for several reasons. The area grew into a popular winter vacation spot for wealthy people from northern states. The Florida Keys were attractive to farmers for the year-round growing season. Then the fashion industry in New York, London, and Paris dictated that egret plumes were a must for stylish women's hats, and milliners looked to the Everglades as the source of plumes.

By the early 1900s, large-scale developers had devised schemes to drain the Everglades and provide more land for development. It was a multipronged assault on the irreplaceable wetland: they dug canals to divert water to the ocean, built levees to keep water out of developed areas, and planted thirsty exotic trees to drink up water. The methods worked over much of the Everglades. Little did they realize their near-sighted actions would ruin a perfect system created by nature.

Another self-appointed savior was Henry Flagler, who dreamed of creating a quick passage for travel from the mainland to Havana. His idea was to extend the Florida East Coast Railroad from Miami to Key West, where a ferry would deliver the passengers across the short watery stretch to Havana. Flagler was an old man with plenty of money to finance the construction and a desire to do something sensational with his last years.

Originally, Flagler planned this route to go overland from Miami to Cape Sable and then mostly over water across Florida Bay to Key West. His engineers tried for two years to find a route through the Everglades to Cape Sable. But the land was too mucky to support a railroad. Then Flagler sent his engineers to test the Florida Keys. They reported that the route was possible, so Flagler approved it.

Spend a minute now contemplating what the Everglades would be like today if Flagler had succeeded in his initial route. The railroad tracks would cut across what is now Everglades National Park. Houses, hotels, stores, roads, and farms would probably line the entire route, and more of the Everglades would have been drained to prevent flooding. Flamingo would be a bustling metropolitan port like Miami. The Everglades would not exist as we know it today, even in its current sorry state. It's a small consolation that the Everglades was spared at the expense of the Keys.

The railroad construction was begun in 1904 and completed in Key West in 1912. Since Key West was the most populated town in Florida at the turn of the century, there was not enough land for the terminal station. So 134 acres were created by pumping mud and marl from the Gulf of Mexico.

The engineers originally wanted to connect all the Keys with ramparts (causeways), with no more than six miles of bridges. But the local people protested, claiming it would prevent the flow of seawater between the islands during storms and cause the water to flood over the islands instead. They were proven right during the 1909 and 1935 hurricanes, and that is why there are so many bridges on the Overseas Highway. The longest one, the Seven-Mile Bridge in Marathon, is the longest bridge of its kind in the world.

The big hurricane of 1935 was the last curtain for the railroad. So much was destroyed that the cost to rebuild was too great. The railroad had already been losing money, and it had facilitated a loss of population in the Keys (the impoverished locals had a way to leave, and many never returned). In 1938, the railroad bed was converted into a road, which is still the only road that goes to Key West. Portions of the old track are still visible along the middle and lower Keys.

A QUICK LOOK AROUND THE MAINLAND

The two outstanding topographic features of southern Florida are the amount of surface water and the flatness of the terrain. Combined, they make the tip of the peninsula look like a giant, shallow lake at certain times of the year. Actually, it is a giant, shallow, and very slowly moving river. The name "Everglades" has come to mean "river of grass." Historically, the Everglades began at the southern end of Lake Okeechobee, where the water overflowed the banks and gradually drifted south to Florida Bay and the Gulf of Mexico. The topographical gradient is so small — only one or two inches per mile — that early white settlers didn't even know the water flowed.

West of the Everglades basin is Big Cypress Swamp, one of the largest remaining wilderness areas in Florida. It has a slightly higher elevation than the Everglades basin. Although it contains marshes, it is predominantly forested with cypresses and pines. It is underlain by the fossiliferous Tamiami limestone. The hydroperiod (the amount of time the area is covered by water) is shorter than in the Everglades, leaving marl instead of peat for the soil. Old growth pine stands contain small populations of the endangered red-cockaded woodpecker. Because of limited accessibility in the Big Cypress, less exploration has been done here than in the Everglades, and less is known about the flora and fauna.

A rock ridge composed of limestone outcroppings extends from Miami southwest to Long Pine Key in Everglades National Park. This region of higher elevation between the coast and the interior marshes was preferred for development and farms because of the lack of flooding. The highest elevations in Homestead are about 13 feet above sea level and in Miami about 23 feet above sea level. The latter can clearly be seen by driving along South Bayshore Drive in the Silver Bluff area of Miami (between Coconut Grove and the Rickenbacker Causeway). The old shoreline, which abutted the limestone bluffs, can be seen in the yards of the houses on the west side of the road.

The ridge prevents most of the Everglades water from flowing east into Biscayne Bay. A few rivers, such as the Miami and New Rivers, penetrate the ridge and allow some water to pass. But the remaining water backs up against the western side of the ridge. Historically, the water pressure pushed through the limestone in some places, creating high volume springs that flowed into Biscayne Bay. The decrease in water level over the past 70 years has caused the springs to cease flowing. The rivers are now entirely channelized.

The huge pool of water that collects west of the ridge — the real Everglades — not only flows southward but also *downward*. By percolating through the porous limestone, it recharges the underlying Biscayne aquifer. Most of south Florida's residents, farmers, and industries depend on this aquifer, and therefore the Everglades, for their water.

The immigration of Europeans and early colonists caused some development to begin in south Florida, but it wasn't until the 1900s that serious environmental degradation began. Huge dredges dug canals to drain the water from the Everglades, creating more farmland. The fill from the canals was used to build levees for flood protection and roads. The series of canals, levees, and pumping stations that now criss-cross the southern Florida peninsula have changed the face of the Everglades. In some places the water no longer flows. In others, the hydroperiod has decreased so much by water being drained, that the peat is exposed and fires ravage the fertile soil. Complications too numerous to elaborate on here have arisen because of the juxtaposition of a sensitive wetland with a burgeoning metropolis.

A QUICK LOOK AROUND THE FLORIDA KEYS

The word "key" as it relates geographically to south Florida originated from the Spanish word *cayo* for "little island" or "island reef." It is used for all small marine islands in south Florida. When capitalized, it refers specifically to the group of developed islands that make up the chain from Key Largo to Key West. The dozens of islands that shape this archipelago stretch about 125 miles from Key Largo to Key West. Actually, that is what is linked by road and 42 bridges, but there are undeveloped and unconnected islands on both ends.

The islands are made of limestone in several forms. Exposed very recently geologically, these 5000-year-old islands are barely separate from the sea. They rise on the average 2-4 feet above sea level, with the highest islands (Key Largo, Plantation Key, Windley Key, Lignumvitae, and Big Pine) rising only up to 18 feet. Actually, the landfills create the highest land now in the Keys.

From Soldier Key in the north to part of Big Pine Key in the south, the substrate rock is Key Largo limestone, an old coral reef. Fossilized remnants of coral skeletons can be easily seen on surface rocks in many places on the upper Keys. Look for a place, even a parking lot on U.S. 1 in Key Largo, that has rocks on the ground and you will probably see striations from former coral colonies. From Big Pine south to Key West, the rock is called Miami Oolite, named for the tiny calcareous spheres that look like eggs or ooids. Note on a map the difference in shape between the two groups of islands.

It is the difference in substrate between the Upper and Lower Keys that determines the availability of fresh water on the islands. In the Upper Keys, the Key Largo limestone is permeable and rain water quickly soaks through to mix with the brackish groundwater. There are few fresh water wells or ponds in the Upper Keys. In the Lower Keys, the dense Miami Oolite retains water which sits in pools or "lenses" above the denser salt water. The pinelands of the Lower Keys exist because of the availability of fresh water. Many mammals, reptiles, and amphibians not found in the Upper Keys can survive in the Lower Keys because of the fresh water. The Key deer and Key mud turtle are examples.

You may notice that it rains less in the Keys than on the mainland. Frequently in the summer you can drive from earth-shaking thunderstorms in Florida City south across the "18-Mile-Stretch" (a colloquial name for the section of U.S. 1 south of Florida City to the drawbridge at Jewfish Creek near Key Largo), and when you arrive in Key Largo the sun is shining. Because the air and ground are both drier, there are very few natural sources of fresh water on the Keys. The public water supply is piped from Florida City to Key West, a distance of 135 miles. Virtually every person on the islands is dependent on this one aqueduct. The aqueduct is mostly buried, but you can see it where it crosses the bridges. Now you can understand why fresh water is expensive and precious in the Keys.

The vegetation of the Keys is distinctly West Indian. Since the Keys are islands, the most likely way for seeds to reach them would be by drifting on the ocean or the wind. Most of the West Indian plants are adapted to those forms of dispersal, but most of the mainland ones are not. Furthermore, the most likely species to survive would be ones adapted to island features, like salty air. The climate resembles that of the West Indies more than that of the mainland. One's overall impression of the Keys is that one is on a Caribbean island.

As a group, the most distinctive trees are the graceful palms. Some botanists would argue that palms aren't trees, since they are monocots and lack a true woody structure. But they are tree-like in form and function and are considered trees by most people. There are only eight species native to south Florida. The coconut palm, so common in this area, is not one of them. Many species of palms have been introduced and thrive in the mild climate.

The animal life, however, brings a northerner back to reality. You will recognize many species from the mainland of Florida: opossums, raccoons, rat snakes, green treefrogs, spadefoot toads, ospreys, and mockingbirds, to name a few. Aside from the birds and insects, which could fly to the islands from far away, other animals were restricted to shorter distances and perhaps less intentional methods of transportation. Mammals, except bats, either swam island-hopping fashion or drifted on flotsam. Some of them may have walked during extremely low tides and sea levels. Most reptiles probably also arrived this way. Small mammals, reptiles, amphibians, and flightless insects probably hitched rides on floating logs or were carried by hurricanes. More recently, humans have aided dispersal (intentionally and unintentionally) with roads, ships, and other methods. Through the pet trade, humans have brought species from all over the world that subsequently escaped and established themselves. The wildlife present now is a blend of three parts continental, two parts West Indian, and one part totally bizarre.

Key limes, a local specialty, are actually of Mexican origin. The lime trees were imported to the Keys by botanist Henry Perrine in the 1800s and have become commercially important. The small, round yellow fruits are used for the famous Key Lime Pie.

On a drive down the "18-Mile-Stretch" from November to March you are likely to pass roseate spoonbills and other wading birds. Another road, called the Card Sound Road (SR 905A), leads from Florida City to North Key Largo. This was the original road and is less traveled and more picturesque than U.S. 1. The southern end, near where Card Sound Road intersects with SR 905, may harbor a well-concealed crocodile in the shallow water around the mangroves.

ECOLOGICAL EFFECTS OF HURRICANE ANDREW ON SOUTH FLORIDA

On August 24, 1992, one of the most powerful storms in United States history wreaked havoc on the southern tip of the Florida peninsula. Roaring in from the Atlantic Ocean at sustained wind speeds near 150 miles per hour and gusts over 175, Hurricane Andrew was the worst natural disaster ever to befall the country. That honor was acquired primarily by the size of the financial damage estimate and the number of people left homeless. But how did nature do?

Recall that hurricanes are spawned as the waters in the ocean warm up during the northern hemisphere's summer (see "Hurricanes" under "Local Precautions" above). If the water becomes too warm, the ocean's creatures will become physically stressed or will die. To remove the tremendous amount of energy stored in the warm ocean, the heat must rise. As it rises, it creates a well-defined air mass that gathers strength when it passes over more warm water. The objective is to move the heat to somewhere else, such as the colder North Atlantic waters. Considering the primary ecological function of a hurricane, Andrew was a success.

If the air mass is strong, it may become defined into a circular wind pattern, with the strongest winds near the center. In the center itself, called the eye, there is no wind, and the barometric pressure is extremely low. At the edge of the eye, the wind begins abruptly at the "eye wall." The wall is a sheer vertical face of wind rising like a column tens of thousands of feet above the ocean. It is along this wall that the strongest winds are sustained. In the northern hemisphere, the wind always travels counter-clockwise around the eye.

As Andrew approached the Florida coast, it was traveling due west. It made landfall in Homestead, about 25 miles south of Miami (see map on the next page). The winds in the first half of the storm, therefore, came from the north. After the eye passed by, the winds shifted 180° and came from the south.

The high winds pushed a wall of water, called a storm surge, across the ocean. Storm surges often cause more damage than the winds in a hurricane, but that was not true of Andrew. The highest surge was 16.9 feet near Perrine and smaller surges extended for a relatively short distance north to Miami Beach and south to North Key Largo. Perhaps because the storm sprinted past so quickly (its forward speed was about twice that of most hurricanes), it did not linger long enough to pound the coast. Furthermore, the natural barriers presented by the coral reefs and mangrove shores performed their functions as nature intended.

As the storm moved across the land, it did not waver in direction or intensity. It left a swath about 25 miles wide across the southern Everglades. Its path of destruction began around Homestead Air Force Base in the east, then continued west through Homestead and surrounding towns, to the main entrance of Everglades National Park. In the park, it struck Chekika, Pine Island, Royal Palm, Long Pine Key, Pinelands, Pa-hay-okee, and Shark Valley areas.

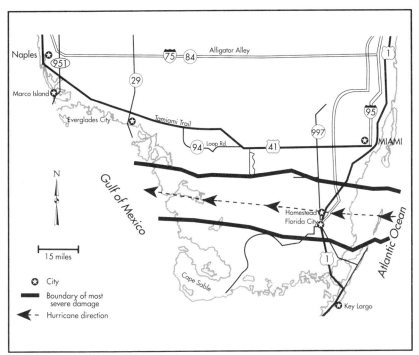

Hurricane Andrew's path as it traveled from east to west across south Florida, August 24, 1992. Dashed line shows center of storm. Boundary includes eye plus eye wall. Damage also occurred outside boundary. Hurricane track information is courtesy of South Florida Water Management District and National Weather Service.

Effects on terrestrial habitats

In a totally natural environment, a hurricane accomplishes beneficial functions in the areas it strikes. These include sweeping accumulated leaf litter from the ground to allow seedlings to sprout, dumping needed rain before the start of the dry season, and flushing the estuaries that have become choked with vegetation. The native vegetation has adapted to hurricanes. For example, some have flexible trunks and some can releaf quickly. When unnatural factors are added, a hurricane can become an ecological disaster. That is what happened with Andrew.

Much of the mangroves that once existed along the coast south of Miami had been destroyed by development years before. Those trees would have absorbed the shock of the storm surge and prevented coastal erosion. Of the mangroves that were left, the worst damage was

35

to the western shore of Biscayne Bay, where 85-90% were destroyed. The worst mangrove damage in Everglades National Park occurred from Shark Point to Lopez River on the west coast. Many trees were uprooted.

The hardwood hammocks were also severely damaged. Many trees were windthrown (blown over), many were snapped off at the trunk, and all were denuded 5 or 10 feet above the ground. The trees that were left standing were reduced to only the thickest branches. Many of the native trees, such as gumbo-limbo, will survive if not further assaulted by freezes or droughts in the near future. For many years to come, the skeletons of the windthrown trees will be visible in Everglades and Biscayne National Parks, Castellow Hammock, and Matheson Hammock.

The pinelands may have survived slightly better. Although many trees were snapped off or windthrown, about 20-50% of them remained intact with only the loss of needles. The slash pines seemed an obvious example of a native tree that had adapted to hurricanes. Evidence of pineland damage can be seen in Navy Wells Pineland Preserve and Everglades National Park.

The ecological problems created by humans and merely assisted by Andrew may be south Florida's worst enemy. Hazardous wastes in the form of paints, solvents, cleaners, batteries, and pesticides were scattered on the ground, after the storm swept them out of garages and porches. Underground fuel tanks leaked. Some of the toxic wastes landed in the canals that lace the area. In the aftermath, some people used the storm as an excuse to dump toxics anywhere. They laughed at "No Littering" laws (the signs were gone). Debris became a major problem so, in a humanitarian move, the Secretary of the Department of Environmental Regulation issued an emergency order to ease restrictions on waste disposal and open burning of debris. Open fires burned all over town, as many as 80 with permits even into October. Severe smog resulted in respiratory problems for the residents. Air quality standards over Everglades National Park were undoubtedly violated. Furthermore, the scores of backyard swimming pools and hot tubs that had filled with debris became giant stagnant cesspools, perfect for the proliferation of mosquitoes. The mosquito control folks called in the big guns — the insecticide bombing planes. Even the military got into the aerial spraying business. The few butterflies that had quietly slipped back in a few days after the storm vanished after the spraying. Another alleged health threat involved rats, which feasted on the piles of garbage.

Perhaps the greatest fear that environmentalists have for the future as a result of Andrew is the uncontrollable spread of plants introduced by humans. Prior to the storm, melaleuca and Brazilian pepper were already threatening the faunal integrity of the Everglades. Those two species, which thrive after disturbance, may have received the added boost they needed to outcompete the native plants beyond our ability to recover them.

Effects on wildlife

At the end of August, there is typically a lull in wildlife activities in south Florida. That timing, plus the lack of flooding, saved much of the wildlife from harm. For example, wading birds had finished nesting, so presumably no nests were destroyed. Bald eagle nesting generally commences in mid-October and had not yet begun. True, some nests from previous years (which the faithful eagles reuse) were destroyed, but the birds could build new ones. Most snail kites were farther north, out of the path of the storm. It is feared, however, that red-cockaded woodpeckers in Big Cypress, already an isolated colony, lost vital nesting trees.

All 23 radio-collared Florida panthers survived and had normal movement patterns after the storm. White-tailed deer fawns were already 5-6 months old and self-sufficient.

A small but insignificant number of alligator eggs may have been destroyed. Crocodiles had already hatched, and most of their nests were outside the severely impacted area. Sea turtle nests in Biscayne National Park and some on Cape Sable in Everglades National Park were destroyed, but the majority of sea turtle nests were located in counties farther north of the impacted area. Some sand deposited on Cape Sable may help future turtle nesting.

Two invertebrate species may have suffered delayed mortality due to the defoliation of the host trees. Tree snails lost the shade cover that keeps them sheltered from the intense sunlight. The Schaus' swallow-tail butterflies were not at their breeding area on Elliott Key and North Key Largo at the time of the storm, but the pupae were. The effect of salt spray and lack of shade is unknown. If most or all of the pupae were killed, the species could be extinct. The fate of the butterfly is a good example of how quickly a species can become extinct. Biologists fear letting a species become too few or restricted geographically, because one catastrophe can erase it forever.

A major problem, the introduction of exotic animals to the wild, may not manifest itself for several years. The hurricane's winds ripped open the cages of thousands of non-native animals that were in zoos, tourist attractions, and private homes. Dozens of state wildlife officers from all over Florida were immediately sent to the ravaged area to capture the animals. Some escapees were dangerous, but most were helpless. Some will never be caught and will adapt and reproduce, creating unknown ecological repercussions.

Effects on marine waters

The coral reefs suffered damage to 60-foot depths in the worst areas, such as Triumph Reef near Elliott Key. Large brain and star corals broke off and rolled like bowling balls. In the shallow reefs, soft corals ripped from the bottom and staghorn and elkhorn branches snapped off. All were covered with a layer of silt. The worst damage seemed to be at the artificial reefs, where ships had been sunk to provide a substrate for coral to anchor to. Since the wrecks themselves were not anchored, they crashed around the ocean bottom, scraping all delicate sea life in their paths.

Other marine problems included increased turbidity for many days after the storm, leakage from the oil and gas tanks of sunken boats, and coastline erosion.

There was little disturbance to the seagrass beds in Florida Bay. Local environmentalists lamented that the hurricane did not flush out Florida Bay with fresh water as needed. That would have been one positive aspect of hosting a major hurricane. It would have ripped out the dying seagrass and created room for healthier recolonizing grasses.

Scientists will be assessing the effects of Hurricane Andrew on south Florida for many years. There will be visible signs of the hurricane for 50 years, such as windthrown trees and snapped off trunks. You can assess the effects in your own way when you visit the impacted areas. On the following pages, those areas are marked with a hurricane symbol 🌀 near the end of the section. The severity of the impact is described. Most parks reopened within a few months after the hurricane. You should call in advance to any place that was severely impacted to confirm that the facilities are operational.

II.
HABITATS

Elkhorn coral

CORAL REEF

Coral reefs are extremely valuable and complex marine ecosystems existing only in the warmer ocean waters of the world. They buffer the adjacent shorelines from storm waves, giving stability to the soil and vegetation, and they concentrate highly productive and diverse marine life.

The only coral reefs in the continental United States are off the south Florida coast. Although occasional corals may be found north to about latitude 30°, reef development reaches its peak in the Florida Keys archipelago, where the warm Florida Current flows. Corals flourish on the eastern sides of continents, because the water is usually warmer from ocean currents. Clear water, with salinities about 35 parts per thousand, temperatures between 68-86°F (20-30°C), and a good food supply are the controlling environmental factors. Water clarity is essen-

39

tial because an integral part of the reef-building coral organism is the one-celled alga known as zooxanthella, which requires sunlight to be able to photosynthesize. Thus, the clearer the water, the deeper the corals can live.

Corals are animals belonging to a group known as the coelenterates, along with jellyfish, anemones, and hydroids; they are radially symmetrical. They have two life stages: asexual sessile polyps and sexual free-swimming medusae. The stony corals that form the backbone of the coral reef have hard, calcareous skeletons of calcium carbonate secreted by the soft polyp. Each polyp looks like a small sea anemone, with its base attached to a little limy cup that it hides in during the day. Unless you go snorkeling or diving at night, all you'll see is the rocklike limestone skeleton.

The coral reefs gained notoriety with the early European explorers and traders (particularly the Spaniards visiting Mexico) because of the danger of wrecking on the shallow "rocks." Many lives and cargoes were lost. Some early Keys residents supported themselves by salvaging shipments of gold, silver, and other valuables. Today, treasure hunters spend fortunes and lifetimes searching for the leftovers. While this may seem harmless enough, rarely can they sift and rake through the sediment without agitating and destroying the sea bottom life.

The Florida Keys reefs are the number one diving destination in the world. Not even the Great Barrier Reef in Australia garners as many underwater explorers. The Florida reefs are home to about 400-500 species of fish and numerous invertebrates, many of them extremely colorful, and all worth at least a glassbottom boat or snorkel trip. Along with the benign-sounding names of angelfish, trumpetfish, butterflyfish, and rock beauties, a few names conjure up apprehension: barracuda, moray eel, southern stingray, and tiger shark.

Barracudas always look as if they are about to strike, but in reality they must swim with their mouths open to breathe. Barracudas have rarely been reported to attack humans, and incidents usually occurred when the water was murky or the person was wearing something shiny. Moray eels are dangerous only if you stick your hand in their hiding holes or crevices. Stingrays are a problem only if you step on them, so watch where you walk in shallow water. They camouflage beautifully, so you must be observant. And sharks are also very maligned. The rare shark attacks generally occur in murky water, when the victim is wearing contrasting tones, when there is blood or chum present, or when the victim is thrashing around. In general, with a little common sense, the reef is a safe and enjoyable place to be.

On the other side of the coin, are the reefs safe from humans? Divers and snorkelers often don't realize how easily they can kill coral. Touching the surface of a coral head can injure the protective mucous membrane. Because water clarity is so essential, kicking up silt is also extremely destructive to coral. In heavily used areas, whole patches of coral have been killed, often by people trying to be considerate but bumping or kicking them by accident.

All corals, soft and hard, are protected by law from collecting. The coral souvenirs found in the local gift shops are imported from other countries, such as the Philippines.

You can see the coral reefs by visiting Biscayne National Park, Dry Tortugas National Park, Bahia Honda State Park, and John Pennekamp Coral Reef State Park.

Pneumatophores of black mangrove

MANGROVE

Four tree species in Florida are collectively considered mangroves: red mangrove, black mangrove, white mangrove, and buttonwood. Only red mangrove, however, is in the mangrove family (Rhizophoraceae). All four share the common traits of being very tolerant of salinity and water level changes. Thus they thrive in tidal zones and represent the transition between the sawgrass marshes and the ocean. Black and white mangroves have mechanisms to excrete salt (you can see the salt glands at the base

41

of each white mangrove leaf), while red mangroves don't allow salt to enter their tissues. Thus, they do not need salt water and can thrive in freshwater habitats, though they are rarely found there because they are outcompeted by freshwater-adapted trees.

Red, black, and white mangroves have seeds, called propagules, that begin germination while still on the tree. Mangrove propagules and roots can anchor well only on low-energy shorelines — that is, shorelines with such shallow slopes that the waves and tides are barely noticeable. Much of Florida, especially the southwest coast, is like that. Another environmental requirement is a warm climate. Together, these reasons make south Florida home to the most extensive mangrove swamps in the United States.

Mangrove systems are vital as rich nursery grounds for fish and invertebrates, such as snook, tarpon, mullet, mangrove snapper, spiny lobster, pink shrimp, oyster, and blue crab. Many birds nest on mangrove trees, such as wood storks, roseate spoonbills, brown pelicans, and white-crowned pigeons.

Red mangrove trees are easily recognized by their prop roots which resemble a spider's legs. Black mangroves (and occasionally white mangroves) have pencil-like root appendages, called pneumatophores, that grow under the tree like new shoots of asparagus. Buttonwoods have no distinguishing root structures.

Mangrove trees are protected from human destruction by Florida law because of their vital roles as nursery grounds and shoreline stabilizers. Good places to see mangroves are the Ten Thousand Islands and Florida Bay in Everglades National Park, Biscayne National Park, John Pennekamp Coral Reef State Park, Rookery Bay, Long Key State Recreation Area, and Collier-Seminole State Park.

Cypress dome

CYPRESS

Scattered throughout the freshwater wetlands of southern Florida, particularly in Big Cypress National Preserve, Corkscrew Swamp Sanctuary, Fakahatchee Strand State Preserve, and Everglades National Park, are vast stands of conifers known locally as cypresses, although they are not true cypresses but bald-cypresses. The name "Big Bald-Cypress National Preserve" just wouldn't have the same ring. Although they are conifers, cypresses shed their needles around November each year (hence look bald) and sprout new ones in February or March. Taxonomists argue whether the pond-cypress is a separate species or a variety of bald-cypress.

Cypresses grow best with their roots in water and are the most flood-tolerant freshwater trees in Florida. Two of their most recognizable characteristics, the swelling buttresses and spindly "knees," are adaptations to their watery environment. The knees are projections of the roots that emerge from the water, probably to assist with respiration when the oxygen levels surrounding the roots are low. Although the seeds need to soak in water, they won't germinate under water.

Cypresses in south Florida are often found growing in one of two types of arrangements: domes and strands. Cypress domes are small, circular concentrations of cypress trees in a pond-like situation. The tallest trees are in the center where the water and soil are deepest, and the shortest trees are around the edges, giving a dome-like silhouette from a distance. Cypress strands are long and narrow, sometimes many miles in length. Their alignment generally indicates the direction of water flow during high-water periods. Fakahatchee Strand is an excellent example.

Vast cypress swamps across the southeastern United States were logged for their rot-resistant lumber. Cypress lumbering is still big business in some areas. The largest and oldest trees left are in Corkscrew Swamp, fortunately protected in perpetuity by the National Audubon Society. Some species that use cypress habitats are swallow-tailed kites, turkeys, deer, otters, panthers, and bobcats.

Slash pines

PINELAND

Much of central and northern Florida is covered by pine forests, but the pinelands of south Florida are different. They are associated with the south

Florida rocklands and are restricted to outcroppings of limestone. These limestone ridges have the highest elevations in the area.

Three main areas have pine rocklands: the Miami Ridge (from Miami to Long Pine Key), the lower Florida Keys, and Big Cypress Swamp. The Miami Ridge, composed of Miami limestone, is the largest outcropping. The lower Keys (from Big Pine to Key West) are also on Miami limestone. In Big Cypress, the older Tamiami limestone is exposed.

The bedrock in pinelands is often exposed, and the soils are very shallow. Numerous pits, pinnacles, and solution holes are formed when the acidic leaf litter, mixing with rain water, dissolves the limestone. This is a very characteristic feature. The early settlers had to plant their crops in the solution holes, the only places with deep enough soil.

Essential to the continual regeneration and success of the slash pines is fire. Without the lightning-caused fires that swept through the pines over the centuries, the pinelands would have reverted to hardwoods. Much of the original pinelands have been lost that way, since we newcomers have suppressed fires. The suppression has been direct in many cases and indirect in many others. The networks of roads, canals, and farms throughout the area have served as effective firebreaks. Natural resource managers in parks containing pinelands (such as Everglades and Big Cypress) practice controlled burning, however, to keep the pines regenerating.

Another major destroyer of pinelands has been lumbering. Unfortunately for the slash pine found in south Florida, its wood is virtually insect- and rot-resistant, making it a blessed building material in south Florida. So much of early Miami and Homestead depended on this tree for building that it is known locally as "Dade County pine."

The understory vegetation of the pinelands must have fire-resistant roots or seeds to be able to regenerate quickly after fire. Saw palmetto, velvetseed, willow bustic, tetrazygia, varnish leaf, and myrsine are common. Coontie formerly was more common. Much of the vegetation is West Indian. Pinelands can be seen in Everglades National Park, Big Cypress National Preserve, Navy Wells Pineland Preserve, and National Key Deer Refuge.

Sawgrass marsh with basking alligator

SAWGRASS MARSH

The Everglades is a vast freshwater marsh generally known as the sawgrass marsh. Some of it is characterized by deep organic soils (peat) and hydroperiods of over nine months. Where hydroperiods are slightly shorter, marl substrates may form instead of peat. Sawgrass is the most common plant, but many other plants grow also. The name sawgrass is both accurate and misleading. The blades do indeed have saw-like edges, but the plant is a sedge, not a grass. Sawgrass may grow ten feet tall.

Mixed in with the sawgrass are spike rush, bladderwort, pickerel-weed, muhly grass, and many other wetland plants. Another species, the cattail, is becoming a scourge in the sawgrass marshes. Thriving on the added nutrients released upstream by the agricultural practices around Lake Okeechobee, the cattails are outcompeting the sawgrasses. This is devastating to the natural community because cattails deplete dissolved oxygen and can form such dense stands that wildlife movement and usage is impaired. A major conservation effort is underway to change farming practices to reduce the added nutrient load to the Everglades.

Sawgrass marshes can be seen in Everglades National Park, Big Cypress National Preserve, Southern Glades Wildlife and Environmental Area, and Fakahatchee Strand State Preserve.

Hardwood hammock

HAMMOCK

Hammocks are "islands" of trees generally growing on higher elevations than the surrounding landscape, or on lower elevations in pines
where greater moisture reduces fire threats. They have evolved from
lack of fire exposure and are the upland climax community. They grow
on rich organic soils and are generally densely canopied and diverse in
flora. Hammocks occur as bay heads, rock reefs, or tropical hardwood
hammocks.

Bayheads, small clumps of hardwoods in the freshwater marshes,
consist of such trees as redbay, sweet bay, wax myrtle, and coco-plum.
Bayheads are found in the sloughs of Everglades National Park and Big
Cypress National Preserve. From the air, their characteristic teardrop
shape is apparent. The teardrop forms when water flowing down the
slough washes detritus from the upstream end and deposits it at the
downstream end.

Rock reefs are ridges of limestone that create higher elevations that
allow hardwood trees to flourish. From a bird's-eye view, a rock reef
looks like a giant snake of trees crawling through the marsh. Rock Reef
Pass in Everglades National Park is a good example.

Tropical hardwood hammocks, which exist from Miami south to the
Keys, are dense stands of primarily West Indian trees. They are the only

47

tropical hardwood forests in the continental United States and are probably the most endangered habitat in the country. Their demise began in the 1500s when early Spaniards began leveling the giant mahogany trees for shipment back to Europe. West Indian mahoganies, native to south Florida, have valuable wood. They are now on the state's threatened plants list. The current land-grab and development boom in this resort area is destroying what's left of this geographically limited habitat. Conservation groups must work very hard to save the remaining tropical hardwood hammocks. Everglades National Park, Castellow Hammock, Crane Point Hammock, Matheson Hammock, Biscayne National Park, and Lignumvitae Key all have tropical hardwood hammocks.

III.
A PEEK AT THE SPECIAL WILDLIFE

TREE SNAILS

Bejeweling our south Florida tropical hardwood hammocks are the colorful tree snails (*Liguus fasciatus*). There are 58 named color forms of *L. fasciatus*, some of which have vanished forever. These native

Tree snail

snails, about two inches long, were once found from Collier and Broward counties southward to and including the Florida Keys.

General habitat destruction has eliminated many hammocks and the tree snails that depend on them. Development has destroyed hammocks outside park boundaries. In undeveloped areas, hammocks have burned because poor water management practices artificially simulate droughts that cause hotter and more widespread fires then the hammocks can withstand.

Tree snails grow during the wet season, mainly from May to September, adding more spirals of color. They feed on fungi, lichens, and mold growing on the bark of wild-tamarind, Jamaica dogwood, and other smooth-barked trees. Their role in the ecosystem is to clean mold and algae from trees. Courtship and mating occur from late June to September, and since tree snails are hermaphroditic (individuals possess both male and female sex organs), they need only find another tree snail to reproduce. Eggs are laid in the leaf mould in early fall and hatch at the beginning of the next rainy season.

During the dry winter months, the snails aestivate to protect their bodies from moisture loss by sealing themselves tightly to a tree. Removing a snail at this time will break the protective seal and may cause the snail to die. Unless you see a tree snail actively crawling around, *do not touch it.* Occasionally a warm winter rain will reactivate a snail temporarily.

SPINY LOBSTERS

Unlike their northern cousins, spiny lobsters (*Panulirus argus*) have no pincers. Spiny lobsters are just as tasty, but the meat lies mainly in the tails. The name comes from the spines on the antennas and carapace.

Harvesting by commercial and sport lobsterers is permitted. The harvesting season runs from August to March 30, during which any person possessing a Florida saltwater fishing license and a lobster stamp may collect lobsters. Sport lobsterers can use nooses, nets, or other noninjuring devices except traps. Traps are used only by commercial lobsterers and may be seen during the off-season (April-July) stacked along the roadside in the Keys. Since egg-bearing and undersized lobsters must be released, such injurious methods of capture as spearing are not permitted.

Lobsters may also be caught by snorkeling or scuba diving. Most people are ecologically conscientious when they capture lobsters. Some, however, are careless or destructive. During the day, these nocturnal creatures hide under ledges with their sensory feelers exposed. At the first sign of trouble, a lobster will withdraw as completely as possible into the rocks, making it difficult to extricate it. Impatient humans have torn the rocks open to free a lobster. Sometimes the rocks destroyed are actually living coral. People have even poured bleach into the rocks to drive lobsters out. Repeated poking and prodding at a group of lobsters may drive them out of hiding to walk across exposed sea bottom to find a safer place. This harassment makes them easy prey for sharks and other large predators.

The most conscientious way to capture a lobster is to: 1) learn to judge the relative size of a lobster by its antenna length, so you leave undersized ones alone; 2) try only two or three times to catch a lobster (after that, your chances of success decrease and you will be only be harassing it); and 3) leave the area if you see that the lobsters are becoming agitated and may try to flee for other cover. Check for egg clusters on the abdomens and immediately release any egg-bearing females.

Until 1992, the last full weekend in July every year was the opening weekend of the state's sport lobstering season. The mania that surrounded it was phenomenal. It is probably safe to say that it was traditionally the busiest weekend of the year in the Keys. Local merchants planned for it months in advance. Diving equipment and motel rooms were all taken. Travel on U.S. 1 slowed to a crawl. In 1992, the state changed the season to begin in midweek, hoping to avoid the insanity of that intense two-day harvest. But the federal season (in waters three miles or more offshore) still begins that last weekend, so the situation is not much improved.

CONCHS

If you want to sound like a local, make sure to pronounce this "conks," ignoring the "h." You'll hear the word frequently, especially in the Keys. Queen conchs (*Strombus gigas*) are large marine snails, sometimes weighing as much as five pounds, found in shallow seagrass beds and sandy bottoms from southern Florida to the West Indies.

For centuries before Europeans arrived, conchs were harvested for food by the native people. The shells were used for tools, bowls, and ornaments. With the influx of white people to the southern end of the peninsula, conch harvesting reached exorbitant levels. Conchs were a staple diet for the early settlers to the Keys. In fact, a person who was born and raised in the Keys is referred to as a "conch."

Queen conchs were also collected as souvenirs for tourists. Since 1985, conchs have been completely protected in Florida, because the conch population had reached critically low numbers. They are still harvested in the Bahamas and West Indies, the current source of conch sold in Florida.

Conchs are considered a delicacy by some people. Other people feel that their reputation is undeserved. True, it is a local specialty, but that is not equivalent to a delicacy. Conch meat is tough and rather bland. It has to be pounded into oblivion (or "cracked" as the locals call it) and spiced to the hilt to be tender and tasty enough to qualify as a delicacy. Cracked conch (pounded and breaded), conch fritters, and conch chowder (usually spicy) are the three most frequent conch items on local menus.

FLORIDA PANTHERS

While settlers from the 1600s to 1900s were systematically destroying the wilderness haunts of the panthers and hunting them almost to extinction (they were hunted for bounty until 1950), a small population survived in the untamed Everglades and Big Cypress. The Florida panther (*Felis concolor coryi*) is a subspecies of the mountain lion (or cougar), which once roamed almost every habitat from the Atlantic to the Pacific oceans. In 1958 the panther became protected in Florida, and in 1967 the U.S. Fish and Wildlife Service listed it as endangered. Today, only 30-50 panthers roam Florida, all from Lake Okeechobee south to Long Pine Key. The number is not increasing in spite of intensive cooperative efforts by the U.S. Fish and Wildlife Service, Florida Game and Freshwater Fish Commission (FGFWFC), the National Park Service at Everglades National Park and Big Cypress National Preserve, and other agencies. Radio-tagged panthers are being tracked by National Park Service staff in Big Cypress and Everglades National Park and the FGFWFC. A captive breeding program has been established by the agencies listed above and will be conducted by zoos in Florida.

Known mortality is due primarily to collisions with automobiles and malnutrition. Of 21 panther deaths investigated from 1978 to 1988, 11 were the result of motor vehicle hits. Most occurred on Alligator Alley (Interstate 75) and Tamiami Trail (U.S. 41), which is the reason the nighttime speed limit on those roads is 10 mph less than the daytime limit. When you drive on either road, be *very* cautious of panthers trying to cross. The situation has been improved with the new wildlife underpasses on Alligator Alley. The Department of Transportation incorporated the underpasses beneath the interstate to allow panthers to cross safely, and evidence from FGFWFC shows that they are using them.

A decrease in the number of white-tailed deer (the preferred diet) has caused the panthers to feed on smaller prey (such as raccoons and young alligators) in some areas. Panthers may survive on small prey items, but they are not likely to reproduce. Studies have shown that a female panther needs large prey items like deer to reproduce and raise her cubs. Another problem is arising with the switch from large to small prey. The fresh waters of the Everglades are contaminated with mercury, which becomes concentrated in predators of aquatic animals, such as raccoons, otters, and gators. Panthers that feed on such animals will acquire contamination themselves. In the Shark Slough drainage area of Everglades National Park, mercury levels of necropsied panthers have been at the toxic level and are responsible for at least one death.

Florida panthers resemble western mountain lions, with a few minor differences. Panthers are more red than the tawny mountain lions, have a "cowlick" in the middle of their backs, and have a sharp bend in the distal end of their tails. They also are slightly smaller, with females weighing about 50-100 lbs. and males 100-140 lbs. Other subspecies introduced or escaped into Florida have intergraded with the native cats, so some individuals do not carry the above traits.

DOLPHINS

Anyone who spends a little time in a canoe or motorboat in the warm shallow waters of Florida Bay, Whitewater Bay, or the Gulf Coast is likely to catch a glimpse of these beautiful creatures. Many people are treated to an even grander spectacle when the dolphins approach their boat. Such dolphins are either engrossed in feeding or are curious about the boat. Dolphins will occasionally drive fish into the shallow water around the tiny mangrove islands in Florida Bay, trapping the fish for easy feeding.

The Atlantic bottle-nosed dolphin is the most likely species of cetacean to be seen in these waters. This is the dolphin made famous by the television show "Flipper" that was filmed partly in the Keys. They are extremely intelligent animals; some scientists believe they are even more intelligent than humans.

Don't be alarmed if you find yourself staring at a menu in a seafood restaurant in south Florida and see "dolphin" as the catch of the day. That dolphin is a common fish harvested locally for human consumption. The bottle-nosed dolphin is a mammal that enjoys protection from intentional commercial harvesting. Many people also know it as a porpoise, although it is not a true porpoise.

Dolphins are common in Florida Bay and the Ten Thousand Islands year-round. Canoeists often see them. If you camp on a beach, such as at Cape Sable, Flamingo's walk-in sites, or the island campsites, you may hear a dolphin spouting at night when it surfaces to breathe.

MANATEES

One of the most treasured experiences a naturalist can have in Florida is to see a manatee. You could go to the Seaquarium in Miami or the Epcot Center in Orlando if you want to guarantee a close-up view, or you can take your chances and patience to the shallow south Florida coast and try to see one in the wild.

Manatees may be visible in south Florida any month of the year. The colder the winter, the more likely it is to find them around. They are sensitive to cold water, and a prolonged cold spell may drive them down from farther north in Florida.

Manatees are also known as "sea cows" because they are giant marine mammals that graze on underwater vegetation. They are even more harmless than cattle, because they have no hooves or horns to inflict injury. In fact, manatees are so defenseless and nonaggressive that they fall easy prey to humans. They lack defensive mechanisms because, as adults, they have no natural predators; most of the large sharks remain off-shore in deeper water than the manatees.

The greatest danger to manatees in the last hundred years is from humans. The early settlers in the Keys depended on manatees for fresh meat, since there was little land for raising cattle. A waterway through a patch of mangroves near Plantation Key is known as "Cowpens Cut," because (before refrigeration became a part of Keys life) the local people would trap manatees in the waterway by blocking the ends. The manatees would survive in this cow pen until their captors needed fresh meat.

Manatees are protected from hunting now, but they face more modern dangers. One is from motor boats. Since manatees are mammals, they must breathe air, so they forage in shallow water where they can surface easily to breathe. This puts them squarely in the path of the thousands of motor boats whose deadly propellers and hulls killed 51 in 1989 and 50 in 1990. In 1991, a record 68 manatees died from human-related causes. Out of a population of about 1800 in the U.S., that is a high percentage.

Finding a manatee will be a real challenge. Most manatees in Everglades National Park dwell along the mangrove-lined rivers and creeks between Flamingo and Everglades City. Thus, canoeing the Wilderness Waterway may provide some encounters. Try asking the rangers at Everglades or Biscayne National Parks if any have been seen recently. Occasionally manatees loll around the Flamingo Marina. They also frequent the canals in the Keys where the residents treat them to fresh water from garden hoses. Because we humans have restricted the flow of fresh water coming down from the Everglades into Florida Bay and have destroyed the natural springs, manatees can sometimes be stressed for fresh drinking water. Although it is very tempting to attract a manatee by feeding or watering it, *it is illegal* and should not be done. Feeding and watering causes them to lose fear of humans and linger around canals and docks. This places them dangerously close to boats.

If you are fortunate enough to encounter manatees while you are canoeing, don't panic. They are very docile and will swim sluggishly around you. If you make a sudden move that startles them, you'll be amazed at the energy they will display when they turn tail and flee. It is legal to swim with these gentle giants as long as you do not alter their behavior; for example, you can't cause them to swim in a direction other than that in which they were headed.

ALLIGATORS & CROCODILES

Few creatures in North America evoke as much fear and curiosity as the two largest native reptiles, the American alligator and the American crocodile. So much myth and mystery surrounds them.

Alligators are found from North Carolina to Florida and west across the Gulf states to Texas. They number in the millions. Alligators prefer fresh water, although occasionally they'll be found swimming in salt water around the Ten Thousand Islands, Flamingo, and so on. Crocodiles, which number 500-600 and are endangered, have a limited U.S. range of southern Florida. They prefer salt water, but will occasionally wander into fresh water, never venturing far from the sea.

Differences in appearance are subtle. An alligator's skin color is black (although it often appears and is depicted as green), while a crocodile's is gray. A gator has a wide snout, while a croc has a narrow one with the large fourth tooth from the lower jaw protruding when the mouth is closed.

Neither species is especially dangerous to humans. The local crocs are not the same species as the so-called man-eaters of Australia, Africa, and India. Crocs and gators are generally nonaggressive to humans (see "Alligators" under "Local Precautions").

Alligators disperse during the wet season and may be difficult to locate. During the dry season, they are easily seen at the Anhinga Trail, Eco Pond, Shark Valley, Big Cypress Bend, and Corkscrew Swamp Sanctuary. Crocodiles are quite rare and always difficult to find. Your best, but not necessarily reliable, bet is to drive down Card Sound Road (the road from Florida City to North Key Largo) and stop just before the intersection with SR 905. There is a group of mangrove ponds known as the Crocodile Lakes. Look from the road with binoculars for a croc's head, preferably on a sunny day when the reptiles are basking. Also try the Buttonwood Canal by the Flamingo Marina or West Lake in Everglades National Park.

RAPTORS

Many of the local raptors are familiar to people from other parts of North America because the birds have migrated from those parts. Red-shouldered hawks, kestrels, and ospreys are three examples. Our resident red-shouldered hawks, however, differ slightly in appearance by having very pale heads.

Many raptors pass by the region as they migrate further south to Central and South America. The peninsula of Cape Florida and the string of Florida Keys create the typical bottleneck that concentrates raptors before setting off across the Straits of Florida. Reluctant to leave the thermals, resting places, and prey that the land provides, the migrating raptors often linger around Cape Florida State Recreation Area and Boot Key in Marathon during September and October. A few species of special interest and where to find them are highlighted here.

Snail kites are present in south Florida throughout the year, although most may disperse to Lake Okeechobee and central Florida during periods of extended drought in the Everglades. Look for them along the Tamiami Trail, especially near the Miccosukee restaurant by the Shark Valley entrance to Everglades National Park. Swallow-tailed kites are fairly common between March and August over pinelands and cypress and mangrove swamps.

Peregrine falcons may be seen in winter from the Observation Deck at Flamingo hunting over the mud flats or around concentrations of shorebirds on Cape Sable. Peregrines, merlins, and kestrels are often seen on Cape Florida and in the Keys during October.

Burrowing owls may be seen at Kendall-Tamiami, Homestead General, and Marathon airports. For safety reasons, however, people are not allowed to walk around most parts of the airports. Therefore, get permission from the airport manager before walking off any road or parking lot. A safer way to see burrowing owls is to go to Sombrero Beach in Marathon (if southbound, turn left at K-mart, across from Crane Point Hammock Museum at MM 50). The owls nest at the park from February to August. Observe the ropes around the burrows; you can see into the nests from the ropes.

Ospreys have fortunately recovered since their perilous decline in the 1950s and 1960s. They may be seen anywhere along the sea coast, Florida Bay, canals, lakes, and ponds. They often build their large stick nests atop utility poles; nests can be seen along U.S. 1 in the Keys. The nesting season is from December to May.

Bald eagles also have recovered since suffering the same fate as the ospreys and brown pelicans in the 1950s. Bald eagles can be seen year-round near bodies of water where they hunt for fish or steal prey from ospreys. Eagles nest on the larger islands in Florida Bay and the coastal prairies of Everglades National Park. Bald eagles may be seen around Mahogany Hammock because they roost near there (see Mahogany Hammock under "Everglades National Park").

WADING BIRDS

One of the great attractions the Everglades holds for many people is the promise of seeing large flocks of graceful and colorful egrets, ibises, herons, spoonbills, and storks painting the sky at dusk. The protection of such flocks was one reason part of the region was set aside as a national park.

Prior to human intervention, approximately 100,000 pairs of wading birds nested in the southern Everglades. Now it may be only 10,000 pairs in a good year, a reduction of 90%. Part of the decrease was caused by the practice, in the late 1800s to early 1900s, of killing the birds during the breeding season to collect plumes for sale to the fashion moguls. Some species recovered, but some (like the reddish egret) have maintained low populations. The decrease has primarily been caused by water management practices that altered the quality, quantity, and timing of water that flowed into the Everglades. Those practices still continue and still affect wading birds.

Enough wading birds remain in the Everglades to make a thrilling sight. Species you are most likely to see are: great blue heron, great white heron, great egret, snowy egret, little blue heron, tricolored heron, green-backed heron, black-crowned night heron, white ibis, roseate spoonbill, and wood stork. A small group of flamingos occasionally feeds in the mud flats off Snake Bight and Sandy Key in northwest Florida Bay, but this is the northern edge of their range and their occurrences here are sporadic. Debate exists over the origin of the flamingos in Everglades National Park; they may be escapees from a tourist attraction or wanderers from Cuba or the Bahamas.

The best time to see wading birds is from November to June, when the decreasing water level concentrates the birds around their aquatic prey, and winter migrants are also present. The best places to look are the mud flats at Flamingo, Eco Pond at dawn or dusk, the Shark Valley Tower Road, the Ten Thousand Islands at Everglades City, the Anhinga Trail, and the "18-Mile Stretch" of U.S. 1 between MM 108 and MM 111. Wood storks usually nest at Corkscrew Swamp Sanctuary from January to June. If local foraging or water conditions prevent nesting, they should still be in the area.

EXOTIC ANIMALS AND PLANTS

For several reasons, south Florida is host to scores of plant and animal species that are not native to the area. These are known to biologists as exotic species. Some of these live nearly innocuous lives, but the majority interfere with the native ecological balance. A few are extreme pests that must be eliminated or we will face ecological disaster.

One reason for exotic animal presence is that Miami is a major port of entry from Central and South America and the West Indies. Animals intended for the pet trade occasionally escape while docked or are released by the shippers if the animals were illegally obtained and the authorities are closing in. Another reason is that the mild climate allows many people to keep exotic pets in screened-in porches year-round, so there is a high concentration of exotic pets. Occasionally these escape or are released when the owners tire of caring for them. Many of these animals can survive and even reproduce around the Miami suburbs. Some exotic animals survive because the plants they feed on here were also introduced from their native land.

Parrots, snakes, and lizards are three types of animals that seem to take to the Miami suburbs with ease. Great flocks of monk parrots, budgerigars, canary-winged parakeets, yellow-headed parrots, and red-crowned parrots (some of which destroy fruit crops) can be found in the skies and trees of greater Miami. Also established are muscovy ducks, red-whiskered bulbuls, and hill and common mynas. Established lizards include brown anoles, Cuban knight anoles, Mediterranean geckos, ashy geckos, and tokay geckos. Other exotic herps found in the area include the marine toad, boa constrictor, and python. The only widely established exotic snake is the Brahminy blind snake. The brown anole seems to have outcompeted the native green anole in this area; the former is rampant, while the latter is rarely seen.

Plants are introduced from tropical and subtropical areas around the world and are cultivated in south Florida gardens. Most of the trees and shrubs in Miami and other south Florida cities are exotic, often planted for their colorful flowers. A number of plants were introduced for functions that were desirable at the time, such as coastal windbreaks and swamp straws (a sarcastic nickname for the melaleuca, a tree that sucks up more than its share of water from the ground). These formerly "beneficial" plants have now been deemed pests.

Three exotic plants make the local conservationists' "most wanted to kill" list. They are melaleuca, Brazilian pepper, and Australian-pine.

Melaleuca (also called punk tree or cajeput) was introduced to Miami in 1906 during the early swamp-draining era. A striking tree with papery white bark, melaleuca can soak up as much as five times more water through its roots than our native vegetation can. Seeds of this tree were allegedly broadcast-spread by air over the Everglades in the 1930s to facilitate draining the marsh. A large stand of melaleucas can steal water from and crowd out native plants, thereby out-competing them. Its phenomenal growth and reproductive rates, coupled with the variety of habitats it can grow in and the difficulty in killing it, make melaleuca one of the most formidable enemies the Everglades faces today. Currently, there are no known methods of large-scale eradication of these swamp straws, except for herbicides. Fortunately, melaleuca was added to the Federal Noxious Weed List in 1992, the first "weed" to be added in over 12 years. Henceforth, transportation of the plant into the U.S. and between states requires a permit from the U.S. Department of Agriculture and other restrictions to prevent its spread. Stands of melaleuca can be seen along Krome Avenue between Homestead and the Tamiami Trail and along the Tamiami Trail west of Krome.

Brazilian pepper is a fast-growing, quick-spreading small tree from Brazil. Its clusters of bright red berries do provide food for raccoons, robins, and other animals, but this benefit does not outweigh the detrimental properties. It grows as an extraordinarily dense under-story tree, impenetrable by all but the smallest animals. Brazilian pepper is now one of the most common plants along the roadsides of Ever-glades National Park and the Keys as well as the interior regions, where it is also called Florida holly. Once Brazilian pepper becomes estab-lished, it is virtually impossible to eradicate, since it is resistant to fires, floods, and droughts. The seeds are spread effectively by the birds and mammals that feed on the fruits.

Australian-pine, also known as Casuarina, is from Australia but is not a true pine. Its wispy needles and small cone-like fruits are reminiscent of pine trees. Australian-pines were introduced as soil retainers and windbreaks along the coast and canals. They, too, outcompete native trees but their weak branches make nesting risky for large birds, such as swallow-tailed kites. Kites prefer to nest on the native slash pines. The roots of Australian-pine growing along the beaches interfere with sea turtle and crocodile nesting. Australian-pine seeds are valueless as wildlife food.

The National Park Service and state and county agencies have exotic plant removal programs aimed at these three species plus many more. It's a never-ending battle to eliminate plants that grow faster than they can be removed.

IV.
NATURAL AREAS: THE MAINLAND

EVERGLADES NATIONAL PARK

THE NAME "EVERGLADES" CONJURES up images in tourists' minds of vast tangled jungles with vines and snakes dripping from the trees. Park rangers frequently hear visitors comment, "This isn't like I pictured." Indeed, the Everglades does have vine-covered jungles, but they are not vast, and the snakes don't drip from trees. The "jungles" are mostly in the form of isolated tree islands and mangrove stands. The two major habitat types are the open freshwater marshes and the coastal mangroves.

The Everglades is a unique ecosystem — there is no other like it anywhere in the world. That is why so many people (starting with Ernest Coe in 1928) led the fight to protect it, culminating with its dedication as a national park in 1947.

Many other honors have been bestowed upon it: the park was designated an International Biosphere Reserve in 1976, a World Heritage Site in 1979 (by United Nations Educational, Scientific, and Cultural Organization, "UNESCO"), and a Wilderness of International Significance in 1987; two canoe trails were designated as National Trails in 1981. There is no doubt the Everglades has played and will continue to play a major role in Florida's mental and environmental health.

Everglades National Park plays another unique role. It was the first national park to be established at the mouth of a water system, rather than at the source. Most parks are at the headwaters of rivers (like Glacier, Yellowstone, Grand Teton, and Yosemite), where the water is pure and the main administrative problem is the overabundance of visitors. Everglades National Park is at the end of a water system that has environmental insults thrown at it every step of the way, causing major ecological problems.

Less than 20 percent of the original Everglades region is contained within the park boundaries. The included area encompasses 1,506,309 acres of wilderness: 572,200 acres of marsh, 220,200 acres of coastal areas, 230,100 acres of mangroves, and 484,200 acres of Florida Bay and the Gulf of Mexico. This total acreage includes the newest addition (dedicated in 1989) to Everglades National Park, the "East Everglades," a 107,600-acre freshwater marsh northwest of Homestead. This undeveloped area was cut off from the natural flow of water by levees and canals, which in turn blocked water to Shark and Taylor Sloughs. The acquisition of this land will mean sheet flow can be restored, and it is a major step toward saving the Everglades. Included in the newly acquired area is the former Chekika State Recreation Area in Homestead.

Fifteen species of animals found in the park are endangered. They are the American crocodile, green turtle, Atlantic Ridley turtle, hawksbill turtle, leatherback turtle, peregrine falcon, Cape Sable seaside sparrow, snail kite, southern bald eagle, wood stork, Florida panther, West Indian manatee, Key Largo wood rat, Key Largo cotton mouse, and Schaus' swallowtail butterfly. The red-cockaded woodpecker has been extirpated from the park. The rich variety of plants and animals includes approximately 400 species of birds, 25 mammals, 60 amphibians and reptiles, 125 fish, 120 trees, and 1000 flowering plants. More than 25 types of orchids grow in the park.

The 137-mile coastline attracts many people for the saltwater fishing. Others come for the excitement of seeing alligators, flocks of wood storks, and other fascinating animals. Still others come to camp in the solitude of the Ten Thousand Islands. Visitation has steadily increased from 123,405 people in 1950 to 1,002,109 in 1990.

The duration of your stay depends on how much time you have, since you can easily fill a two-week stay. If you have only a day in the winter, you should at least see the Anhinga and Gumbo Limbo Trails at Royal Palm. If you have only a day in the summer, you may be better off canoeing away from land and the mosquitoes at Flamingo or taking a boat trip to the Ten Thousand Islands at Everglades City. A two-day trip should include an overnight stay at the quiet outpost of Flamingo, with a canoe trip or boat tour. Hopefully, you will have at least a week, with time to see Royal Palm, Flamingo, Shark Valley, and Everglades City. Take advantage of the ranger-led trips and programs to learn about the Everglades. Wildlife observing, canoeing, fishing, hiking, and photographing opportunities are excellent.

During your visit, keep these regulations in mind: 1) All plants and animals (whole or part) are protected and collection is not permitted. An exception is fish, because fishing is allowed in the park. Another exception is that a maximum of one quart of unoccupied sea shells may be collected per person per day (check carefully for hermit crabs inside). As the National Park Service says, "Take only pictures, leave only footprints." 2) Do not feed the wildlife, because it creates nuisance or dangerous animal situations.

Because of the magnitude of the park's resources and facilities, each area will be described separately below.

Location, Mailing Address and Phone

There are four land entrances (Florida City, Shark Valley, Everglades City, Chekika). Key Largo is currently just a ranger station, although plans are in the works for an Interpretive Center there in the future. The main park entrance is west of Florida City on SR 9336 about 10 miles southwest of the intersection of SW 344th St. (Palm Dr.) and U.S. 1. Chekika, Everglades City, Flamingo, Long Pine Key, Royal Palm, and Shark Valley are regions of the park that are covered separately below.

P.O. Box 279, Homestead, FL 33030 (305) 242-7700. This address is for all regions and entrances of the park.

Facilities and Activities

Camping, nature trails, hiking trails, birding, canoeing, boat tours, tram tours, boat and canoe rentals, bicycle rentals, ranger activities, freshwater and saltwater fishing, boating, lodging and restaurant, wildlife observation areas, bicycling, visitor centers, marina, gift shops. There are no airboat tours in the park.

Literature is available in Spanish, German, and French at the main and Shark Valley Visitor Centers. Visitors should stop at the Visitor Center serving the area they are about to explore to gather the tour schedules, trail maps, and other helpful materials. A handout called "Accessibility" will help handicapped people to get the most from the park's facilities. Visitor Centers are at the main park entrance, Royal Palm, Flamingo, Shark Valley, and Everglades City. In the near future, Chekika will have a fully functioning visitor center. Operations (such as tours and naturalist programs) are reduced during the summer, so call ahead to confirm schedules.

Camping

Three campgrounds, one at Long Pine Key, one at Flamingo, and one at Chekika, provide basic camping facilities. Winter camping stays are limited to 14 days and summer camping is limited to 30 days. Although the campgrounds are open year-round, the summer heat, insects, and thunderstorms can be intense. Few people brave an overnight camping stay. Summer camping (approximately May 1 to mid-November) is free, but tentsites are reduced in number (never a problem) and ranger assistance is reduced.

Long Pine Key

The Long Pine Key campground turnoff is located 3.8 miles past the Entrance Station on the Main Park Road. There are 108 sites, each with a picnic table and grill. There are scattered drinking water spigots but no camper hookups for water, electricity, or sewage. A sewage dumping station is located at the campground entrance. Bathrooms are handicapped accessible. There are no showers.

Camping is pleasant under the shady slash pine trees. You're more likely to be kept awake by a barred owl than by your neighboring campers. The lake next to the loop road usually has alligators. Several hiking trails through the pinelands originate from the campground.

Flamingo

At the end of the Main Park Road, past the Visitor Center complex and lodge, is another campground. It is divided into two sections: the 235 drive-in sites and the 60 walk-in sites. The drive-in sites are similar to Long Pine Key in that you drive your car to your site. The sites are more open and sunny than Long Pine Key. Each site has a table and grill. There are no hookups, but there is a sewage dumping station. This is the only camping area that has showers. But be prepared — they are cold water only and they are "open air," so take your shower before a cold front hits! The bathrooms are handicapped accessible, and drinking water spigots are provided.

The walk-in sites are great for car-camping. Picture a large grassy field sprinkled with palm trees, perched next to Florida Bay. The parking lot where you leave your car is at most a few hundred yards away. You can pick a spot near your car or near the bay. From your tentsite, you can see reddish egrets dancing drunkenly for prey in the shallow water, a bald eagle stealing food from an osprey overhead, a cornsnake sliding down from an arboreal hiding place, and dolphins spouting plumes of vapor as they surface. Redbellied woodpeckers love the coconut palms and can easily be identified by their trilling calls. Each site has a grill and table, and bathrooms are nearby. Don't leave any food unattended on your picnic table or you will learn just how fast turkey vultures, crows, and raccoons can steal a sandwich. Walk-in sites are closed in summer.

Chekika

This newly-acquired campground is reached from SR 997 in Homestead. There are 20 sites, obtained on a first-come basis. There is a group site for which a reservation can be made.

Backcountry Sites

There are 48 designated primitive backcountry sites, accessible only by canoe or motor boat, from Everglades City to Flamingo. These are either chickees, ground sites, or beach sites.

Chickees (named after the Miccosukee word for house) are 10-foot by 12-foot wooden platforms on stilts over water, in areas where there is no high ground available. They are suitable for self-supporting tents or open-air sleeping. The chickees have roofs and chemical toilets. The maximum group size is six people. Some are double chickees, with enough room for two groups. There is even one chickee at Pearl Bay (a four-mile canoe trip from the Main Park Road) that is adapted for wheelchairs: it has an accessible toilet, railings, stair ramp, and a boat slip for canoe stability.

The ground sites are on relatively high ground away from the coast. Some are located on old Indian middens (like Willy Willy), which is the reason the ground is higher there. They have docks, chemical toilets, and picnic tables, but no pavilions. Beach sites are on beautiful shell beaches, with open views and cooling breezes, but no tables and most have no toilets — a good trade-off! Remember to pitch your tent above the high tide line.

The backcountry sites are within easy canoeing distance from each other (some are as little as a mile apart). However, conditions can be difficult (high winds, strong currents, heavy rains, getting lost), so you must get a backcountry permit from a ranger. These are free and are available at the Flamingo and Everglades City Ranger Stations.

Camping is permitted in Florida Bay at three sites only: North Nest Key, Carl Ross Key, and Rabbit Key. These are beach sites and the permits may be obtained free from Flamingo or Key Largo Ranger Stations. Length of stay limits vary for each site from one to seven nights during the peak visitor season (December 1 to April 30). During the summer, mosquitoes and no-see-ums can make camping unbearable, so visitation drops off; however, you still need a permit. Call the Key Largo Ranger Station (305-852-5119) to inquire about permits.

Campfires are permitted only at some beach sites below the storm surge line. Driftwood on the ground may be used for fires. At all other sites, fires are permitted only in camping stoves; no grills are provided at the sites. Particularly at the ground and beach sites, raccoons spell trouble for your food — they are relentless in their pursuit of it. You should have a hard-sided cooler (styrofoam does not work) or a way to keep food out of reach of the raccoons. Raccoons will also chew through soft-sided water containers, particularly in the dry season.

Lodging

The only lodging within the park is at Flamingo. All other main visitor areas are near enough to towns to be easily accessible to motels.

The Flamingo Lodge, located between the marina and the camp-ground at Flamingo, offers 102 air-conditioned modern rooms with full services (phone 305-253-2241 or 813-695-3101). The screened-in pool, for lodge guests only, represents the only safe swimming in the park (gators and sharks prevent swimming in the fresh and salt waters, respectively). The lodge also maintains 24 cottages, with separate bedrooms and living rooms, that are excellent for families. Each cottage contains a fully-equipped kitchen (refrigerator, stove, oven, sink, dishes, dish towel and soap, utensils), so you need only bring your food. A laundromat with coin machines allows guests to do their own laundry. Due to the lack of visitors in the summer, only part of the lodge remains open. The full-service dates are November 1 to April 30, and reduced services are May to October. The peak rates are from December 15 to April 30, lower rates are November 1 to December 14, and lowest rates are May 1 to October 31. Summer weekend rates are slightly higher than weekday rates. No pets are allowed in the lodge or cottages.

The restaurant at Flamingo flaunts a spectacular view of Florida Bay, with eagles, pelicans, and egrets visible during dining (theirs and yours). It is the only restaurant this author keeps a bird list for! The atmosphere is so relaxing and unique that people drive from Miami just to have dinner here. Reservations are required. Make them early in the day, because they fill up fast and you may have a very late dinner. But, like the lodge, summer visitation drops off too much, so the restaurant has reduced service from May 1 to October 31. Salads, pizza, sand-wiches and drinks are available year-round at the Buttonwood Lounge (located beneath the restaurant) and the marina serves snacks.

Fishing

About one third of Everglades National Park is water, and fishing has always been popular. Noncommercial fishing is permitted in the park and must follow park fishing regulations. A freshwater license is needed to fish in Nine-Mile Pond and all waters northward along the Main Park Road or to possess freshwater fish caught in brackish waters. This license must be purchased outside the park, since none are sold within the park. You will need a saltwater license for Florida Bay, the Gulf of Mexico, Long Sound, Little Blackwater Sound, and Blackwater

Sound. You can purchase a saltwater license at the Flamingo Marina (same phone as Flamingo Lodge above).

Due to mercury found in largemouth bass, a problem the park scientists and administrators are currently investigating, the park has issued the following warning: "Do not eat bass caught north of the Main Park Road. Do not eat bass caught south of the Main Park Road more than once a week. Children and pregnant women should not eat any bass." This warning does not apply to saltwater fish. Some of the main freshwater ponds are posted with warning signs. Too bad the otters and gators can't read.

Areas closed to fishing because they are strictly wildlife observation ponds include the ponds by the main Visitor Center and Royal Palm Visitor Center area and trails, Taylor Slough, Mrazek Pond, Eco Pond, along the Shark Valley tram road, and at the Flamingo Marina during daylight hours.

The lucky saltwater angler may land any one of the following fish: snook, spotted seatrout, redfish, mangrove snapper, sheepshead, and black drum. Tarpon, ladyfish, and shark are also good possibilities, as well as dozens of other species. Guides are available for hire by calling the Flamingo Marina.

Boating

The boat ramps located at Flamingo (Florida Bay side and Buttonwood Canal side), Little Blackwater Sound, Paurotis Pond, West Lake, and Everglades City are free. Southern Florida Bay is accessible from the Keys via boat ramps at marinas or at public ramps and may not be free.

Some areas are off-limits to boats (including canoes). Boats are prohibited from landing on all of the little mangrove islands in Florida Bay, with the exceptions of Carl Ross, Little Rabbit, North Nest, and Bradley Keys (Bradley Key only during daylight hours). This is to protect the nesting birds and other wildlife. A crocodile refuge exists in northeast Florida Bay; therefore, there are seasonal restrictions on when boats are allowed in the waters of Little Madeira and Joe Bays or in the waters of the back bays from Little Madeira Bay east to U.S. 1. Boats are allowed to land on any of the keys in the Ten Thousand Islands, except the southern part of Pavilion Key.

Motors are prohibited from some parts of the park, including all freshwater lakes. Prohibited brackish areas include: the canoe trails of Bear Lake, Noble Hammock, Coot Bay Pond, and Mud Lake; Raulerson's Marsh, the southern part of Hell's Bay canoe trail, and the creek at the southeastern end of West Lake through to Garfield Bight. On West

Lake, only motors of 5.5 horsepower or less are permitted. "No Wake" zones exist around Everglades City, Flamingo, and Key Largo and must be observed. Waterskiing and "jet-skiing" are prohibited throughout the park. Coast Guard regulations require that all watercraft carry a personal flotation device, quickly accessible, for each person on board.

The Marina at Flamingo, operated by TW Services, has slips with water and electric hookups for at least 50 boats. It also has gas pumps at the dock. Skiffs and canoes can be rented at the Marina.

Birding

The vastness of the park, the warm climate, and the rich variety of habitats and plants contribute to the exceptional birding enjoyed by visitors to Everglades National Park. As of 1990, the park's bird list included 350 species. Birds from temperate North America and the tropical Caribbean thrive in South Florida. Tropical storms blow accidentals from far out at sea.

There is no telling where an interesting bird may show up. The following easily accessible places are the most reliable to start with: Anhinga Trail, Mahogany Hammock, West Lake, Snake Bight Trail, the mud flats in front of the Flamingo Visitor Center, Eco Pond, and the Shark Valley Tram Road.

The use of audiotape recordings to attract birds is prohibited within the park. Such tapes interfere with the birds' natural activities.

Pets

Must be on a six-foot leash, must not be left unattended; not allowed on trails, in buildings, in amphitheaters, or on boat and tram tours.

MAIN PARK ENTRANCE

From the north: take Florida's Turnpike Extension south to the end in Florida City. Turn right onto SW 344th St. (Palm Dr.) and follow the signs on SR 9336 to Everglades National Park. From the Keys: Take U.S. 1 to first traffic light in Florida City at SW 344th St. (Palm Dr.), turn left and follow the signs on SR 9336.

Facilities and Activites

Visitor Center

The Visitor Center is located on the right, before the Entrance Station, and is open 8:00 AM to 5:00 PM daily. Information for any part of the park can be obtained here. A large selection of books about the Everglades (natural and human history) is for sale. In the auditorium a 15-minute movie on the Everglades is presented and there is a large display of tree snail shells.

Outside the Visitor Center are two marshy ponds that attract many birds. Spend a few minutes, especially early in the morning, and you might see alligators, wading birds, and ospreys, with swallow-tailed kites present from March to August. Also visit the native plant garden by the parking lot. This is a good place to take a restroom break before heading to Flamingo.

ROYAL PALM

Enter the park from Florida City on SR 9336. Turn left off the Main Park Road about two miles past the Entrance Station.

Facilities and Activities

Visitor center, birding and other wildlife viewing, nature trails, photographic opportunities.

Royal Palm was the nucleus of the new national park in 1947. It was the site of the first state park in Florida, formed in 1916 by the Florida Federation of Women's Clubs to preserve the fabulous hammock at Paradise Key with its stately native royal palms. The state gave it to the National Park Service in 1947.

Visitor Center

Static displays by the very creative artist Charles Harper illustrate the intricate web of life in Taylor Slough. You must look closely at each display to catch all the characters in the web. It will take only 5 or 10 minutes to study the displays ---and don't forget to look at the ceiling. The attached small gift shop sells Everglades books, field guides, and souvenirs. Restrooms are available. Vending machines dispense snacks and drinks.

Anhinga Trail

Certainly the most famous trail in the park, the Anhinga Trail is one of the most famous trails in the National Park system. One of the reasons is the ease in reaching it from a major metropolitan area. Another is the ease of walking it. Most thrilling of all is the reward of fantastic views of wildlife found few other places in the country.

What makes this trail so attractive to wildlife? If you look on the official Everglades National Park map, you'll see that Taylor Slough flows through the Royal Palm area. The slough is a region of slightly deeper water than the surrounding area. During the dry season, much of the water in the Everglades disappears through evaporation, transpiration, and run-off to the sea. Water always remains in the sloughs, like Taylor and Shark River sloughs. Wildlife is forced to concentrate around these watering holes.

The Anhinga Trail passes right over the water where these concentrations are. Through the years, the animals have become habituated to the presence of humans on the trail. They seem to know that the wingless two-legged creatures stay within a certain territory and won't bother them. In fact, the anhinga (the bird the trail was named for), even nests within plain view of the trail! Visitors have observed courtship displays, eggs, fluffy pink chicks, and awkward fledglings without disturbing the birds.

The wildlife concentrations begin around November or December, depending on the local water levels. From January to April, visitors may be treated to excellent views of alligators, frogs, snakes, turtles, gar fish, ospreys, anhingas, herons, bitterns, raccoons, deer, marsh rabbits, and much more. The anhingas generally nest beginning in January or February. Look for these birds swimming gracefully underwater, then watch them climb onto a branch and spread their wings to dry and warm themselves. During the winter, the pond at the start of the trail is a sure place to find alligators.

The trail is only a half mile long, but you won't want to hurry around it. Most of the trail is actually a boardwalk. The only part over dry land is where the old Ingraham Highway (the original route of the Homestead-to-Flamingo road) passed. Notice the cypress dugout canoe in the pond by the Visitor Center. You can watch anhingas spear bass underwater, purple gallinules step lightly on lily pads and rummage for insects, and soft-shelled turtles glide silently by. Look for black racers, rough green snakes, and water snakes. Short-tailed hawks have been seen soaring overhead from October to March.

You will be comforted to know that, since the trail is mostly open, mosquitoes are less pesky here than on most other trails in the park. The trade-off is that it is often very hot in the sun. So, just as mamma says not to salt your food before you taste it, refrain from applying insect repellent until you get to the trail and are sure you'll need it. Bring a sun hat and sun block, though.

The openness of the trail is due to the fact that it courses through the sawgrass marsh. This is an excellent place to see sawgrass close up and even touch it. Beware of its telltale name — the blade's edge can cut your skin like a knife. Other common plants are willow, cocoplum, and pond apple.

Photographing opportunities are wonderful, and you don't even need a long telephoto lens (unless you want a photo of an alligator's eye). Because the habitat is open, slow-speed film is usually sufficient. An inexpensive instant-type camera will work well here.

Check the announcement board by the Visitor Center for the schedule of ranger activities. Rangers give talks in the shade by the benches and lead groups around the trail every day. This trail is easily accessible to the handicapped. No bicycles allowed.

Gumbo Limbo Trail

A few yards to the right of the start of the Anhinga Trail is the beginning of the Gumbo Limbo Trail. Quite the opposite of the Anhinga Trail, the Gumbo Limbo is cool, shady, and buggy. This narrow paved footpath, also a half mile long, wanders through the Paradise Key hammock. The hammock is densely vegetated by West Indian hardwood hammock trees, orchids, bromeliads, ferns, and lianas, lending a jungle feel to the trail. Look for tree snails, anole lizards, and golden orb-weaver spiders. Some common plants are strangler fig, lancewood, poisonwood, wild-tamarind, and pigeon-plum.

The unusual name of this trail comes from a tree of the same name. Plenty of gumbo-limbos inhabit the hammock, displaying their satiny bronze bark to the visitors. Although the hammock is lush with epiphytic plants, you won't find them attached to gumbo-limbos. This is because the bark is smooth and flakes off too easily, like birch bark, so the plants can't get a good grip. Epiphytes like to grow on fissured and firmly attached bark.

Because the vegetation grows densely, the mosquitoes find a haven from intense sun and debilitating breezes in the summer. Photographers will have a more difficult task in capturing the plants and animals on this trail. Most of the animals are the small types (that is, songbirds and tree snails rather than great blue herons and alligators). The filtered sunlight will make metering tricky, and the closeness of the subjects will make focusing harder. Slow-speed film, tripods, and even flash units are handy here. Handicapped accessible. No bicycles.

Best Time of Year

December to April. The anhingas nest from late January to April.

LONG PINE KEY

Enter the park from Florida City on SR 9336. Turn left at the sign for Long Pine Key, 3.8 miles past the Entrance Station on the Main Park Road.

Facilites and Activities

Campground, picnic area, fishing pond, nature trails, and bicycling.

The main draw for people to Long Pine Key is the campground (see "Campgrounds" above). But there are other reasons to go, even if you're not camping. Miles of shady trails offer excellent hiking and bicycling. Botanizing is exceptional, with about 30 species of plants found here and nowhere else. Located in a large stand of slash pines, the habitat is maintained by periodic prescribed burns conducted by the National Park Service.

Long Pine Key Trail

Just before the fee station at the campground entrance is the beginning of this trail. Walk to or park by Gate 4. The gate is locked, and only Park Service vehicles are allowed past it. Human feet, bicycles, and horses are the permitted alternatives. The trail is an unpaved fire road that the rangers occasionally use, so it is wide, hardpacked, and passable by bicycle. In the summer, there can be large puddles from rain and large clouds from mosquitoes. Winter is beautiful hiking weather and the trail will most likely be dry. From Gate 4 to the end of the trail at the Main Park Road (Gate 8), the trail is seven miles long. You can return the same way, walk along the Main Park Road, or find another (but longer) trail back.

The trail heads west from Gate 4. It passes alternately through tall pine stands and open marshes. There are a few turns, and occasional side trails intersect, but the main trail is obvious. Besides the slash pine, you should see the small satinleaf trees, one of the most beautiful tree species in the park. The leaves are dark green above and shiny bronze underneath. When the wind blows, the satiny undersides shine in the sun. Other common species are beauty berry, rough velvetseed, tetrazygia, and willow bustic.

The trail ends at the small Pine Glades Lake, near Gate 8 on the Main Park Road. The lake is open to fishing but is posted with warnings of mercury-contaminated fish. It is five miles along the main road from Pine Glades Lake to the turnoff to Long Pine Key Campground.

Pinelands Trail

This trail is located 2.1 miles west of the entrance to Long Pine Key Campground on the Main Park Road. Look for the sign "Pine Land" with a parking lot on the right. The trail is a half-mile loop through typical slash pine habitat. Although the trail is gentle enough to walk on, the ground beside the trail is treacherous. The soil is shallow, and the limestone substrate rock pokes through numerous places. The limestone is pock-marked from dissolving by rainwater mixed with acidic plant matter. Most solution holes are very small, hardly noticeable. Occasional ones are a foot or more across and several feet deep. Picture the early explorers trying to hike across this unforgiving land. The larger solution holes serve as refuges during the dry season for small fish and other aquatic organisms. The holes may be the only places left with drinking water for deer, panther, northern bobwhite quail, and other terrestrial creatures.

The predominant shrub-like palm forming the understory is saw palmetto. Look also for tetrazygia, wild-tamarind, satinleaf, and beauty berry. The trail is punctuated with interpretive signs about the plants and animals. Handicapped people should use caution, since the solution holes are not railed off.

Other Trails

Several other trails originate at the Long Pine Key Campground. One starts at Gate 3, directly opposite the gate for the Long Pine Key Trail above. This trail runs east, with two right turns along the way. The first right turn takes you on a three-mile round-trip hike. The second right is a five-mile round-trip. Both require walking a short distance on a paved road (Research Center Road).

Research Center Road

Formerly called "Long Pine Key Road" by the locals, this 4-mile stretch of paved road (accessible from Royal Palm Road) leads to the Research Center for Everglades National Park. The Research Center is the working office for the many biologists and hydrologists who are seeking ways to understand and protect the Everglades. There is nothing for a visitor to see in either of the two buildings at the end of Research Center Road, and the presence of visitors may distract the staff.

The road is of interest to people looking for wildlife. You may see a white-tailed deer, bobwhite quail, gray fox, pygmy rattlesnake, Everglades racer, barn owl, or glass lizard. Panthers and black bears have been seen on this road within the last few years. However, there may be no more panthers in this area now. The road is a popular wildlife crossing, so keep the 45 mph maximum speed limit in mind at all times. Rangers patrol this road (and other park roads) frequently for speeding cars. Even at 45 mph, you will miss a lot of the wildlife, so it is better to keep your speed slower. Unfortunately, too many wild animals have become victims of four-wheeled predators.

Hidden Lake

Named for its seclusion, this lake is not on the main tourist list. You can find it by turning off the Main Park Road onto the Royal Palm Road, then turning right towards the Research Center Road, and going straight past the turnoff for the Research Center (see sign for Hidden Lake). The road becomes unpaved. Look for Gate 13 off the left side of the road 0.3 miles past the turnoff to Research Center Road. Park your car and walk the short distance in to the pond. The pond is good for quiet wildlife observations. There are no facilities, no interpretive signs, and no provisions for handicapped people. Programs at the nearby Interpretive Center are by reservation only.

Old Ingraham Highway

The original highway, built in 1922, was the first land link to Flamingo. Before that, Flamingo residents traveled by boat, usually to Key West for supplies. When the Park Service rerouted part of the road, they closed this section to vehicular traffic. It is now a good hiking and bicycling road.

To find the start of the road, turn off the Main Park Road at Royal Palm, make the first right (as if you're going to the Research Center), but keep going straight past Research Center Road. Pass the gate for Hidden Lake on the unpaved road. At one mile past the turnoff for Research Center Road, Gate 15 crosses the road and blocks through traffic for vehicles. The only vehicles allowed are the Park Service and utility companies (the latter maintain the power lines along the road). Start from the gate on foot or bicycle. The flat graded road is suitable even for touring bikes. The road continues for 11 miles.

This road through the marsh would not be here but for the grace of the canal that parallels the road, created by digging for fill. Look through the trees on the north side of the road and you will see the canal. The canal is the reason you may see semi-aquatic animals cross your path, such as otters, alligators, water snakes, anhingas, and turtles. It's a good hike to take in the dry season, when wildlife is concentrated around watering holes.

At the end of the road, the trail appears to end. However, the persistent hiker can continue on a small foot path for three more miles to the Main Park Road at Sweet Bay Pond. Bicyclists will have a difficult, but not impossible, time getting through. It will probably be necessary to walk your bike at least part way. These last three miles were bulldozed to allow the water to flow across the marsh. The power lines disappear underground here. Don't attempt this last three-mile section unless it is a very dry year.

MAIN PARK ROAD FROM ROCK REEF PASS TO BUTTONWOOD CANAL

Stay on the Main Park Road from the Main Park entrance.

Facilities and Activities

Many people see Everglades National Park only from a road, usually from this one. The National Park Service has established stops along the road at all the main habitat types to provide people with convenient places to view the land. Some of the stops have only interpretive signs, but some have trails with interpretive signs. Allow extra time on your drive to Flamingo to stop at these trails. The distances given below in brackets are measured from the Entrance Station.

Rock Reef Pass

[10.7 miles]

This is marked by a sign on the road bragging that the elevation is three feet. Although Coloradoans may snicker, this is not an insignificant landmark. In this flat land, just barely above sea level, *every inch* counts. On both sides of the road, the trees grow on this narrow strip of higher land. From the air, this narrow band of trees looks like an anaconda snaking through the marsh. It is the slight extra elevation above the adjacent marsh that keeps the trees' roots dry enough to grow here and not in the adjacent marsh. Changes in the Everglades are indeed subtle!

Pa-hay-okee Overlook

[12.2 miles]

A short boardwalk (0.2 miles) leads to a two-story observation platform that overlooks the sawgrass prairie. In fact, the name Pa-hay-okee means "Grassy Waters" in the Seminole language. The panoramic view includes tree islands (hammocks), wading birds, and hawks. It is an excellent spot for using your binoculars, spotting scope, and camera. At certain times of the year, brush fires and thunderstorms can be seen in the distance.

Along the boardwalk leading to the platform, look over the railing into the sawgrass for the white shells of the apple snails (*Pomacea paludosa*) about 1.5 inches in diameter. These are the famed snails that the endangered snail kites feed on exclusively.

Interpretive signs explain the ecology of the sawgrass prairie. The observation platform is not accessible to wheelchairs, although the short trail to the base of the platform is.

Along the Main Park Road near Pa-hay-okee Overlook, you will start to see stunted cypress trees. These are dwarf pond-cypresses (a variety of bald-cypress) that may be over 100 years old but only 15 feet tall. Their growth is limited by the depth of water there; generally, the taller cypresses grow in deeper water. You can bet that where you see taller cypresses next to shorter ones, the water is deeper under the taller ones. Most visitors see these trees in the winter when they lack their foliage. The needles are dropped in the autumn at the start of the dry season, theoretically to conserve moisture.

Mahogany Hammock

[19.3 miles]

To many people, Mahogany Hammock is what the Everglades is supposed to look like — dense and jungly, with vines strangling every tree. This is a fascinating trail, one of the most interesting places in the park that's easily accessible. The trail is actually a boardwalk, a half-mile long, through the interior of one of the largest tropical hardwood hammocks in the park. The hammock's name is derived from

Mahogany

the huge mahogany tree along the boardwalk that is the U.S. champion (that is, the largest mahogany in the United States). There are also numerous smaller mahoganies in the hammock.

At the "doorway" into the hammock, notice the clump of skinny palms with fan-shaped leaves on the right side. These are the state-threatened paurotis palms, native to southern Florida and restricted to the transitional (brackish) marshes between the fresh water and the estuary.

Notice the bromeliads, orchids, and ferns growing in the upper branches of the mahoganies and live oaks. This microhabitat of plants creates places for tree frogs, anoles, insects, and snakes to find food, water, and hiding places without ever descending to the ground. Most of the ferns in the upper branches are resurrection ferns. In the dry season, these ferns dehydrate and wither into brown leaves that look dead. But a soaking rainfall will saturate these plants and allow them to "resurrect" into vibrant, green, growing plants.

As you stroll through the hammock, keep an eye peeled for anoles, warblers, and tree snails. The snails may be on a tree trunk or on the boardwalk. Don't even touch a tree snail, for touching it may cause it to break its moisture seal, which in the dry season will kill it. In winter, white-crowned pigeons are occasionally found feeding here; they are common in the summer. The hammock is also a reliable place to see and hear barred owls. Be patient, and look and listen quietly for them.

If you visit in the dry season, you will see vines, ferns, bromeliads, and orchids, and the hammock will look quite dense. However, the summer rains really spur the growth in the hammock, and the lush vegetation in July, August, and September is phenomenal.

From June to September be prepared for mosquitoes. The boardwalk is accessible by wheelchair; proceed counterclockwise for easiest approach to the two moderately steep inclines.

The pines across the Main Park Road from Mahogany Hammock are a traditional roost for bald eagles. At dawn, they depart the pines, heading south to the lakes and bays. At dusk, they return from the south, and you should see the eagles as they approach. December and January are the best months and evening is the best time for viewing the eagles.

In the summer, a few sandhill cranes return to the marsh around Mahogany Hammock. Look for them along the Main Park Road near the Mahogany Hammock turnoff.

Paurotis Pond

[23.9 miles]

This small artificial pond was named for the paurotis palms on the island. The pond has a ramp for small hand-propelled boats. A boat is only needed to get you onto the water for fishing, since you can't go anywhere with it. There are picnic tables at the pond's edge. This pond is more a fishing pond than anything else, although you can't eat the bass due to mercury contamination (see "Fishing" on page 66 above).

West Lake

[30.3 miles]

A nature trail and canoe trail originate here; see page 85 for canoeing information. The nature trail is a boardwalk (less than 0.5 miles long) that bisects a mangrove stand. The four tree species collectively known as mangroves can be seen from the boardwalk. During the wet season, this section can be very buggy. The boardwalk ventures out onto the open water of West Lake. The breeze can be very refreshing. So can the view in late winter, with hundreds of ducks of at least half a dozen species. Alligators, coots, and wading birds are commonly seen. In fact, West Lake is a great place to sit and watch the water — a lot goes on because of the abundant life beneath the water's surface. Redfish, snook, mullet, and other fish need this brackish lake for feeding.

Interpretive signs along the trail explain the mangrove ecosystem. The only restroom facilities between Long Pine Key and Flamingo are located here (handicapped accessible). The trail is handicapped accessible (one moderately steep incline).

Snake Bight Trail

[32.7 miles]

The old road to Snake Bight formerly served a fishing camp on Florida Bay. The road is 1.8 miles long and terminates at a boardwalk on the edge of Florida Bay. The boardwalk is an exceptional place for birding most of the year. It is tidally influenced, rather than seasonally influenced, meaning you must catch the right tides for good birding. An outgoing or low tide is best; a high tide is worst. Shorebirds and wading birds (including roseate spoonbills) use this shallow, rich, protected edge of the bay as a feeding ground. It is here that the best views of flamingos have been seen from land over recent years.

Along the trail are excellent opportunities to view wildlife. Alligators find this trail a convenient place to rest. If you see one, keep your distance, since it can fool you with its sluggish appearance. Snakes are common, and treefrogs can be found in the bromeliads. Warblers and other birds, such as mangrove cuckoos, are active here. Bobcats prowl frequently. Perhaps the best known inhabitant of the Snake Bight Trail is the mosquito. If mosquitoes are anywhere around, they'll show up here first.

From December to April the road is also used by the concession for tram tours. The trams have mosquito netting over the windows and a narrator to explain the sights. Just prior to the first tram tour of the year, the Park Service mows the vegetation that has grown on the road since the previous year. For several months before the tours commence, vegetation can get tall, so watch out for chiggers. If you want to take the tram tour, inquire at the gift shop at Flamingo. Bicycles permitted.

Mrazek Pond

[33.6 miles]

Park Ranger Vincent Mrazek must have had a glorious view of wading birds as he gazed out over this pond in the 1950s and 1960s. Judging by the activity almost 40 years later, it must have been quite a sight. Mrazek Pond is one of those special birding spots that almost every local birder and every birder who has been to the park knows about. Finding it and getting to it couldn't be easier. The pond is immediately alongside the Main Park Road.

The birds seem to habituate to people watching quietly from the grassy shore, so it's easy to observe them feeding and resting. Some of them get too close to focus a telephoto lens! In fact, Mrazek Pond is known even more as a photographic hotspot than for birding. Probably more photos of wading birds have been published from here than from Anhinga Trail, which is saying a lot. The nice part is that you don't have to lug your camera gear far.

The bad news is that the avian activity doesn't last all year. The peak months are December to March, when water levels in the park are dropping. Sometimes the activity is reduced to a hectic few weeks during those months, when it seems like every wading bird from Cape Sable to Taylor Slough is visiting. You're likely to see great egrets, snowy egrets, great white herons, great blue herons, little blue herons, tricolored herons, roseate spoonbills, wood storks, white ibises, green-backed herons, white pelicans, black skimmers, common moorhens, rails, blue-winged teal and other ducks, alligators, turtles, and maybe even a bobcat. The birds disappear when their feeding frenzies have depleted the fish populations. In drought years, the pond may dry completely in late winter.

This is a wildlife observation pond, so no boating or fishing is permitted. The viewing area is easily handicapped-accessible.

Coot Bay Pond

[34.0 miles]

Just past Mrazek Pond is the small channel, known as Coot Bay Pond, leading from the Main Park Road to Coot Bay. In late winter and spring, it is a good place to watch ducks and wading birds. There are picnic tables and there is a place to launch canoes.

Rowdy Bend Trail

[34.7 miles]

This old road winds through stands of buttonwood trees and coastal prairie for 2.6 miles and ends at the Snake Bight Trail. Buttonwoods were used by the early South Florida settlers for making charcoal for cooking. Cactus and yucca grow here because of the lack of fresh water. Wet and buggy in summer. Not recommended for bicycles.

Christian Point Trail

[36.6 miles]

Remnants of a buttonwood forest are evident along the trail, where the weathered trunks that once surrendered to a hurricane lie prone on the coastal prairie. The trail is 1.8 miles one way and ends at the western part of Snake Bight. Ospreys are usually seen along this trail. Keep your eyes open for a rare indigo snake, the longest snake in Florida. Wet and buggy in summer. Not recommended for bicycles.

Best Time of Year

December to May for the trails; they are usually too buggy and wet the rest of the year.

FLAMINGO

Go to the end of the Main Park Road, 37 miles from the main park entrance.

Flamingo was a quiet fishing village in the late 1800s. No roads led to it; it was accessible only by boat. Families built houses on stilts and farmed small patches of land. A few of the crops they grew were bananas, tomatoes, sugar cane, and squash. They made charcoal from buttonwood trees for shipment to Key West. Every few years a hurricane would level most of the houses and destroy the crops, so the village never grew very large. In fact, after the road from Florida City was completed in 1922 and villagers discovered a way *out*, more people left than arrived. It may go without saying that living with the mosquitoes was pure torture much of the year. Smudge pots inside the houses were a way of life.

Some Flamingo residents made a living by plume hunting. Many of the colonies of birds the plume hunters sought were near Flamingo. Around the turn of the century, the killing of egrets, herons, and spoonbills for their feathers was very lucrative. The long breeding plumes of the great egret brought $32.00 an ounce (more than gold cost). In 1905, National Audubon Society warden Guy Bradley, who lived in Flamingo, was shot to death by plume hunters while protecting a colony of birds. His death stirred a major crusade, sparked several years earlier by women outraged that the birds were killed for so worthless a purpose. In 1910, the governor of New York signed a landmark bill making the sale of plumes illegal in that state. The political attack against the center of the plume market in New York City effectively curtailed much of the slaughter.

The town was named in 1893, when residents had to identify the post office they had requested. Knowing their town was unique and rather hellish, they wanted to name it something exotic and distinctive. A flock of a thousand flamingos, probably from the Bahamas, had been seen on Cape Sable a few years previously and lent their name to the town. Since then, only a handful of flamingos are seen occasionally in Florida Bay.

Since 1947, when the Park Service became caretakers, the village has included only Park Service and concession employees, their families, and tourists.

Facilities and Activities

Campground, lodge, marina, restaurant, nature trails, hiking trails, boat tours, tram tours, bicycling, naturalist programs, canoeing, visitor center, museum, boat rentals, canoe rentals, bicycle rentals, fishing, boating, boat ramps, birding and other wildlife viewing.

During the winter season, the rangers lead numerous walks, slogs, canoe trips, and lectures. At the amphitheater next to the walk-in campsites, expert scientists and naturalists present slide shows every evening. Schedules can be found at the ranger station information desk.

The concession may be contacted (for Flamingo Lodge, boat tours and rentals, canoe and skiff rentals, bike rentals, fishing guides, tram tours, marina and store, restaurant, gift shop) by writing to T.W. Services, Inc., P.O. Box 428, Flamingo, FL 33030 or calling (305) 253-2241 (813-695-3101 from Everglades City).

The campground and lodge were discussed above (see "Camping" and "Lodging").

Marina and Store

The marina is open seven days a week. It offers automobile and boat fuel pumps, boat ramps to the Florida Bay side and to the Buttonwood Canal side, rental skiffs and canoes, and the marina store. The latter is actually a general store. You can buy groceries, basic boating and camping equipment, fishing bait and tackle, books, and souvenirs. The snack bar at the marina store is useful in the summer when the restaurant is closed. You can rent a bicycle or sign up for the boat tours. There are restrooms and showers. Boaters can pay for overnight docking here (electric hook-ups are available).

Canoes and motor skiffs are rentable by the hour, half-day, and full day. Reservations are accepted for canoes. Skiffs may be used only on the Whitewater Bay side (not in Florida Bay). For a total water experience, you can rent a houseboat that sleeps 6-8 people for up to a week. Houseboat renters can rent a canoe for a discount and bring it on the houseboat for exploring shallow places.

Boat Tours

There are three types of boat tours, all operated by the concession (fees charged). The very large capacity "Bald Eagle" and "Pelican" pontoon boats operate in Florida Bay and Whitewater Bay and cruise for two hours. A tour guide explains about Florida Bay and the wildlife you will see. The six-passenger "Osprey" and "Dolphin" seek out the shallower backwaters. The trips on the smaller boats go to Hell's Bay and Joe River and last four hours. The boat captains know where to find interesting wildlife. The sailboat "Windfall" is a 57-foot sloop that sails into Florida Bay for the sunset every evening in the winter. Reservations are required for all boat tours.

Visitor Center Complex

The Visitor Center complex near the marina includes a ranger station, museum, observation deck, and gift shop, as well as the restaurant and lounge. Go to the ranger station if you need to plan a backcountry trip or get a permit. Information on ranger-led activities is also posted there. In summer, the ranger station desk may be closed, and you may have to "self-register" for a backcountry permit. Next to the ranger station is a small museum with exhibits of local Everglades ecology.

The observation deck is a great place to be at low tide. Wading birds and shore birds are abundant and easily observed. Pelicans, ospreys, terns, skimmers, cormorants, and gulls round out the complement of birds. In most years, a pair of bald eagles nest on a small mangrove island just offshore and are visible from the deck. Peregrine falcons hunt for shorebirds and ducks over the mud flats in the winter. Bottle-nosed dolphins are frequently seen in the bay by Flamingo.

The Gift Shop (beneath the restaurant) has a wide assortment of gifts and souvenirs. It is closed in summer, usually from May 1 to October 31. Register for the tram tours to Snake Bight here. The tours run three times a day from about mid-November to Easter. The trip lasts 1 1/2 hours.

Walking Trails
Bear Lake Trail

Go to Bear Lake Road on the west side of the Buttonwood Canal and turn north. The trail head is at the north end of Bear Lake Road, 1.8 miles from the Main Park Road. The trail parallels the Homestead Canal through dense mangroves and other hardwoods. The canal was so named because it connected Cape Sable with Homestead. The fill for the trail was obtained from dredging the canal in the 1920s. Birding will probably be concentrated on passerines and other small woodland birds, particularly warblers in winter. Photography will require fast film and short lenses. The trail is 1.6 miles one way.

Eco Pond

Located between the marina and the campground on the main road, this eight-acre freshwater pond is an excellent place for observing wildlife. The treated effluent from Flamingo is discharged into this shallow evaporation pond. The 0.2-mile loop trail

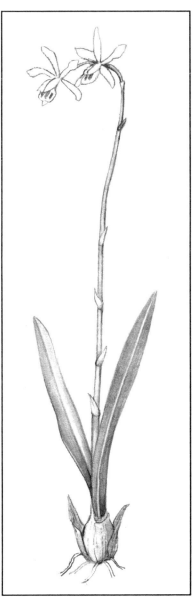

Butterfly orchid

circumnavigates the cattail-dominated pond. From the observation platform at the beginning of the trail, you can watch herons hunting for fish, gators hunting for herons, and raccoons hunting for just about anything. The ramp leading to the observation platform was completed in January 1992 for handicapped-accessibility. Eco Pond is a popular roost for white ibis and roseate spoonbills, so try to be there at sunset or sunrise. Look for rails, smooth-billed anis, painted buntings, baby gators, frogs, and bobcat tracks around the pond. Fishing is reserved for the animals.

Guy Bradley Trail

If you're looking for a shortcut by foot or bicycle from the campground to the marina, take this one-mile trail located at the eastern end of the campground, by the amphitheater. It meanders partly along the shore and gives a good view of the mud flats at low tide where you may see a reddish egret. Marsh rabbits often feed along the trail.

Bayshore Loop

This trail begins at the very western end of the drive-in campground Loop C, where the Coastal Prairie Trail starts. It's a 0.4-mile unmarked loop that goes from the Coastal Prairie Trail to the shore of Florida Bay. To find it, turn left at the sign "Coastal Prairie Trail" that's part way down the Coastal Prairie Trail. Florida box turtles are frequently seen. In summer it is muddy and overgrown. It's a convenient walk from the campground.

Coastal Prairie Trail

This trail, which follows an old roadbed beginning at the western end of the campground, goes through buttonwood forests and coastal prairie. There is little shade and the breeze never seems to reach here. It is often hot, humid, buggy, and wet. On a cool winter day, none of these are a problem, and the trail is delightful. Salt-tolerant plants (like saltwort, glasswort, prickly-pear cactus, sea purslane, yucca, and coral bean) dominate. A hardy backpacker can hike to Clubhouse Beach at the trail's end (7.5 miles) to camp. The white sand beach is beautiful, and with the prairie behind and the mangroves on either side, you can feel quite isolated. Bring plenty of drinking water; there are no facilities. Bicycles are permitted.

Canoe Trails

Nine Mile Pond

This is a nice trip for the summer months, when the water level is high, since mosquitoes are less prevalent here. The trail is a 5.2-mile loop and takes about four hours to complete. The National Park Service distributes an excellent printed guide for this trail that is coordinated with numbered signposts, so be sure to ask for one at the Visitor Center. Watch for immature bald eagles here. Motors are prohibited.

Noble Hammock

The trail originally was used during Prohibition by bootleggers going to their stills in the hammocks. The three-mile loop is marked with numbered floats and takes about three hours. Low water may present a problem during the dry season. Narrow passages and tight corners make this trail tricky for novices. Motors are prohibited.

Hell's Bay

You'll understand the origin of this trail's name when you paddle your way through the dense mangroves, cutting through spider webs, clouds of mosquitoes, and branches masking the trail. The trail is marked with floats. The distance is 3.0 miles to Lard Can, the first campsite (about two hours). About a half-mile farther is the Pearl Bay Chickee, and about two miles past Pearl Bay is the Hell's Bay Chickee. Not for novice canoeists.

West Lake

A 7.7-mile trail starts from the launch by the West Lake Interpretive Shelter. The trail first crosses a long stretch of open lake, making for windy paddling much of the time. Then the marked trail progresses through a series of smaller lakes connected by creeks and terminates at Garfield Bight. A campsite with no improvements is located at Garfield Bight. Allow about seven hours travel time one way.

Coot Bay

There are two places to launch a canoe headed for Bear Lake. One is at the Flamingo Marina and the other is at the north end of Bear Lake Road. The latter saves about 2.2 miles of paddling. The Buttonwood Canal is straight and easy paddling, a good choice for novice canoeists or windy days. Coot Bay is open and can be windy. Canoeists can continue to Mud Lake then circle back via the Bear Lake Canoe Trail to Bear Lake Road. That loop is 4.8 miles long.

The bay is named for a past era when coots, aquatic chicken-like birds, were abundant here. They fed on the aquatic vegetation that was wiped out when the canal was built because the canal allowed saltwater intrusion. The salinity has been reduced since 1982, when the "plug" (a concrete dike) was installed at the Florida Bay end of the canal to prevent further intrusion.

Bear Lake

As with the Coot Bay Trail, there are two possible launch sites: the Flamingo marina and the north end of Bear Lake Road. The choice of the Bear Lake Road parking area saves about 2.2 miles of paddling and a short portage. From the Bear Lake Road, it's about 1.6 miles to Bear Lake along a narrow mangrove-lined canal. The canal was dug in 1922 to drain Cape Sable and provide access to the Cape. Motors are not permitted on Bear Lake Canal.

Cape Sable

Experienced canoeists who desire a two- to three-day camping trip can continue past Bear Lake to Cape Sable. The total distance from Bear Lake Road to Cape Sable is 12 miles and includes a second portage on East Cape Canal. Parts of the western stretch can be impassable during the dry season (check with a ranger). The destination is a campsite on East Cape, which means a paddle of about 1.1 miles on open Gulf of Mexico waters (not recommended for novices). Camping on Cape Sable is very remote and peaceful. Aside from an old dock, there are no reminders of civilization. Look closely at the sand on the beach; it's made of broken shells, not quartz like most other beaches.

Florida Bay

Canoeing on Florida Bay can be wonderful or miserable, depending on the weather and tides. Check with a ranger or concession employee about those two factors before setting out into Florida Bay. Winds and tides can be very strong and thunderstorms can make it hazardous to be out in the open. Low tides can strand you for hours. The concession will not rent canoes for the bay side on windy days.

On calm days, when the water is called "flat" by the locals, canoeing on shallow Florida Bay presents an unbeatable way to see flocks of wading birds and shorebirds. Dolphins are frequently seen around Flamingo. Manatees and sea turtles are possibilities. Small sharks (such as black-tipped, bonnethead, and lemon) are common; their dorsal fins break the surface, revealing their presence. They pose no threat to people in canoes, but it is not advisable to wade in the shallow water.

Much of Florida Bay, including the Flamingo area, is covered by seagrass. There are three common kinds of seagrasses here: turtle grass (*Thalassia testudinum*), manatee grass (*Syringodium filiforme*), and shoal grass (*Halodule wrightii*). Turtle grass, with flat blades up to a half inch wide, is grazed by green sea turtles. Manatee grass, which (along with other seagrasses) is grazed by manatees, has leaves that are round in cross-section. Shoal grass, with very narrow flat leaves, is important as an early colonizer of disturbed underwater sites.

During daylight hours, boaters are permitted to land on Bradley Key. This is a worthwhile and easy destination. The island was named for Guy Bradley, the Audubon warden who was killed nearby while protecting a colony of wading birds from plume hunters. Boaters may not land on any other island in this area. Another destination is Snake Bight, the cove to the east of Flamingo. At low tide, hundreds of wading and shore birds gather to feed on the mud flats laden with invertebrates.

Boating

Flamingo is a popular launch site for small, shallow draft motor boats. There are two ramps: the Florida Bay ramp and the Whitewater Bay ramp on the Buttonwood Canal. There is no fee for launching.

Although Florida Bay was once connected to Whitewater Bay by the Buttonwood Canal, passage is now blocked by the dike that keeps salt water from intruding into the mostly fresh canal. A boater who wishes to pass through Flamingo from one bay to the other, and who doesn't have a boat trailer at Flamingo, must have the boat mechanically hoisted over the dike at the marina (fee charged).

Florida Bay is shallow and laced with mud banks. At low tide, much of the bay is exposed, and the sight of thousands of wading birds and shorebirds feeding on the invertebrates and trapped fish is spectacular. The shallow water attracts small sharks, rays, dolphins, sea turtles, and occasionally a manatee. Local boaters learn to "read the water." That is, they can tell by the size of the waves and the water's color if they are about to hit a shoal. A newcomer to Florida Bay boating should get a nautical chart at the marina and stick close to port.

Boaters must observe "No Wake" signs. These are posted in areas where wakes (tracks of waves) would cause erosion, endanger manatees, or jeopardize canoeists. Always slow to no-wake speed when passing close to canoes so they don't get swamped.

Fishing

All year long the lure of saltwater fishing draws people to Flamingo. Locals make frequent weekend trips for sport or to stock their freezers. For those who prefer shallow calm water and light tackle to deep sea fishing, Florida Bay is the perfect place.

The most sought-after food fish are snook, redfish, spotted seatrout, black drum, mangrove snapper, tripletail, and sheepshead. Other popular targets are tarpon and ladyfish. The warm shallow waters of Florida Bay are a rich nursery for invertebrates (such as shrimp, crabs, lobsters, and mollusks) and larval fish. This gives the larger gamefish plenty to feed on.

An easy (but not cheap) way for a novice to do some good fishing is to hire a fishing guide. This can be done by calling the Flamingo Marina. Marina staff will make the arrangements and all you have to do is show up at the Marina at the appointed time.

Best Time of Year

December to April for most activities. Mosquitoes and heat keep many people away in the summer.

CHEKIKA

6 miles west of SR 997 (Krome Ave.) on SW 168th St. (Richard St.), north of Homestead.

This is the most recent addition to Everglades National Park. The 640 acres that was formerly Chekika State Recreation Area was turned over to the National Park Service on October 1, 1991. This encourages visitor access to the eastern part of the Everglades to see a tropical hardwood hammock surrounded by sawgrass marsh. Visitors traveling between the main park entrance and Shark Valley or Everglades City will find a convenient place to camp or have a picnic lunch. Only a few of the previous regulations changed; hunting and possession of weapons are now prohibited.

The area was named for the famous Seminole, Chief Chekika. Chekika was hanged in 1840 in a nearby hammock by Lt. Col. William Harney in revenge for several earlier attacks by the Seminoles.

As late as 1903, local Indian families camped in the high ground of the hammock. In 1943, oil prospectors drilled 1,250 feet into the underlying aquifer and struck water instead of oil. The resulting artesian well released 2.5 million gallons of sulphurous water a day. The deep well was later capped and replaced by a shallower, less sulphurous one.

Facilities and Activities

Campground, nature trail, boardwalk, swimming, fishing and picnicking.

The changeover from state land to National Park Service land will bring changes not finalized at the time of this printing. Interpretive services will probably benefit the most. The Hammock Trail is currently a short footpath through a hardwood hammock, labeled with interpretive signs. It is not handicapped-accessible. A boardwalk crossing the sawgrass is also labeled with interpretive signs. The swimming area was created by directing the artesian well into a natural depression. The water now is recirculated to prevent contamination downstream with the unnaturally sulphurous water. The fishing is in freshwater. See "Campgrounds" above for information on camping.

Best Time of Year

December to April for most activities. Summer is popular for swimming.

SHARK VALLEY

On Tamiami Trail, 18 miles west of the intersection of the Trail with Krome Ave. (SR 997). Phone (305) 221-8776 for National Park Service information; (305) 221-8455 for concession information (tram tours, bicycle rentals).

Shark Valley is at the northern boundary of Everglades National Park. It provides access for visitors to the Shark River Slough, a wide but shallow and slowly moving body of water that supports much wildlife. It is easily reachable from Miami and Naples. Too many visitors to Everglades National Park head only to Flamingo or Royal Palm and miss this part of the Everglades. A trip around the Lookout Tower Road, whether by tram or bicycle, is a good way to see alligators and wading birds.

Facilities And Activities

Visitor center, bicycling, bicycle rentals, nature trails, birding and other wildlife viewing, naturalist programs, tram ride and observation tower.

Visitor Center

This small center contains educational displays of a freshwater aquarium with fish, crayfish, and salamanders plus skulls of alligators, otters, gar fish, raccoons, and deer. Items for sale include local human and natural history books, slides, videos, and film. At the Visitor Center, you can obtain the schedule for the many ranger-led programs offered. These include a 3.5-hour bicycle tour to the observation tower, a three-hour get-your-feet-wet "Slough Slog" to a gator hole or hammock, a 45-minute walk on an elevated boardwalk, or a 20-minute sit-down talk next to the Visitor Center. Programs are free.

Vending machines for chips, snacks, and soft drinks provide the only food on the premises. Across the Tamiami Trail from the entrance station is a restaurant, run by the Miccosukees, which serves Miccosukee and American food. The marsh behind the restaurant is a good place to check for snail kites.

Trails

Lookout Tower Road

The main "trail," if you can call it that, is the 15-mile loop road that leads to the Observation Tower. The road was built by Humbel Oil (now Exxon) in 1946 for oil drilling. It is paved and is seven miles on the straight (western) side and eight miles on the wiggly (eastern) side. Plenty of gators, including babies, can be seen at close range; look in the culverts on the side of the road. Wood storks, deer, otters, water snakes, snail kites, and many other animals can be seen. The road intercepts Shark Slough and is the only way most people will get to see the slough. A slough is a slow-moving channel in the marsh that has slightly deeper water than the rest of the marsh. It holds water longer (has a longer hydroperiod), looks greener from the air, and serves as a refuge for wildlife when other areas dry up. Shark Slough is the largest slough in the park.

The only motorized vehicles allowed are the tour trams and ranger patrol cars. Visitors can travel the road one of three ways: taking the tram, riding a bicycle, or walking. Due to the openness and heat, not many people choose to walk the entire length, although many people walk shorter segments. The tram is the most popular way.

The two-hour tram tours are run by the concession seven days a week all year (weather permitting). The trams are covered on top (so they are shady) but are open-sided for good viewing (so you may get wet if it rains). The tram makes a half-hour stop at the Observation Tower (see below) and riders are encouraged to disembark and ascend the ramp to the tower. Occasional stops are made elsewhere if the guide sees something interesting, but riders must stay on the tram. Reservations are suggested from December to March. Tickets are available at the Tram Tour Office (fee charged). Call first for departure times, since they vary seasonally. In the busy season, the schedule includes moonlight and early morning tram tours.

An excellent way to see and feel the Everglades more closely is by bicycle. Many people ride the 15-mile road. Visitors can bring their own bicycles or they can rent them from the concession. Specify if you want a bike with a basket for carrying your field guides and lunch. Bicycling is easy on the flat terrain, but it can get very hot. Bring plenty of drinking water and a sun hat. Don't attempt to bicycle if there are thunderstorms around. You will not be safe from lightning on a bicycle as you would be in a car, and there is little protective cover along the road. Allow at least two to three hours to pedal the route.

Bobcat Trail

A short walk from the parking lot is a 0.25-mile boardwalk that connects the two legs of the Tower Road. The boardwalk trail leads to the bayhead habitat and is punctuated by interpretive trail signs. A small gazebo midway along the trail provides a place to rest and enjoy the quiet. Look for rails, particularly the king rail, along the boardwalk. Handicapped accessible.

Otter Trail

A 0.5-mile walk along the western leg of the Tower Road (from the parking lot) will bring you to the start of the Otter Trail, which is about one mile long. It is a narrow footpath through a hammock, also with interpretive signs, and emerges on the same side of the Tower Road.

Observation Tower Trail

Originally built as a fire tower, the current observation tower was remodeled in the 1960s for park visitors. A long spiral ramp (handicapped accessible) now leads to the top of the 65-foot tower, which yields a glorious panoramic view of the Shark Slough. This is one of the more popular photography spots in the park. During the spring months, the drying of the glades forces gators, turtles, fish, and other wildlife to concentrate in the water at the base of the tower. Several dozen gators may be seen at once. The trees surrounding the tower also serve as a diurnal roost for yellow-crowned night herons. At the base of the tower are restrooms and drinking water.

The Tower Trail, a small side trail near the base of the Observation Tower, is 0.25 miles long. It is good for observing butterflies and great blue herons and for photography.

Best Time of Year

December to April, the dry season, because wildlife will be concentrated in the water along the road and the weather is cooler. In the summer, however, high water levels may drive snakes, frogs, and mammals onto the roads and trails.

EVERGLADES CITY

The Gulf Coast Ranger Station in Everglades City is on SR 29, 4.8 miles south of the intersection with Tamiami Trail. For park information, call (813) 695-3311 or (305) 242-7700. For concession information (boat tours, canoe rentals), call (813) 695-2591 (800-445-7724 in Florida), or write Everglades National Park Boat Tours, P.O. Box 119, Everglades, FL 33929.

Tucked up in the northwest corner of Everglades National Park is a region called the Ten Thousand Islands. Named for the myriad of small, irregularly shaped mangrove islands, this area is popular with canoeists and anglers. It is a vast wilderness in which it is easy to find solitude. Wildlife abounds here. Manatees, dolphins, alligators, rays, sharks, sea turtles, spoonbills, and white ibises are visible at certain times of the year. This is a water-oriented area; there are mangrove islands, but no land for trails. You'll just have to find a boat if you want to see this area.

Facilities and Activities

Canoeing and canoe rentals, boating, fishing, boat tours, visitor center, and gift shop.

Visitor Center

The Visitor Center is a ranger station where information can be obtained. There are two audio-visual presentations available on request. This is where boaters and canoeists get back-country permits and maps. The Visitor Center is located on the second floor of the building and is not accessible to the handicapped. Handicapped people should ask on the first floor for park information.

The concession authorized by the Park Service operates the gift shop on the first floor. It sells souvenirs, Seminole crafts, and a small assortment of books. Vending machines dispense sandwiches, snacks, and drinks. For more substantial meals, there are restaurants across the street.

Boat Tours

Two boat tours make it easy for people to see the Everglades coast by water. The "Ten Thousand Island Boat Tour" is a 1 3/4-hour trip through the coastal mangrove islands and estuaries. The "Kingston Key Boat Tour" is a ranger-led 2 1/2-hour trip and includes a 30-minute walk on the beach at Kingston Key as well as cruising through the mangrove islands. The concession charges a fee for these boat tours and will assist with wheelchairs.

Canoeing

Canoeing is an excellent way to see the Ten Thousand Islands. Trips of several hours to several days can be planned. This is the northern terminus of the Wilderness Waterway, a 99-mile canoe trail to Flamingo (see "Wilderness Waterway" below).

All canoe trips should be carefully planned in advance. Proper safety equipment includes a Coast Guard-approved personal flotation device for each person. The Coast Guard recommends all boaters bring a current NOAA nautical chart covering their route and vicinity. The chart for the Everglades City area day trips is #11430 ("Lostmans River to Wiggins

Pass"). For the Wilderness Waterway trip, you would also need #11432 ("Lostmans River to Shark River") and #11433 ("Whitewater Bay"). The National Park Service recommends each person bring at least one gallon of water per day planned, plus enough for one extra day. Since strong tides can greatly impede your progress, check with a ranger for the local tide schedule.

Day trips don't require a backcountry permit, but it is best to check with a ranger before departing for the latest information on tides, winds, and storms. Tides can be very strong, and combined with a head wind, it can be impossible for a strong canoeist to make headway. There aren't many places to pull over and rest either. The mangroves can be confusing to navigate if you deviate from a marked trail or visibility decreases. However, with careful planning, you can make sure the tides are with you and enjoy a most delightful canoe trip.

Day Trips

The National Park Service distributes printed guides with maps for canoe day trips. The trips will be briefly described in the next two paragraphs for advanced planning, but you should ask the Park Service for these guides when you arrive or send for them earlier (request the canoe guides for Everglades City). You can bring your own canoe or rent one at the concession at the Ranger Station. You can launch at the Ranger Station or at Outdoor Resorts on Chokoloskee Island (Outdoor Resorts also rents canoes).

The Sandfly Island trip will take about 2 1/2 hours paddling time (round-trip). Sandfly Island is about two miles from the Ranger Station, across open water. It will take longer if you circumnavigate the island (which is sheltered). There is a dock at the near end, with a nature trail on the island, so get out and stretch your legs. The Chokoloskee Bay Loop is almost entirely open water with no reliable place to land and rest. It is also about 2 1/2 hours paddling time.

If you prefer an "inland" canoe trip, you can choose several routes through narrow mangrove and sawgrass channels. You can leave either from an access road on the Tamiami Trail (about 11 miles east of Everglades City), from the Gulf Coast Ranger Station, or from Chokoloskee. The Turner River trip takes about five hours from Tamiami Trail to Chokoloskee and is not a loop (so an upriver return or alternate transportation back to your car must be planned). From Everglades City or Chokoloskee, you can take a shorter loop through Halfway Creek and Left Hand Turner River. This will take about three hours, depending on wind and tides. Due to the intense mosquito population, the inland trips are best avoided in summer.

There are other nice routes for day trips that you can plan yourself using a nautical chart. The rangers at Gulf Coast Ranger Station will be glad to help you plan a route.

Overnight Trips

Numerous combinations of routes can be used to plan overnight trips. In fact, there are too many to describe here. The backcountry chickees and campsites are strategically placed by the Park Service for overnight convenience (see "Backcountry sites" under "Camping" above). As mentioned above, you need a permit from a ranger to stay at a backcountry site. During the busy winter season, you will have a better chance of getting the backcountry camping site of your choice if you avoid holidays and begin on a weekday. Loop trips are the most sensible, rather than one-way trips.

Wilderness Waterway

For those super-adventurous, super-experienced canoeists with 7-10 days available for serious canoeing, there is the Wilderness Waterway. It's a 99-mile marked canoe trail between Everglades City and Flamingo. Even though the numbers on the markers begin at Flamingo, the trail can be traveled just as easily from the other direction.

Paddling along the waterway, you'll pass seemingly endless miles of mangroves. Concealed in the tangle of living trunks and prop roots are the skeletal ghosts of giant mangroves, destroyed in the hurricanes of 1960, 1965, and 1992. Some died by having their branches stripped bare of leaves.

Occasionally, a shell mound will create enough elevation for a change of vegetation. The shell mounds were built by the Calusa Indians, who lived along the southwest coast possibly as early as 1450 B.C. These indigenous people depended on shellfish, primarily oysters, clams, and conchs. They piled the empty shells into huge mounds. Some were burial sites, some were refuse piles, and some were structured for habitation. The latter mounds reached extraordinary proportions. The town of Chokoloskee, at the northern end of the Wilderness Waterway, is built on a 150-acre shell mound that is 20 feet high. Sandfly Island, west of Chokoloskee, is a 75-acre shell mound. While clams have since been depleted by canneries early in this century, the oysters are still abundant. This will be gratingly obvious every time your canoe scrapes over an oyster bar.

The trail bisects some of the wildest country left in the eastern United States. That is why people who are looking for solitude and wilderness head for this unique trail. It is also why anyone who undertakes this journey must be experienced, well-prepared, and willing to take a risk. Risks are mostly in the form of strong tides, high winds, choppy water, lightning, sun exposure, hypothermia, lack of drinking water, and getting lost. The last one is not a problem if you keep the markers in site. If you explore off the trail or encounter poor visibility, you can easily get confused in the tangle of mangrove islands. As for drinking water, there is no source from Everglades City to Flamingo. All boaters must carry their own in heavy duty (preferably hard-sided) containers that won't puncture and will be secure from raccoons. During the dry season, the lack of fresh water can drive raccoons and other animals to seek it from humans. Raccoons can chew through soft-sided containers.

The campsites (chickees and ground sites) are spaced at irregular intervals along the trail. Some are as little as a mile apart and some have almost ten-mile gaps. Since most campsites are slightly off the marked trail, they can be difficult to find. They are marked on the NOAA nautical charts #11430, 11432, and 11433. Be sure to get the Park Service brochure "Backcountry Trip Planner" that explains where the campsites are.

A long-distance trip like this must be planned well in advance. Since the trail is not a loop, you will need to arrange transportation from your destination back to your car, unless you plan to paddle the 99 miles back! The drive around by land between Flamingo and Everglades City is about 3 1/2 hours.

Plan your Wilderness Waterway trip carefully. The Park Service brochure "Introduction to Canoeing the Everglades" includes an excellent checklist of items to carry. You'll have to get permits for the campsites (see "Backcountry Sites" under "Camping"). You can also buy a book called "A Guide to the Wilderness Waterway of the Everglades National Park" (by William G. Truesdell) from The Florida National Parks and Monuments Association. Write to the Association at P.O. Box 279, Homestead, FL 33030 or call them at (305) 247-1216 for ordering information.

Fishing and Boating

Fishing is extremely popular around the Ten Thousand Islands. Snook, cobia, redfish, spotted seatrout, and mangrove snapper are some local favorites. Fishing guides can be contacted by calling the Everglades City Chamber of Commerce at (813) 696-3941. Boats can be launched at the Baron Marina on SR 29 in Everglades City (813 - 695-3591) or at Outdoor Resorts in Chokoloskee (at the end of the causeway between Everglades City and Chokoloskee; (813-695-2881).

If you bring your own boat, you had better be good at reading the local nautical charts. The water is so full of shoals, it's almost impossible to drive in a straight line. During extremely low tides, boating to or from Chokoloskee may be impossible for several hours.

Best Time Of Year

Generally, November to April. Winter has fewer mosquitoes, cooler temperatures, less rain, and more wading birds. In the summer, though, waters are calmer for boating and fishing. Some National Park Service programs may not be run during the summer.

 HURRICANE ANDREW UPDATE

In spite of its immense size, all of the park was affected in some way. The center of the storm cut a 25-mile swath from east to west through the center of the park, so the northern and southern edges showed the least effect. The main entrance area was severely damaged. That included the main Visitor Center, the Royal Palm Visitor Center, Anhinga Trail, Gumbo Limbo Trail, Pinelands Trail, Long Pine Key Campground, Pa-hay-okee Overlook, and undeveloped areas west of Pa-hay-okee. The observation tower and boardwalk at Shark Valley were damaged. Mahogany Hammock did not have as much damage from Andrew as it did from Hurricane Donna in 1960; the latter's effects were still evident when Andrew hit. Also within the intense wind area was Chekika. Flamingo, however, was basically unaffected because it was slightly to the south of the eye wall. As the storm swept westward across the sawgrass marshes, it blew away the periphyton mats that protect minute organisms. Trees on the tree islands were denuded, broken apart, or windthrown. At the western edge, the mangroves were stripped of leaves or uprooted. Most of the park remained closed for about three months, and facilities and services were limited for several months afterward.

The Atlantic bottle-nosed dolphin is a common fishlike mammal of shallow south Florida marine waters, such as Florida Bay. [Larry Lipsky] **1**

Two Key deer nuzzle each other on Big Pine Key. [Larry Lipsky] **2**

Isolated Lignumvitae Key is relatively pristine. Just inland from the dock (at island's right) is the tall tower of the windmill that previously generated power for the resident family.
[Larry Lipsky]   **3**

A visitor studies the view of the mangroves from the observation tower at Long Key State Park.
[Larry Lipsky]   **4**

The common salt marsh mosquito gorges itself on human blood. Actual body size is about one-quarter inch.
[Grover L. Larkins]   **5**

A male snail kite balances on a branch as it eats its staple food, the apple snail. [Rob Bennetts] **6**

A sawgrass marsh extends to the horizon, while two alligators bask in the foreground. [Larry Lipsky] **7**

Greater flamingos occasionally appear in Florida Bay. Those pictured were at Sandy Key in Everglades National Park. They are not known to nest in the wild in Florida. [Grover L. Larkins]

A sleek river otter emerges from the water at Shark Valley.
[Grover L. Larkins]   **9**

A limpkin, which can be recognized at night by its piercing cry, wades in swamps feeding on snails.
[Grover L. Larkins]   **10**

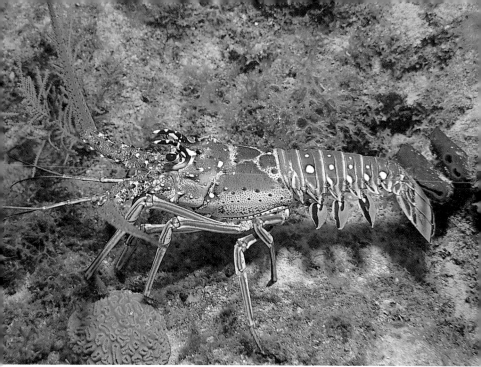

A spiny lobster scavenges for food on a coral reef. [Larry Lipsky] **11**

One of the most captivating fish of the coral reef is the queen angelfish, named for the halolike marking on its forehead. [Larry Lipsky] **12**

In its head-up and motionless stance, the American bittern camouflages beautifully with the reeds and grasses of its typical habitat.
[Grover L. Larkins]   **13**

A bald eagle devours its finned prey.
[Grover L. Larkins]   **14**

A female alligator guards her nest, a mound of decomposing sawgrass, rushes, and other aquatic plants. [Susan D. Jewell]   **15**

The spectacular roseate spoonbill uses its spatulate bill to sift through muddy water for small fish and shrimp. [Larry Lipsky]   **16**

A survivor in stone if nothing else, this Florida panther surveys the damage to the Gumbo Limbo hammock at Royal Palm (Everglades National Park) caused by Hurricane Andrew. Note the two fallen royal palms on the grass. [Susan D. Jewell]   **17**

Dulled in color beside the vivid red fire sponge, the bluestriped grunts, French grunts, and yellow goatfish school together on a coral reef. [Larry Lipsky]   **18**

This large tree island in the southern Everglades is surrounded by sawgrass.
[Susan D. Jewell]
19

Atop a nest of sticks, an osprey dines on a fish. [Larry Lipsky]   **20**

Fakahatchee Strand State Preserve staff have intentionally set this low-energy, carefully watched fire to keep ground debris from accumulating and causing an uncontrollable destructive fire. [Susan D. Jewell]   **21**

The town of Tavernier is surrounded by mangroves. The narrow undeveloped mangrove island in the background contains a channel that early settlers blocked at both ends to trap manatees (Cowpen's Cut). [Larry Lipsky] **22**

The Florida Keys are renowned for their spectacular sunsets, owed partially to the humid air. Here, two brown pelicans glide over Florida Bay near the old Florida East Coast Railroad tracks. [Larry Lipsky] **23**

An American crocodile basks on an algae-covered rock in the C-111 canal. Note the gray skin color, the narrow snout, and the protruding fourth tooth in the lower jaw that distinguishes it from an alligator.
[Grover L. Larkins]
24

Red touch yellow kills a ellow" is the adage that arns of the poisonous oral snake. Note the ed and yellow bands at touch each other nd the black nose onfirming this is a oral snake.
Grover L. Larkins]
25

The West Indian manatee is such a slow-moving creature that algae can grow on its back.
[Larry Lipsky]   **26**

A better adjective could not be found to describe the striking colors of the painted bunting, which winters in south Florida. Pictured is a male of the species; the female is a drab greenish yellow. [Grover L. Larkins]

27

A sea wall protects Fort Jefferson on Garden Key in Dry Tortugas National Park. In the clear shallow moat between the fort and the sea wall, many fascinating marine animals can be observed. [Susan D. Jewell]   **28**

A wood stork flashes its wings to startle prey, making foraging easier. [Grover L. Larkins]   **29**

In the open cypress marshes
of the Everglades, a hefty
cowhorn orchid flowers
in the spring.
[Susan D. Jewell]   **30**

This burrowing owl, with its characteristically long legs, stands beside its burrow that contains litter the owl collected.
[Larry Lipsky] **31**

A male anhinga preens its feathers. The colorful eye ring indicates it is in breeding condition.
[Larry Lipsky] **32**

A hungry brood keeps this female anhinga busy at the Anhinga Trail (Everglades National Park). Her fluffy chicks stick their heads into her mouth to retrieve the fish she's swallowed.
[Grover L. Larkins] **33**

Of the many orchids native to Florida, the grass-pink (*Calopogon*) is one of the most beautiful. [Grover L. Larkins]   **34**

Brown noddies perch on prickly pear cactus on Bush Key at Dry Tortugas National Park. [Susan D. Jewell]   **35**

Birders and photographers gather on the bank of the famed Mrazek Pond (Everglades National Park) to watch wading birds feeding on the concentrations of fish. [Larry Lipsky]

Barred owls are a
common sight at
Mahogany Hammock
and Corkscrew
Swamp. Their
"who-cooks-for-you"
call can be heard
often at night.
[Grover L. Larkins]
37

Black skimmers, here at rest, feed by flying barely above the water, skimming the surface
with their long lower bills to feel for fish. [Grover L. Larkins]   **38**

BISCAYNE NATIONAL PARK

THE MAINLAND

TRULY ONE OF THE UNDISCOVERED GEMS of the National Park system! In 1968, President Lyndon Johnson turned the barrier islands into a national monument to protect them from inevitable development. After an enlargement in 1974, and another in 1980, it became a national park. Ironically, the coral reef, the northernmost in North America, was not the original concern. Now it is the main attraction, and rightfully so. Farther down the Keys, the barrier islands (such as Key Largo, Plantation Key, and Upper Matecumbe) are developed and cause pollution problems to the adjacent reef. Here, since the barrier islands are almost totally pristine, the coral is healthy and the water crystal clear. Compared with the Pennekamp Park area, there are fewer boaters.

Besides the 44 barrier islands and the reef, the park protects 14 continuous miles of mangrove shoreline, the longest uninterrupted stretch of mangroves along the eastern coast of Florida. But of the 181,500 acres the park encompasses, 95% is water. Newcomers to the park arrive at Convoy Point, the mainland "jumping off" point, take one look at the parking lot, the Visitor Center, the boat dock, and the store, and say "Is this it?" Most emphatically "No!" But you have to find your way onto or into the water to see the best part. Fortunately, the National Park Service makes that easy. Take advantage of the opportunity to see this gorgeous reef by snorkeling or taking a glassbottom boat trip, and try a canoe trip along the mangrove shoreline. You may see manatees or dolphins or the colorful tropical fish. Biscayne Bay is a sanctuary for spiny lobsters, a regional delicacy.

The park has hosted nine species of endangered animals. They are the American crocodile, hawksbill turtle, green turtle, leatherback turtle, wood stork, southern bald eagle, peregrine falcon, West Indian manatee, and Schaus' swallowtail butterfly.

Location, Mailing Address and Phone

9700 SW 328th St. (North Canal Dr.), Homestead. Convoy Point is 9 miles east of Homestead. From the north, follow the signs from Florida's Turnpike or U.S. 1. From the Keys, follow the signs on U.S. 1, turning right onto SW 328th St. (Lucy St.)

For National Park Service information, write P.O. Box 1369, Homestead, FL 33090-1369. For concession information, write Biscayne National Underwater Park Co., P.O. Box 1270, Homestead, FL 33090-1270.

For Park Service information, call (305) 247-PARK (247-7275). For concession information, call (305) 247-2400.

Facilities and Activities

Swimming, snorkeling, diving, glassbottom boat, picnicking, canoeing, hiking, camping, fishing, interpretive programs. No admission fee; there are fees for concession tours and rentals. Note: There are no overnight lodging accommodations at the park.

Visitor Centers

Convoy Point

Hours are 8:30 AM – 5:00 PM. It's a small center now, but in 1994 the new center will be ready. Currently, there are a few displays about the reef, and two saltwater tanks with native reef fish and anemones. A small selection of books, including marine field guides, is for sale (the adjacent concession fills the gap; see below). The new center will be an expanded version.

An eight-minute slide show on Biscayne National Park ecosystems is shown as requested in the auditorium. A slide program on the area's cultural history and a closed-caption slide program are also available on request.

Elliott Key

The Visitor Center on Elliott Key operates a little differently because of the infrequent visitation. It has restrooms (handicapped accessible), a small screened-in picnic area, and a few static displays. There are no telephones on the island. In the winter (usually Christmas to Easter), it is staffed by an interpretive ranger or volunteer intermittently on weekends. It functions more as a ranger station than a visitor center, because of the infrequent visitation.

Canoeing

You can bring your own or rent one from the concession. You can canoe along the shore, around the mangroves, and to nearby islands by yourself. On winter weekends, an interpretive ranger leads a guided canoe trip. There is no charge for this guided trip, but you must have a canoe (which may mean renting one). The trips leave fairly reliably around 9:00 AM (call ahead for reservations).

If you canoe on your own, be careful of the tides, since the currents can be very strong. Check with a ranger for the tide schedule and plan your trip so you paddle with the current. Also watch for strong winds and choppy waters that are frequent in the winter. Although it is possible to paddle from Convoy Point to Elliott Key (about nine miles), it is not recommended. You must be an experienced canoeist, familiar with ocean currents and waves, and in good physical condition. Rather than navigate due east from Convoy Point, a better route would be to go south along the shore to the Arsenicker Keys, then east toward Totten Key, then north along the barrier islands to your destination (such as camping on Elliott Key). This is a longer route, but keeps you closer to land and should be safer and more scenic. Watch for passing motorboats that may swamp your canoe.

Boating

Visitors with their own motor boats will find much to see and do. Fishing for tarpon, grouper, snook, and so on is very popular, and it's easy to find snorkeling hot spots on your own. Mooring buoys are provided at several places around the reef; they are there to protect the coral, since it is illegal to anchor on coral. If no mooring buoys are available, you must anchor on sand. Due to the shallowness of Biscayne Bay and the reef, you should carry a NOAA nautical chart (#11451, "Miami to Marathon and Florida Bay," available at Convoy Point) with you. The adjacent Homestead Bayfront Park (a county park) has a boat launch and gas dock; there are no such facilities in Biscayne National Park.

There are 66 slips in the harbor by the Visitor Center on Elliott Key. They are free, available on a first-come basis, for day use or overnight. Docks are also available at Adams (day use only) and Boca Chita Keys.

Swimming

There are many places to swim, although the area you can get to without a boat (at Convoy Point) is small. The coral reef must be reached by boat. There are swimming areas at Elliott Key, both oceanside and bayside. The bayside area is sheltered and shallow, with seagrass and barracudas, grunts, and snappers commonly seen. Swimming is prohibited in the harbors, "No Wake" zones, and marked channels.

Fishing

Fishing in the park is entirely saltwater and is very popular with local people. Since most of the park is water, there is ample room for everyone to fish. From Convoy Point, you can fish on the jetty opposite the marked channel and catch such fish as barracuda, grunt, mangrove snapper, and snook. There is no bait for sale at the park, but you can go to the adjacent Homestead Bayfront Park to buy bait. Fishing is prohibited in the harbors, "No Wake" zones, and marked channels. You must have a Florida saltwater fishing license, available at most tackle shops in town (not sold at the park).

Trails

If you can get to Elliott Key, allow time to hike around. A loop trail, about 1.5 miles round-trip, with a section of boardwalk on the ocean side, begins on the bayside near the Visitor Center. It has interpretive

Sea grape

signs about the natural and human history of Elliott Key. It meanders through a West Indian hardwood hammock and mangroves. The mangrove land crabs (*Ucides cordatus*) scurry around by the dozens under the mangroves, above the tide line. The vivid purple and orange shells of these land crabs are a spectacular sight.

There is a much longer straight trail (the old road) running almost the entire length of the seven-mile island. From the Visitor Center, the trail goes for 2.5 miles north and 4.5 miles south. The habitat is tropical hammock, and many native hardwoods can be found.

There is also a half-mile loop trail on Adams Key. It doesn't have interpretive signs, but it penetrates a hardwood hammock (with seven-year-apple, white stopper, pigeon-plum, poisonwood, canker-tree) and openings (with buttonwood, bay-cedar, and sea ox-eye daisy). Adams Key is partially composed of fill pumped up from the ocean floor. That's why you'll see piles of clamshells on the island, resembling an Indian midden. Camping on Adams is reserved for school groups.

During the autumn and spring raptor, passerine, and shorebird migrations, Elliott and Adams are resting and foraging places, thus also great for birding. Birding is good all winter. In fact, a LaSagra's Flycatcher has been seen on Elliot during several recent winters.

Biscayne National Park is one of the few remaining places left to see the Schaus' swallowtail butterfly (*Papilio aristodemus ponceanus*), listed as endangered since 1975 by the state and federal governments. The chief contributor to the species' demise is the long-term destruction of native hardwoods, like torchwood and wild-lime, on which it specializes. Since 1972, aerial spraying of pesticides targeted at mosquitoes is also contributing to the destruction. This beautiful butterfly, about 3.5 inches across, is black with yellow diagonal bands and black tails edged with yellow. The adults usually live only three or four days but may survive several weeks. Look for them from late April through mid-July. The islands in Biscayne National Park are possibly the only places left to see this nearly extinct butterfly (a few individual butterflies may still exist on Key Largo).

The Mexican red-bellied squirrel, an introduced mammal, can be seen foraging in the treetops of Elliott Key. This attractive squirrel is black with a rusty-colored belly.

The Jetty

Wayside exhibits line the 370-foot boardwalk and a half-mile breakwater jetty that tread the water from Convoy Point. Fishermen often surf-cast from the non-channel side of the jetty, and the winter shore-birding can be great. White mangrove, sea grape, sea purslane, and sea ox-eye daisy grab a tenuous roothold along the jetty.

Camping

There is no camping on the mainland section (Convoy Point). Camping is allowed on Elliott and Boca Chita Keys; both have tentsites, cooking grills, and bathrooms. You must get to the islands by boat on your own, and it is generally regarded as too far in open water to canoe. Elliott Key has fresh water and showers. Boca Chita has no fresh water or showers. No charge for camping; backcountry permits needed.

If you can get to Elliott Key and you're seeking a little seclusion, get a backcountry permit from the ranger station and hike on the old road north or south from the Elliott Key Visitor Center. You must pack in everything you need (including water) and you must pack it all out (except of course the water). The insects can be nasty on the keys, even in winter, so bring a tent with no-see-um-proof netting.

The concession will bring groups (minimum 30 people) out to the camping areas on Elliott or Boca Chita Keys for overnight camping from autumn through spring. The fee for the boat depends upon the group size. Of course, the boat will return to retrieve you. Make arrangements at least a few weeks in advance.

Concession Tours and Rentals

The Biscayne National Underwater Park Company offers ways for almost everyone to enjoy the coral reef. At the store at Convoy Point, you can reserve space on the glassbottom boat or the snorkel and dive boat. While there are regularly scheduled tours, you can also arrange special group tours in advance. You should make reservations and check schedules in advance for all trips, either in person or by phone: (305) 247-2400. All trips leave from Convoy Point and may be cancelled due to weather.

There is one snorkel trip a day, departing at 1:30 PM, seven days a week. The cost of the trip includes equipment (you can bring your own, but you don't save any money). The trip lasts four hours, and about half of that is in-the-water time. *Do not touch the coral*, because touching can kill it. Enjoy watching the colorful angelfish, parrotfish, blue tangs, and butterflyfish. You may even see a complacent nurse shark.

The concession maintains full diving instruction and certification facilities, including a "resort course." The latter is the cheapest and quickest way to get you scuba diving safely (a half day of instruction and one dive; price varies by group size). This is good if you're not sure you'll like diving, only have a little time, or think you'll never go diving again but want to go once. You will not get certified this way. If you're already certified, you can go on their two-tank dives. Equipment is also for sale. There is one dive trip a day (on the snorkel boat). You'll see some of the thousands of patch reefs that have formed on the oceanside near Elliott Key. A patch reef is a small, circular coral reef (usually only a few hundred yards in diameter) surrounded by a ring of sand. The concession has two 53-foot vessels that can carry 49 passengers each. The boats are custom-built for the reef, with recessed propellers to prevent turbulence to and siltation of the reef. The 28-inch draft is small for a boat that size and allows it to venture into very shallow water without scraping the coral. A National Park Service interpretive ranger will be on board each trip to narrate about the reef. The trips leave at 10:00 AM seven days a week and are three hours long. The boat has a boarding ramp made for wheelchairs.

Canoeists can rent 17-foot aluminum canoes by the hour (two-hour minimum), half day, whole day, or overnight. For an extra fee, you can rent a car-top carrier and take the canoe outside the park. For a small additional fee, basic canoeing instruction is also available (enough to get a newcomer going).

Miscellaneous

Windsurfing is permitted and conditions are often excellent, but you must bring your own equipment (no rentals available). Waterskiing is permitted away from docks and anchorages.

Visitors should come prepared with their own lunches. Food sold here is limited to snacks and soft drinks. There is limited food service at the adjacent county park. The nearest food store or restaurant is in the town of Homestead, about nine miles west. Expansion of park facilities in a few years may include more food services.

Best Time of Year

January to April have the fewest insects and the driest weather. Ocean water temperature and clarity are best from April to October (for swimming, snorkeling, and diving) but they are generally good year-round. Glassbottom boat trips are good any month, since the reef is more protected from heavy seas here than off Key Largo. High winds and winter cold fronts can cause boat tours to be cancelled. A popular sailing regatta is held near Elliott Key every year on Columbus Day weekend.

Pets

Allowed on a 6-foot leash, but not in buildings or on concession boats.

 HURRICANE ANDREW UPDATE

The entire park was directly in the path of the worst winds and storm surges. The center of the hurricane made landfall here. Damage to this park was extensive. All buildings (except the old stone ones on the islands) were severely damaged or destroyed. No trees were left standing on Boca Chita Key, and Elliott and Adams Keys had only a few left standing. Most of the park's mangroves were uprooted. There was damage on all reefs, but most appeared minor. The park partially reopened at the end of 1992. Boca Chita won't be open until early to mid 1994. Elliott will be open by press time, and Adams will open shortly after. The Visitor Center will be in a temporary building until late 1994, when the previously planned new Visitor Center will open.

NAVY WELLS PINELAND PRESERVE

SCATTERED THROUGHOUT DADE COUNTY are remnant patches of pinelands. The largest outside of Everglades National Park survived because it happened to be perched atop a very important wellfield. In 1940, the U.S. Navy built an 18-inch diameter pipeline to supply the naval station on Boca Chica, near Key West. The source of the water was a well in Florida City on the mainland 130 miles away. The Florida Keys Aqueduct Authority bought water from the Navy to sell to civilian Keys residents. The 310-acre slash pine preserve surrounds the original wellfield compound. The aqueduct has since been purchased by the Aqueduct Authority and enlarged to meet the growing need for water in the Keys. The Metropolitan Dade County Park and Recreation Department now owns most of the land around the wellfield.

Location, Mailing Address and Phone

192nd Ave. (Tower Rd.) in Florida City. From Krome Ave. or U.S. 1 in Florida City, turn west onto SW 344th St. (Palm Dr.). Turn left at 192nd Ave. (at "Robert Is Here" Fruit Stand), and drive 0.6 miles. The Preserve is on the right, where there is a large sign "Well Field and Treatment Facility" and a smaller sign "Navy Wells Pineland Preserve."

c/o Castellow Hammock Nature Center, 22301 SW 162nd Ave., Goulds, FL 33170. (305) 245-4321 (at Castellow)

Facilities and Activities

Hiking trail. No visitor facilities; minimal public access. No admission fee.

There are several grassy firebreak roads through the preserve. Volunteers of the Florida Trail Association also maintain a hiking trail, beginning at the edge of the field behind the gate near the parking area.

It is a mile long and will be lengthened to three miles as volunteers' time permits. The surficial limestone bedrock makes this a rough trail, complete with frequent poisonwood trees. The pinelands are well preserved because the county conducts prescribed burns in conjunction with the Division of Forestry.

Northern bobwhite quail are common residents. Swallow-tailed kites may be seen from March to August. Eastern indigo snakes may also be seen. This is a good place to see the ancient cycad, coontie. The starchy root of the coontie was a staple food of the Seminoles and Miccosukees. Coontie depends on the Florida atala (*Eumaeus atala florida*), a threatened tropical butterfly, to pollinate it.

Other plants of special interest include silver palm, tetrazygia, pineland jacquemontia, and pineland croton. The croton depends on the Florida leafwing (*Anaea troglodyta floridalis*), a rare butterfly endemic to Florida. Forty-six species of grasses sprout beneath the pines in this preserve. One of them, Florida gamagrass, is endemic to southern Florida.

Best Time Of Year

November - May (the nonmosquito season).

Pets

Allowed.

 HURRICANE ANDREW UPDATE

The pinelands survived remarkably well, considering they were in the most intense winds. Many trees snapped off and many were uprooted, but many also survived. You may have to pick your way around pine logs.

SOUTHERN GLADES WILDLIFE AND ENVIRONMENTAL AREA

THE EVERGLADES INCLUDES MUCH MORE than the area within Everglades National Park boundaries. One of the bordering areas has recently been made available to hikers. The Southern Glades Wildlife and Environmental Area (SGWEA) is state-owned land under the administration of the South Florida Water Management District. It was purchased through the "Save Our Rivers" and "Conservation and Recreation Lands" programs for recreational use. The Florida Game and Freshwater Fish Commission enforces the hunting regulations, but the Florida Department of Natural Resources and the South Florida Water Management District regulate other aspects.

The 26,000 acres contain canals and levees that were created long ago to drain the Everglades and provide flood protection. The dominant habitat is sawgrass marsh with bay heads and cypress domes interspersed.

Location, Mailing Address and Phone

From SW 344th St. (Palm Dr.) in Florida City, drive 5.3 miles south on U.S. 1. Turn right on Dade County Work Camp Rd. (SW 424th St.) at MM 122.5.

c/o Florida Game and Fresh Water Fish Commission, 551 North Military Trail, West Palm Beach, FL 33415   (407) 640-6100 (Florida Game and Fresh Water Fish Commission)

Facilities and Activities

Hiking, bicycling, fishing, hunting. No visitor facilities. No admission fee.

The three trails, totalling 21 miles, are on top of the levees paralleling the canals. The levees were built with the dredge material from the canals and have been used as access to maintain the canals. No trails, then, were newly cut for the change in management plan. The levees are 4-5 feet above the surrounding marsh, affording an open view and dry footing.

The first trail is a mere one-tenth of a mile west of U.S. 1. It is rocky and rough, although suitable for a mountain bike. It is 5.5 miles long, with a turnoff to U.S. 1 halfway down. It can also be reached from the southern end by driving on U.S. 1 to MM 116.4 and turning east into the C-111 canal area (north side of the canal). Go under the bridge and follow the canal west to the beginning of the trail. You may see a crocodile along this canal.

The second trail can be found by driving on Work Camp Road 1.7 miles past the first trail. Work Camp Road becomes unpaved and rather narrow and rough after a mile. The trail is five miles long and slightly smoother for bicycling. The canal banks are more overgrown, so the view is not quite as open.

The third trail is approximately two miles west of the second trail. It is four miles long. A trail is planned by the Game Commission and the Florida Trail Association to connect the three trails at their southern ends.

With careful searching, you may see some of the endangered animals that have been reported in the SGWEA: crocodiles, bald eagles, Cape Sable seaside sparrows, snail kites, peregrine falcons, and wood storks. Also watch for the threateded eastern indigo snakes, least terns, and sandhill cranes. Other animals you may see are bobcats, river otters, white-tailed deer, limpkins, and roseate spoonbills.

In addition to sawgrass, some trees and plants to look for are wax myrtles, redbay, sweet bay, coco-plum, paradise-tree, butterfly orchid, worm-vine orchid, and twisted air plant.

Hunting, fishing, and frogging are permitted. Because this is not a true Wildlife Management Area but an area created for controlled multiple recreational and educational uses, there are more hunting regulations than in a wildlife Management Area.

Best Time of Year

October through April to catch the migrating and overwintering birds. From June to September, wildlife may use the levee roads as corridors, since everything else may be submerged. Be prepared for mosquitoes. Since this is a hunting area, wear bright clothing in the autumn and winter.

Pets

Allowed.

HURRICANE ANDREW UPDATE

The SGWEA was on the southern side of Andrew and incurred intense winds. Trees were uprooted, but there were no visitor facilities to be damaged. The area is open for exploring.

CASTELLOW HAMMOCK NATURE CENTER

CASTELLOW HAMMOCK IS A 60-ACRE NATURE SANCTUARY administered by the MetroDade County Parks & Recreation Department. It was established as an environmental education center in 1974. It boasts of a tropical hammock with over 450 species of plants in an easily accessible area north of Homestead.

Castellow Hammock is probably best known for its wintering painted buntings. People come from all over the country in the winter to watch and photograph these brilliantly colored birds, easily visible from the Nature Center.

Allow about two hours to see the Nature Center, watch the butterfly garden and bird feeder, and walk the trail.

Location, Mailing Address and Phone

A half mile south of SW 216th St. on SW 162nd Ave. It can be difficult to find: look carefully for the "Castellow Hammock" sign on the east side of 162nd Ave.

22301 SW 162nd Ave., Goulds, FL 33170   (305) 245-4321

Facilities and Activities

Nature Center, self-guided nature trail, butterfly garden, educational programs, field trips, picnic tables, childrens' day camp. No admission fee. Fees are charged for educational programs.

Nature Center

The modest Nature Center building houses a small exhibit room with birds' nests, live native reptiles, a hammock display, a tree snail display, and a 150-gallon aquarium with a snapping turtle and other local aquatics. The bird feeder outside is frequented by painted and indigo buntings from October through April and white-winged doves year-round. Ask for their checklists of birds, butterflies, and other animals at Castellow, as well as their handout "Birdwatcher's Guide to South Florida."

Over 70 species of butterflies and skippers have been identified at and around Castellow. Many are tropical and are found nowhere else in the United States. A "butterfly garden" north of the nature center displays plants that attract butterflies, especially interesting for the gardener who is looking for the right butterfly-attracting plants. Examples are necklace pod and firebush. Of course, the garden is the place to see butterflies feeding on those plants, and the best months are September to November. Hummingbirds regularly visit the garden from September to April.

A covered pavilion with picnic tables and grills is available to groups by reservation. Bathrooms are available at the Nature Center.

The park provides special programs and field trips for general public, school, and scout groups. Two examples are "Native Plant Identification Workshop" and "Everglades Wildflower Walk." There is also a summer nature day camp for children.

Nature Trail

You can pick up a printed trail guide at the Nature Center; there is no charge, but return it when you're done. The trail through the hammock is a half mile one way. It is dirt, occasionally rocky and narrow (not handicapped accessible). Some trees likely to be seen along the trail are wild-tamarind, mastic, gumbo-limbo, pigeon-plum, paradise tree, lancewood, and West-Indian cherry. Several national champion trees are in this hammock. The two along the trail are a wild-tamarind 100 feet tall and 8.5 feet in diameter and a mastic. At one of the numbered stops is a limestone solution hole.

The bird list for the park includes 126 species of resident and migratory birds. Besides those already mentioned are mangrove cuckoos, smooth-billed anis, scissor-tailed flycatchers, and purple martins.

Best Time Of Year

In summer, the graceful swallow-tailed kites roost in the hammock, and in the winter the hammock is a roost for black and turkey vultures. Many warblers feed in the hammock during migration. Buntings and hummingbirds are frequent in winter, and butterflies are common in the summer and autumn.

Pets

Not allowed.

HURRICANE ANDREW UPDATE

Castellow was in the center of the worst winds. Damage to the hammock and visitor facilites was severe. The Visitor Center will be leveled and rebuilt. As of press time, no decision has been made on when to reopen the park but it will be approximately late 1993 or early 1994. Birders may still go in 1993 and walk around the open areas looking for buntings and hummingbirds. Call before visiting.

BILL BAGGS CAPE FLORIDA STATE RECREATION AREA

THE MAINLAND

CAPE FLORIDA IS PART OF A LARGE BARRIER ISLAND that protects the mainland. Beaches and dunes are a natural part of the Cape. Because of the Cape's proximity to the dangerous shoals and reefs of the Atlantic Ocean and Biscayne Bay, a lighthouse was built in 1825. Through the bitter Seminole Wars, the lighthouse was alternately lit and darkened.

In 1966, the state bought 406 acres at the south end of Cape Florida and named the new park after a Miami newspaper editor instrumental in getting the area protected.

Cape Florida is primarily a recreational area, with Miamians flocking to the beaches in the summer and the picnic areas on holidays. Much of the native vegetation has been replaced by exotics such as Australian-pine. For a few months in the fall, Cape Florida shines as a birding hotspot. Because migrating birds, particularly warblers and raptors, follow the coastline from the north, they often congregate on the south end before venturing across the water. You may see as many as 20 species of warblers in one day when unfavorable winds or weather frontal systems concentrate migrating birds at coastal sites. Shorebirds frequent the long stretches of beaches.

Location, Mailing Address and Phone

At the southern end of Key Biscayne (southeast Miami). Take the Rickenbacker Causeway from Coconut Grove south to the park entrance.

1200 S. Crandon Blvd., Key Biscayne, FL 33149   (305) 361-5811

Facilities and Activities

Swimming, nature trail, birding, picnicking, fishing, bicycling, historic lighthouse, snack bar. This is a day-use park. Admission fee charged.

A self-guided nature trail cuts through a hammock for about a half mile one way near the swimming beach. Interpretive signs explain about the native vegetation and habitat. A bicycle path circumnavigates most of the park, but joins with the road for a short stretch. The beautiful swimming beach is on the Atlantic Ocean side and is about 1.25 miles long. The seawall along Biscayne Bay is a popular fishing place. Anglers can catch snappers, groupers, jacks, snook, and other game fish.

The lighthouse is an interesting historic site. Tours into the lighthouse are given periodically during the day (fee charged). The lighthouse area is a good place to watch for migrating birds. It's possible they use the lighthouse as a navigational aid, as mariners do.

BEST TIME OF YEAR

September to November for migrating birds. Year-round for all other activities such as swimming and fishing..

PETS

Allowed on a 6-foot leash, but not on beaches or near concessions.

 HURRICANE ANDREW UPDATE

The very southern tip of Cape Florida was at the outer edge of the northern eye wall. Virtually every tree in the park was blown down. Many were the exotic Australian pines, which are not hurricane-adapted. The lighthouse and lighthouse keeper's quarters survived. Due to the major effort of clearing the trees from the roads and trails, the park will remain closed until approximately April, 1993.

BIG CYPRESS NATIONAL PRESERVE

BIG CYPRESS IS A NATIONAL PRESERVE, not a national park, and as such it has fewer restrictions than a national park. The preserve was established partly as a buffer to Everglades National Park and partly for its own ecological and recreational value. An immense international airport and satellite city were almost built here in the early 1970s to ease the burden on Miami International Airport. Environmentalists blocked the original plan but had to settle for a training airport north of Tamiami Trail, the Dade-Collier Training Airport (where commercial jet pilots practice take-offs and landings). Increased cypress logging, cattle ranching, and oil drilling added to the pressures.

The National Park Service was able to acquire 570,000 acres in 1974, but had to make concessions to landowners. These included allowing the existing hunting camps to be retained by the owners, allowing off-road vehicles (such as airboats and swamp buggies), hunting, and environmentally safeguarded mining and oil-drilling. The Big Cypress National Preserve Addition Act, passed by Congress in 1988, will gradually add 146,000 acres to the preserve.

The name "Big Cypress" comes from the extent of the cypress strands, rather than the size of the trees. Most of the preserve consists of bald-cypress, and very little is virgin. Most people see the preserve only from the pavement of Tamiami Trail or Alligator Alley, both of which bisect it. The Florida Trail (an unpaved hiking trail) has its southern terminus here. Pinelands and marshes comprise much of the remaining preserve.

Seven species of endangered animals can be found within the preserve: wood stork, snail kite, southern bald eagle, red-cockaded woodpecker, Cape Sable seaside sparrow, West Indian manatee, and Florida panther. The preserve is the last stronghold in extreme south Florida for the red-cockaded woodpecker and the panther, both of

115

which still breed here.

Location, Mailing Address and Phone

The Oasis Visitor Center is on Tamiami Trail (U.S. 41) in Ochopee, 37 miles west of Krome Ave. and 21 miles east of State Road 29. The Headquarters is on Tamiami Trail, 18 miles west of Oasis. The eastern preserve boundary is 25 miles west of Krome Ave. on Tamiami Trail and the western boundary is just east of (and parallel to) State Road 29.

HCR 61, Star Route Box 110, Ochopee, FL 33943   (813) 695-2000; Oasis Visitor Center (813) 695-4111

Facilities and Activities

Visitor Center, hiking trails, camping. Because this is a national preserve, construction of physical facilities is intentionally minimized. Note: No lodging or food facilities at preserve; nearest food service is at Ochopee (21 miles west).

Visitor Center

The Oasis Visitor Center and Ranger Station can be perused in 20-30 minutes, including the movie. Here you can get backcountry information for camping (permits not required), permits for off-road vehicles (required), and information on where to go and what to see.

Displays in the Visitor Center include tree snails and stuffed animals. A good selection of nature books and videos is sold. The 15-minute movie is shown on request in a small auditorium at the Center and explains the wet-dry season cycle in the Big Cypress area.

Camping

There are five primitive campgrounds along Tamiami Trail, maintained by the National Preserve. All are free, but they have no hookups and no running water; there are chemical toilets in winter only. They are good for self-sufficient camper vehicles and tents and the maximum stay is 30 days.

There are several primitive campgrounds along the Loop Road. Red Bird Lane (located 6.3 miles west of the eastern intersection of Tamiami Trail and Loop Road) and Black Bird Lane (5.5 miles west of the same intersection) each have eight campsites. They serve self-contained camper vehicles and tents.

A new one-acre primitive campground, known as Pineland, consists of 12 sites. It is located 12.5 miles southeast of Monroe Station (where the western end of the Loop Road intersects with the Tamiami Trail).

Tent camping is allowed on the Florida Trail anywhere you can find a dry spot. The safest way for you to ensure having a dry place to sleep is to carry a lightweight string hammock. The two primitive campsites designated on the official map are on higher ground, but they have no shelter or cooking grill. Campfires are permitted with deadwood found on the ground. There is no guaranteed source of drinking water along the trail. You must bring your own potable water or methods to purify water. At the two sites on the park map that indicate drinking water, the pumps have been removed (the park could not guarantee the water was safe). There is no charge for camping in the preserve.

Trails

The well-known Florida Trail begins or ends here, depending on your point of view. It stretches in fits and spurts (that is, with gaps) northward through the Florida peninsula and westward into the Panhandle. The section in Big Cypress (from Tamiami Trail to Alligator Alley) is about 28 miles long. Access at the north end is 38.5 miles west of the Andytown toll plaza or 0.3 miles east of Mile Marker 38. Access from the south end is from the Oasis Visitor Center. It is safer (from vandals) to park your vehicle at the visitor center than at the trailhead on Alligator Alley.

From the visitor center, the trail leads north through cypresses, pinelands, marshes, and hardwood hammocks. Even in the dry season, parts of the trail can be wet. Off-road vehicles are permitted to cross the trail, but they may not traverse it. Keep your eyes open for deer, wild hogs, bald eagles, swallow-tailed and snail kites, alligators, and possibly even a Florida panther. Two primitive campsites are available along the trail (see "Camping" above). A loop day- or overnight-hike of 13 miles or one of 26 miles can be done from Oasis Visitor Center. Let a ranger know your intentions if you're leaving your car parked overnight at Oasis.

Another section of the Florida Trail, seven miles long, is on the south side of Tamiami Trail and across from the visitor center (where you park your car) in an area known as the Loop Road Unit. It is not well-marked on the roadside, and it is not marked at all on the official park map, so it's less known to visitors and less traveled. (Look directly across from the eastern entrance to the parking lot to find this very narrow trail.) Another plus to this section is that off-road vehicles are not permitted anywhere in the Loop Road Unit. It's a beautiful section of trail, with bromeliad-festooned bald-cypresses shading the way. Ask at Oasis if you have trouble finding the trail. The trail is wet until mid or late winter. Contact the Florida Trail Association (see Appendix) for more information on the Big Cypress National Preserve section of the Florida Trail.

Loop Road

One way to see the edge of the Loop Road Unit is by driving the Loop Road. The Loop Road is a 24-mile stretch of narrow road between Forty-Mile Bend (near the Tamiami Ranger Station) and Monroe Station on the Tamiami Trail. The eight miles east of Pinecrest is paved and is gentle on city cars. West of Pinecrest, however, the road is pock marked with potholes and occasional puddles, so expect to average about 15 mph. That means it may take over an hour to drive the unimproved section. You may want to stop occasionally and get out of your car, which is easy to do because there is hardly any traffic. Add a little extra time for this.

Although it appears from the official Big Cypress Preserve map that the Loop Road is entirely within preserve boundaries, this is deceiving. Actually, the Loop Road is a county road (the only Monroe County road on the mainland), and you will see homes of people that live along the road. Please respect the private property owners' rights.

Aside from the homes, the road goes through some wild country, and you may see otters, bobcats, wild turkeys, snakes, wading birds, sandhill cranes, and, rarely, a panther. Just west of Pinecrest is an environmental interpretive center. Its main function is to teach local school children, so there is nothing of interest to the drop-in visitor. The short Hammock Nature Trail (on the north side of the road, opposite the Interpretive Center gate) leads to an old whiskey still and is open to visitors. The trail is narrow (not suited for wheelchairs) and can be covered in a leisurely 15 minutes. You can see strap fern, white stopper, and gumbo-limbo.

This road is worth the trip if you have the time and a car that can take potholes. In the summer, the road may be flooded, so call ahead to the Oasis Visitor Center for the conditions. At any time of the day or night you'll probably see something interesting. If you go at night, make sure your car can make it out on its own.

Turner River Road

Several unpaved graded county roads in the preserve may be worth driving for wildlife viewing. One such road is the Turner River Road (County Road 839) located 14.5 miles west of the Oasis Visitor Center and 4.1 miles east of Big Cypress Headquarters. It runs straight north for about 18 miles, and a "borrow" canal, which provided fill for the road, runs parallel the entire length. This road is not likely to flood but can get dusty or muddy. White ibises roost in the trees beside the canal. Panthers still roam this area, and the very lucky person may catch a glimpse of one.

Best Time of Year

Hiking the Florida Trail is better in the winter and spring (January-April). The summer rains usually flood the trail, and hiking is reduced to slogging through mosquitoes with nary a dry spot to pitch a tent. Driving the Loop Road is good year-round for seeing wildlife, but wet years cause some flooding of the road in summer. Hunting seasons of different types (waterfowl, small game, turkey, archery) run from September to April. But the main big game season (deer and wild hog) occurs during the period from mid-November to January 1 and is not a good time to wander around the preserve. Many hunters park their cars along the Loop Road and set out from there. Call Oasis Visitor Center in advance for local flooding conditions and hunting seasons. *If you hike during deer season, wear bright orange clothing.*

Pets

Allowed at campgrounds on a leash; not allowed on trails or in Visitor Center.

 # HURRICANE ANDREW UPDATE

The southern end of the preserve (south of Tamiami Trail) experienced severe hurricane winds. Damage to buildings (primarily ranger residences) was substantial. The Loop Road was closed for several weeks to clear fallen trees. The hammocks in the southwest (known as the "stairstep" region because of its zigzag border with Everglades National Park) were flattened. One hunting section south of Loop Road was closed for the season to prevent additional stress to the wildlife. The park reopened quickly after the storm.

FAKAHATCHEE STRAND STATE PRESERVE

FAKAHATCHEE STRAND STATE PRESERVE is a recent and very priceless addition to the state park system. It extends from Alligator Alley on the north end to Everglades National Park and the Ten Thousand Islands on the south. The strand, approximately 20 miles long and varying from three to five miles in width, is part of the Big Cypress Swamp. The 74,000-acre preserve contains the largest stand of native royal palms and the greatest variety of native epiphytic orchids, bromeliads, and ferns in North America. Many rare plants are found here.

Although it is now one of the wildest areas left in Florida, traces of old logging operations that ended in the 1950s are evident. The old roads used for logging cypress trees are called "trams" now by the locals. The only old growth cypresses left in the preserve are at Big Cypress Bend. Natural plant communities in the preserve include mixed hardwood swamps, swamp lakes, wet prairies, cypress forests, pine rocklands, oak-palm islands, fresh water marshes, saltwater marshes, and mangrove swamps. Because of this diversity, about 140 bird, 21 mammal, 24 reptile, and 14 amphibian species have been documented in the preserve. Fakahatchee Strand is one of the last strongholds for the Florida panther. Black bears, Everglades mink, bald eagles, and wood storks also live in the preserve.

During the dry season, you can easily spend a day hiking the trams and walking the Big Cypress Bend boardwalk.

Location, Mailing Address and Phone

There are two main accesses. Big Cypress Bend is on the Tamiami Trail, 7 miles west of the junction of Tamiami Trail and SR 29. It is right next to the Indian Village. To find the Headquarters and Janes Scenic Drive from Tamiami Trail: turn north onto SR 29, drive 2.5 miles to County

Road 837 in Copeland. Then turn left onto County Road 837 and drive 1.1 miles, bearing sharply right at the fork in the road, to a small building on the right that is the Fakahatchee Strand State Preserve headquarters (next to the fire tower). If the office is closed, pick up a brochure outside and continue up the road. Almost immediately the road becomes Janes Scenic Drive.

P.O. Box 548, Copeland, FL 33926. (813) 695-4593

Facilities and Activities

Boardwalk, scenic drive, hiking trails, bicycling, guided walks, birding. Note: This preserve is not developed for visitors. No food, water, lodging, restrooms, or other facilities are available. Write in advance for the vertebrate checklist (birds, mammals, amphibians, and reptiles).No admission fee.

Big Cypress Bend

This 2,000-foot (one way) boardwalk is an impressive addition to the state park system. It rivals Corkscrew Swamp Sanctuary's boardwalk on a smaller scale. If you are in the area to see Everglades City, for example, it is well worth a stop at Big Cypress Bend. It has been designated a National Natural Landmark. The boardwalk is not a loop (it ends at a central slough with deeper water), so you return the way you came. Interpretive signs along the way explain about the slough that the boardwalk passes over, the massive old growth cypress trees, the abundant and fascinating epiphytes, other plants, and wildlife. The surface is wide and smooth, suitable for wheelchairs. Preserve brochures are available at this location also.

W.J. Janes Memorial Scenic Drive

Janes Scenic Drive is a well-graded dirt road about 11 miles long. Unless you really know your way around the abandoned roads at the far end (part of the Golden Gate Estates), consider the road a dead end. The Golden Gate Estates is a large-scale development fiasco that left a maze of dozens of unfinished roads in an otherwise wilderness area.

The speed limit is 30 mph. This is to protect the wildlife, such as black bears, deer, panthers, foxes, turtles, and snakes. The lack of automobile traffic makes Janes Drive a good road to ride bicycles.

Hiking

The trams (old dirt logging roads) are scattered at intervals along Janes Drive. They are marked by locked gates, preventing vehicular passage. Most of the trams are overgrown and difficult to hike. Six of

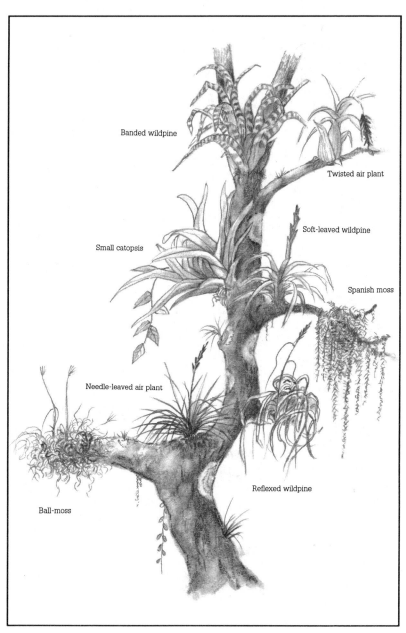

Banded wildpine

Twisted air plant

Soft-leaved wildpine

Small catopsis

Spanish moss

Needle-leaved air plant

Reflexed wildpine

Ball-moss

Bromeliads

the 20 trams have been partially cleared, meaning at least the first few miles of the roads have been cleared of regrowth, and passage by foot is easy. The cleared trams are Gates 2, 7, 12, 16, 19, and 20. Even on the uncleared trams, the trails are obvious, since they are higher than the surrounding land. For specific information on the cleared trams, call the preserve headquarters.

The trams pass through many types of habitats, such as hardwood hammocks and swamps. Some of the more picturesque, such as Gate 7 (4.4 miles from the headquarters), open onto wet prairies. Because of the variety of habitats, it's possible to see many types of wildlife.

Guided Walks

The giant preserve is understaffed, leaving a paucity of natural history programs in this fascinating region. Also, conditions are often too hot and buggy in summer to lead walks. From November to April rangers lead walks through the strand. Call in advance for reservations. The schedule depends on the number of people requesting guided walks. Be prepared for some wet slogging — you may find yourself in waist-high water!

East River Pond

Paralleling the Tamiami Trail is a canal that was created by "borrowing" fill to build the road. Occasionally, more fill was needed and large pits were dug. The pits have filled with water and become ponds. One such pond is in Fakahatchee Strand State Preserve. To find it, drive 5.2 miles west of the intersection of SR 29 on the Tamiami Trail. A small brown sign for the preserve indicates the dirt turnoff on the left.

You can fish here and even launch a small boat. The pond is loaded with alligators. During the early summer (April-June), tricolored herons and snowy egrets may be seen in the mangroves along the pond. They are visible from the water's edge with a spotting scope and provide a good photographic opportunity.

Best Time Of Year

February, March, and April for the driest conditions on the tram roads. November to April for Big Cypress Bend (best concentration of wildlife).

Pets

Not allowed on the Big Cypress Bend boardwalk; allowed elsewhere on a 6-foot leash.

HURRICANE ANDREW UPDATE

The preserve was at the extreme northern edge and did not receive severe winds. Damage from the hurricane was minimal and did not affect visitation. Several trees were toppled on the Big Cypress Bend boardwalk and were subsequently removed. Windthrown trees may still be seen from the trams.

COLLIER-SEMINOLE STATE PARK

EVERYWHERE YOU TURN in this area is something with the Barron Collier name. Barron Collier owned a million acres around here in the 1920s. Part of his holdings included a rare stand of native royal palm trees. Collier reserved this stand for a park. It became a state park in 1947. Before Collier owned the land, it was the home of the Seminole Indians. Some still live nearby. The park's name partly honors these Native Americans.

One of the most impressive historical features in the park is the "walking dredge" displayed near the entrance station. This dredge, a huge affair, was used to dig the Tamiami Canal in the 1920s. The 60-foot-long machine had legs that spanned the width of the yet-to-be-dug canal. The dredge would scoop the ground between its legs, then "walk" along, scooping as it went. The dredged material would be placed alongside the canal and sculpted into a road. Other walking dredges were used to build other canals in south Florida.

The park's 6,423 acres contain diverse habitats: tropical hardwood hammocks, mangroves, cypress swamps, salt marshes, and pine flatwoods. Thus, the wildlife is also diverse. Some of the rare and endangered species of Florida that have been seen here are the bald eagle, wood stork, brown pelican, red-cockaded woodpecker, crocodile, manatee, black bear, and mangrove fox squirrel.

The tropical hardwood hammock contains trees typical of the coasts of the West Indies and Yucatan. Royal palms, which may reach 100 feet tall, grow in this hammock. The mangroves are mostly found in a 4,760-acre wilderness preserve within the state park. This relatively untouched preserve can be explored by canoe.

Location, Mailing Address and Phone

On Tamiami Trail (U.S. 41), 17 miles south of Naples near Marco Island; 8.4 miles east of SR 951, 15.6 miles west of SR 29.

Route 4, Box 848, Naples, FL 33961   (813) 394-3397

Facilities and Activities

Self-guided nature trail, hiking trail, interpretive center, fishing, canoeing, boating and boat ramp, guided boat tours, campground, and primitive camping. Admission fee charged. Fees for camping, boat tours, and rentals are extra.

The 130 campsites are split into two campground areas, one popular for tenting and one for recreational vehicles. One-hour guided pontoon boat tours through the mangroves on the Blackwater River are run year-round. Some ranger-led programs are available only during the winter. Paddleboats can be rented for use in the boat basin. There is a boat ramp at the boat basin from which motorboats can run the Blackwater River to the Ten Thousand Islands.

Interpretive Center

The Interpretive Center is a tiny building that is of more interest than the exhibits it houses. The building is a cypress log block house, a replica of the type used locally during the Seminole Wars by defending whites. Its six sides were made of limestone rocks on the first floor and cypress logs on the second. The interpretive exhibits on local natural and human history are located in the small single room downstairs.

Walking Trails

The Royal Palm Nature Trail

This 0.9-mile self-guided trail wanders through tropical and temperate hardwoods. Large royal palms, Jamaica dogwoods, and gumbo-limbos grow along the trail. The sabal palmettos are hosts for the epiphytic golden polypody and rare shoestring ferns. The trail is partly boardwalk and partly hardpacked dirt (not wheelchair accessible). Interpretive plaques line the trail. A dead-end spur of boardwalk leads to a small observation platform overlooking the salt marsh. During the winter, songbirds that migrated from the north use the hammock for foraging.

Royal palm

Collier-Seminole Hiking Trail

This trail is relatively unknown because it's hard to find. It starts on U.S. 41, 0.7 miles east of the park entrance. The small gate on the north side is unmarked. This is because hikers must register at the entrance station before embarking on the trail. Otherwise, you cannot get through the locked gate.

The 6.5-mile loop trail passes primarily through pine flatwoods and cypress swamps. There is a primitive backpackers' campsite about three miles from the gate. Carry at least a gallon of drinking water per person for an overnight stay.

Canoeing

The mangrove wilderness preserve is accessible by canoe (bring your own or rent one here). The trail is 13.5 miles long and has a primitive campsite for an overnight stay. In the winter, rangers lead three-hour guided canoe trips to Mud Bay, part way along the canoe trail. Manatees are occasionally seen along the trail. Wading birds are common.

Best Time of Year

The nonmosquito season (November-April).

Pets

Allowed on a six-foot leash, but not in camping areas, wilderness areas, or near concessions.

HURRICANE ANDREW UPDATE

The park was on the extreme northern edge of the storm. Damage was minimal and visitor facilities quickly resumed. Some trees were knocked down. Oaks were uprooted and branches were broken off. Most royal palms withstood well, but some were beheaded. The Royal Palm Nature Trail was closed for a while for clearing of debris.

BRIGGS NATURE CENTER & ROOKERY BAY

THE MAINLAND

THE BRIGGS NATURE CENTER IS NESTLED within the 9,400-acre Rookery Bay National Estuarine Reserve (RBNER). It serves as the environmental education arm of the reserve. Although RBNER is administered by the National Oceanic and Atmospheric Administration and the Florida Department of Natural Resources (DNR), the Nature Center is run by a private nonprofit conservation organization in Naples called The Conservancy, Inc. The reserve exists through the dedicated efforts of individuals and organizations (such as the National Audubon Society and The Nature Conservancy). When the area was threatened with development in 1964, a local conservation movement succeeded in halting it temporarily.

To prevent subsequent development threats, this group of individuals, aided again by the above-mentioned organizations, were able to purchase the land and protect it permanently. The Conservancy, Inc. was born of this movement. It continues to be a strong voice for conservation in southwestern Florida (see also NAPLES NATURE CENTER). In 1977, The Conservancy's efforts were rewarded when Rookery Bay was included in the National Estuarine Sanctuary Program.

The protected mangrove estuary is vital to the growth of gamefish, commercial fish, shrimp, crabs, oysters, and snails. These support some of the most stable wading bird colonies ("rookeries") remaining in south Florida. Visitors can see some of the sanctuary from the trails and from boats.

Location, Mailing Address and Phone

Briggs Nature Center is located on Shell Island Rd., between Naples and Marco Island. From Tamiami Trail (U.S. 1), take SR 951 south

3 miles to Shell Island Rd. (look for Nature Center sign); turn right and drive about a mile to the Nature Center.
401 Shell Island Rd., Naples, FL 33942   (813) 775-8569

Facilities and Activities
Nature Center, nature trails and boardwalk, canoeing, guided canoe and boat tours, naturalist programs, boat ramp. No admission fee for the Nature Center or trails; fee charged for boardwalk.

Nature Center and Boardwalk
The central attraction inside the small Nature Center is the pair of 230-gallon saltwater tanks supporting estuarine fish, turtles, and other animals. Exhibits explain the local wildlife and ecology, and a small section is devoted to nature books for sale. Outside is a labeled wildflower garden. You may see scrub jays around the Nature Center, evidence of a research project for which they were transplanted here. Scrub jays (a threatened species in Florida) were probably not native to this exact area, but the scrub habitat is suitable.

The highlight of the Center is the one-half-mile boardwalk trail. This is accessible only through the Nature Center, since a fee for the boardwalk is charged. This loop walk enters five ecosystems: oak scrub, bayhead, brackish pond, fringe mangrove, and pine flatwoods. There are interpretive signs along the way, but the excellent "Boardwalk Guide" (available inside the Nature Center)

Red Mangrove

accompanies the numbered posts. A covered observation platform overlooks a brackish pond. A short side trail, called "Birdfeeder Trail," lives up to its name. Birdfeeders have been placed by the trail for birdwatching. Allow about an hour for the boardwalk. A guided tour is also available. Wheelchair accessible.

Trails

Two short trails are located down the road from the Nature Center. To find them, drive on Shell Island Road past the Center. Along the way, watch for wildlife on this graded dirt road. Gopher tortoises and yellow rat snakes are often seen. You'll pass the DNR Marine Laboratory Headquarters at 1.6 miles. Two-tenths of a mile past the Lab, the road ends at a small boat ramp. The trails begin to the left of the ramp.

The Monument Tower Trail follows an old grassy roadbed about a quarter mile one way to a small stone monument dedicated to two local conservationists. There are no interpretive signs and much of the roadside vegetation is exotic, the result of human disturbance.

The Catclaw Trail turns off near the beginning of the Monument Trail. It was designed as a low-impact interpretive trail. It is also about a quarter mile long and not a loop. There isn't enough dry land around here for longer trails. Some of the trees you'll see are saffron-plum, white stopper, white indigo-berry, and red mangrove. The trail's name comes from another small tree you'll see here, the catclaw. The trees have identification tags.

Black Mangrove

Best Time of Year
The nonmosquito season (November - April).

Pets
Not allowed.

131

CORKSCREW SWAMP SANCTUARY

CORKSCREW IS OWNED AND MANAGED by the National Audubon Society and is one of the jewels of its sanctuary system. It was made a "Registered Natural History Landmark" by the U.S. Department of the Interior in 1964. The sanctuary's 11,000 acres protects the largest remaining stand of old growth bald-cypress in the country. Some of the trees are over 500 years old.

The sanctuary would be valuable enough just for protecting the trees, but the real claim-to-fame of the swamp is the wood stork colony that forms almost every year. It has historically been the largest stork colony in the United States. Although the size of the colony has decreased over the years and varies considerably, it is still possible to see 1,000 pairs of storks nesting at the sanctuary in the best years. In 1992, 1800 pairs nested here, with some nests visible from the boardwalk. Nesting depends on water levels in the area; these may fluctuate up to 4.5 feet between the wet and dry seasons. The swamp is accessible by an impressive boardwalk built by the National Audubon Society in 1955. Alligators are an intimate part of this swamp and are frequently seen.

Corkscrew is about a two-hour drive from Homestead. It will take about 2-3 hours to see the visitor center and walk the boardwalk trail, so the trip can be done in one day. Consider combining it with a visit to Everglades City and lodging there overnight or camping at Big Cypress.

Location, Mailing Address and Phone

Located 1.5 miles north and west from County Road 846 in Immokalee. The Sanctuary Road entrance is on County Road 849. It is 14 miles from Immokalee, 21 miles from U.S. 41, and 15 miles from Interstate 75, exit 17.

Strangler fig

Route 6, Box 1875-A, Sanctuary Rd., Naples, FL 33964
(813) 657-3771

Facilities and Activities

Boardwalk nature trail, gift shop, displays, nature programs, birding.

Visitor Center

The building is small, considering the number of visitors that pour through the doors some days. There are plans to expand it. It contains a gift shop that sells an excellent variety of natural history books plus beautiful wildlife tee-shirts, note cards, film, wildlife art prints, and so forth. The exhibit section features a 50-gallon freshwater aquarium with mosquitofish, flagfish, sailfin mollies, and other local native species.

Pick up an illustrated self-guided tour booklet at the Visitor Center before you head out for the boardwalk. There is a small charge if you want to keep the booklet, otherwise you can borrow it for your walk and return it when you're finished. Also ask for the bird checklist. You'll keep busy searching for the 189 birds on the list.

There is a soft-drink vending machine for refreshments; the nearest food is at a convenience store seven miles away.

Boardwalk

The boardwalk at Corkscrew is probably world-famous to birders. This two-mile-long serpentine path has given hundreds of thousands of people the opportunity to view a pristine swamp without damaging it. The boardwalk traverses many habitats: bald-cypress, pine flatwoods, hammocks, willows, wet prairies, marshes, ponds, and lettuce lakes. Orchids, ferns, epiphytes, sawgrass, lichens, palms, and hardwoods are among the many plants you'll find here. In June, the wild hibiscus flowers, including the world's only known variety of wild hibiscus with white flowers.

Alligators, Carolina anoles, southeastern five-lined skinks, and cottonmouth snakes are among the many reptiles found here. Mammals include otters and white-tailed deer. Numerous wading birds, warblers during migration, and other birds can be found. Barred owls and limpkins are seen regularly. Many animals become accustomed to humans and walk on the boardwalk themselves.

At the halfway point, there is an observation platform that overlooks the central prairie — a beautiful view and a good photographic spot. During the stork nesting season, groups of stork nests can be seen in the cypresses surrounding the prairie.

No food, alcohol, or pets are allowed on the boardwalk. The chalkboard at the trailhead lists recent sightings of animals. To walk the boardwalk before the sanctuary opens in the morning, make arrangements in advance (send a letter with intended date).

Truck Tours

Only National Audubon Society chapters (not individual members) are permitted to request truck tours. An Audubon guide will take a minimum of 12 people on the sanctuary's back roads not normally seen by the public. Make arrangements in advance.

Best Time of Year

The famous wood stork colony may start forming any time from December to March, if it forms at all. Nesting should be going strong from February through May. You are likely to see storks during this time. In the winter, when the water levels are decreasing, there are concentrations of wading birds, alligators and snakes. Summer visitors will find much of the wildlife dispersed and rainstorms frequent, but many plants are flowering and the vegetation is lush. Mosquitoes are not as obnoxious here.

Pets: Not allowed.

V.
NATURAL AREAS: THE KEYS

JOHN PENNEKAMP CORAL REEF STATE PARK

APPROPRIATELY, THE NATION'S FIRST UNDERSEA PRESERVE is mostly under water. The park protects part of the only living coral reef in the continental United States. Within this marine sanctuary live 40 species of corals and 650 species of fish. The coral reef is very shallow in places, providing excellent snorkeling and scuba diving opportunities. The park's concession services make it easy for almost everyone to see the colorful reef, either by snorkeling, diving, or glassbottom boat. Other water-related activities are available here, including canoeing, fishing, and swimming. Land-bound facilities include camping and interpretive trails.

The park is named for John Pennekamp, a former associate editor of the Miami Herald, who was instrumental in getting Everglades National Park established. The original plans for the national park called for the boundary to extend south of Florida Bay, across Key Largo, and into the Atlantic Ocean, thus including the reef. Opposition from Florida Keys residents, whose homes would be within the new park boundaries, convinced officials that the only way to get the Everglades preserved was to exclude Key Largo and the reef. Fortunately, the reef was made into a state park shortly after.

Due to the intensive human usage of the reef, this glorious ecosystem is showing signs of stress and declining health. Among the culprits are careless anchoring, propellers striking bottom in shallow water, silting of coral by propeller wash, touching of coral by divers, littering, spilling fuel and oil, bilge pumping, and polluting from land sources. The reef is still beautiful, but please do your part to keep it that way.

Location, Mailing Address and Phone

MM 102.5 oceanside, U.S. 1, Key Largo. About 30 minutes south of Homestead.

For general park information, write P.O. Box 487, Key Largo, FL 33037; for concession information, write Coral Reef Park Company, P.O. Box 1560, Key Largo, FL 33037. For general park information, call (305) 451-1202; for concession information, call (305) 451-1621.

Facilities and Activities

Visitor center, picnic tables, snack bar, gift shop, dive shop, diving and snorkeling boat trips, glassbottom boat trips, boat ramp, swimming, boat rentals, campground. Admission fee charged; fees for camping, boat tours, and rentals are extra.

Visitor Center

Open 8:00 AM to 5:00 PM. This visitor center outclasses all others in our area. The star attraction is the 30,000-gallon saltwater aquarium, called "The Patch Reef Tank," that recreates a coral reef. Visitors can view the tank from all sides. Although the coral is not alive, the fish don't seem to notice. The live occupants include large lobsters, queen and gray angelfish, ocean surgeons, foureye butterflyfish, hogfish, parrotfish, and yellowtail snapper. Lining the visitor center walls are many smaller tanks, including "The Seagrass Community," "The Spiny Lobster," "Threats to the Reef," "The Reef Fish Community," and "The Outer Reef." Static displays explain natural storm protection from the reef and the mangrove community. In the auditorium, 14 different films about the state parks (each 17-45 minutes long) run continuously; there is no set schedule. This is an excellent small seaquarium for all ages and is included with admission into the park. Ask for their bird list, which contains 198 species.

Swimming

There are three designated swimming areas. The main swimming area, near the main parking lot and the visitor center, is somewhat sheltered from the open ocean. It is a roped-off area with an artificial wreck of a Spanish galleon in very shallow water. The wreck attracts grunts, barracuda, hogfish, gray snapper, and other fish, all very easy for the beginning snorkeler to see. In fact, this is one of the few places in the Keys to go snorkeling from shore and see something interesting. Because of the proximity of the swimming area to the muddy mangrove bottoms, upside-down jellyfish flourish here. They are so named because they swim mouth-downward, but flip over when resting on the bottom, exposing their fluttery mantle containing photosynthesizing cells. They can grow to one foot across and can give irritating stings, but they are not a serious problem.

There are two other swimming areas away from the main parking lot. One is more open ocean where the scuba classes go, the other is a sheltered area. Bath houses are available.

Snorkeling and Scuba Diving

You can't see the coral reef by snorkeling from shore. The park concession at the dive shop can set you up with everything you need for snorkeling or diving. Snorkeling and diving trips leave several times daily, weather permitting. You should call ahead to make a reservation (no deposit required) and check the weather forecast. The calmest water is usually in the morning. The light is best at noon because it is from directly overhead, revealing all the colors just below the water's surface. The afternoon trip is often windiest. You can rent (or purchase) all types of snorkeling and diving equipment at the dive shop. Scuba divers must show their certification cards to rent equipment and go on the diving boat. Remember...don't touch the coral!

In a typical 30-minute dive, snorkel, or glassbottom boat trip, you may see as many as 100 species of fish. These are the fish that are the most abundant, active, and diurnal. Many other species are present but are less likely to be seen on a short trip. Some of the common ones are blue tangs, trumpetfish, angelfish, damselfish, parrotfish, barracuda, grunts, butterflyfish, and snappers. Moray eels are common but nocturnal, and stingrays camouflage themselves with the sea bottom.

Glassbottom Boat

A good way for nonsnorkelers and nondivers to see the coral reef is on the 2 1/2-hour glassbottom boat trip operated by the concession. It is more appropriately called a glass-sided boat, distinguishing it from the other glassbottom tour boats in the area. Viewing is excellent. Reservations are suggested. The natural light is best at noon, when the sun's rays are most direct.

The captain will only rarely allow wheelchairs on board; the weather must be very calm, and he will not make a decision until the day of the trip (see "Glassbottom Boat" under "Biscayne National Park" for alternative).

Boating
Motorboats are available to rent. There are 14- to 22-foot boats, requiring a one-hour minimum rental. Sailboats are also for rent. There is a boat ramp and fuel docks if you have your own boat. Don't anchor a boat on coral — it is illegal and extremely damaging to the reef. Anchor on sand patches.

Canoeing
From the canoe launch by the Mangrove Trail, canoeists can wind through narrow mangrove channels or paddle out to the ocean. There are other places to put-in, too, like at the concession where you can rent canoes. Canoeing is a good way to see the park. During the winter season (November to March or April), ranger-naturalists lead several-hour canoe trips.

Trails
There are two short nature trails, one through mangroves and one through a hardwood hammock.

The Mangrove Trail is actually a boardwalk that allows you to walk among the mangrove waterways without getting your feet wet. It's a leisurely 15-minute self-guided walk with interpretive signs along the way. It is excellent place to see red mangroves in their watery environment, particularly for a wheelchair-bound person. There is an observation tower (not handicapped accessible) about 10 feet above the water that is just tall enough to view across the tops of the mangroves.

The Tamarind Trail (near the Entrance Station) is a leisurely 20-minute walk through a tropical hardwood hammock. It's a narrow dirt trail with many roots and rocks (unsuitable for a wheelchair). It is unmarked and has no interpretive signs. It is best to go with a ranger for a guided tour. You will see such trees as pigeon-plum and gumbo-limbo, plus the wild-tamarind for which the trail was named. Some commonly seen birds are warblers (palm, prairie, blackpoll, yellow-throated, and redstarts) and indigo buntings.

Ranger-naturalists lead daily walks in the winter (end of November to March or April). During the off-season, no guided trips are scheduled, but you can often find a ranger to give you a tour on request. Special groups tours can be arranged year-round.

Campground
Twenty-five of the 47 campsites are available by reservation only (call 305-451-1202 no more than 60 days in advance), and the other 22 are on a first-come basis. It is best to arrive by 5:00 PM. There is a

maximum camping period of 14 days and a maximum of eight people per site. The sites are small, but enough for one or two cars and a tent. There are recycling bins for aluminum cans, plastic bottles, and glass.

At one end of the campground is a lagoon-type pond that often has white ibises, great white herons, terns, and other water birds feeding.

Gift Shop and Snack Bar
The snack bar serves sandwiches, drinks, and snacks. The gift shop has a wide assortment of souvenirs.

Best Time of Year

The water temperature from November to April is 70-75°F (21-24°C) at the surface. Except during cold fronts, snorkeling is comfortable. Scuba divers usually wear wet suits since the deeper water is colder. In the winter, cold fronts can cause strong winds, occasionally canceling scheduled boat trips. From May to October, the surf temperature is 80-85°F (26-29°C). Starting in June, thunderstorms and tropical storms can make water-related activities hazardous. The most reliable months for good weather are April and May. These are also low mosquito months. Migrating birds can be seen and a lot of the winter crowds have gone.

Pets

Allowed on a six-foot leash, but not in campground, swimming areas, or buildings.

LIGNUMVITAE KEY STATE BOTANICAL SITE

THIS 280-ACRE ISLAND is a mile across the water from the road. It has some of the highest ground in the Keys (up to 16.5 feet above sea level) but doesn't have a road connecting it to anywhere. The Florida Department of Natural Resources (DNR) took over maintenance of the island in 1971. DNR has preserved the flora in its natural state, making it one of the best remaining examples of a West Indian tropical hammock. DNR staff and volunteers painstakingly removed exotic vegetation that had escaped cultivation from the original residents' landscaping. A few exotic plants have been left around the building for historical value. The only human inhabitant of the island now is the park's manager. Access to the island is by boat only.

The island's name comes from a small tree of the same name, lignum vitae. Lignum vitae, which means "wood of life," is native to Central America, the Antilles, the Bahamas, and extreme southern Florida (mostly the Keys, rarely the mainland). "Wood of Life" was the name dubbed by 16th-century Europeans who thought it was a cure for syphilis and other diseases. The wood, the densest used commercially, does not float. It is so loaded with resins (about 30% of the weight of the wood) and is so self-lubricating that it was once in demand by the shipping industry to make propeller shaft bearings.

Truly blue flowers, such as those borne by the lignum vitae, are uncommon in native North American plants; most of our blue flowers were introduced. The flowers appear in spring and early summer. The tree is small, up to 33 feet tall, and gnarled looking. The opposite, evenly-pinnate compound leaves are evergreen. Lignum vitae trees may grow to be 1000 years old, but they are not common enough to be used commercially any more. In fact, they are on the state's endangered species list.

A recent expansion of park boundaries includes the surrounding waters of Lignumvitae Key, Shell Key, and Indian Key (10,200 acres). This area is now protected from collecting of sponges and tropical fish. It prohibits use of boat motors where the water depth is three feet or less.

For botanists, Lignumvitae Key is well worth the trip from the mainland and the inconvenience of getting to the island. It is perhaps the most pristine example of native tropical hardwoods left in the continental United States. The historical aspects (such as the tour of the house) are also fascinating.

Location, Mailing Address and Phone

Accessible only by boat (tour boat or private). To tour boat dock from the north: Take U.S. 1 south past Islamorada to MM 79.5 on Indian Key Fill. A sign on the right says "State Tour Boat Landing 1000 Feet." Turn right into the parking lot with the sign "Lignumvitae State Botanical Site Tour Boat Monroe Landing." From the south, a sign around MM 80 (just before Indian Key Channel) says "Lignumvitae State Tour Boat Landing 2000 Feet." Turn left into the parking lot. Tourboat leaves at 1:30 PM Thursday - Monday. Note: The 3-hour boat tour of Indian Key State Historic Site leaves from the same dock at 8:30 AM Thursday-Monday.

P.O. Box 1052, Islamorada, FL 33036   (305) 451-7617 or (305) 664-4815

Facilities and Activities

Guided nature walk and tour of historical house, day-use boat dock. Closed Tuesdays and Wednesdays. Fee charged for boat trip and tour. Private boats may dock (free) during daylight hours and passengers can join the 10:30 AM, 1:00 PM, or 2:30 PM guided walks. Most facilities are not handicapped accessible.

Matheson House

This picturesque house was built of coral rock in 1919 by William J. Matheson, who also donated the original land for Matheson Hammock Park (see page 165). It is furnished with original and period furniture and now serves as a ranger station and museum. The windmill that provided power to the residents still stands next to the house; now a generator does that job. Fresh water was, and still is, obtained from cisterns. Cisterns are tanks that are filled with rain water falling on the roofs of buildings. The rain water is funneled through gutters to the tanks. From the tanks, the water is pumped to a modern plumbing system. Water that collects during the summer rainy season is usually enough to last through the winter dry months. Be sparing on your restroom flushes here. Once the water is depleted in the reservoir tank, there will be no more until the next hard rain. Lignumvitae is one of

Lignum vitae

the few places left in the Keys still using cisterns because aerial spraying for mosquitoes contaminates the water elsewhere; spraying is not permitted over Lignumvitae. The Matheson house was built with the hot tropical climate in mind, and the design reflects careful usage of architectural features that take advantage of the cooling breezes.

Trails

There are several trails on the island, but visitors must remain with a tour guide when on any trail. The tour guides are well acquainted with the native plants. Some of the trees you may see are mastic, lancewood, white stopper, saffron-plum, pigeon-plum, wild coffee, sapodilla, and satinleaf. White-tailed deer may be seen in the open areas near the buildings or on the trails. Although they are smaller than mainland deer, they are not the same subspecies as the Key deer.

Reportedly, they are descendants of Michigan stock. In the summer (May-October) white-crowned pigeons are easily seen in the canopy feeding on the fruits of the pigeon-plum, poisonwood, and fig trees.

The trails are wide and level enough for wheelchairs. The tour, including the boat ride, takes about three hours.

Best Time of Year

The dry season, when mosquitoes are fewest (don't forget, there is no artificial mosquito control here).

Pets

Not allowed.

LONG KEY STATE RECREATION AREA

PERCHED ATOP VESTIGES OF ANCIENT CORAL REEFS, Long Key is rich in West Indian vegetation and marine life. Realizing the natural resource and recreational values of the area, the state began to protect it in 1961 and by 1973 it had acquired 965 acres for the park; 116 acres are submerged.

Local saltwater fishing was an attraction that brought world-wide attention when Henry Flagler (builder of the overseas railroad to Key West) established the Long Key Fishing Club in 1906 after the first bridge was completed. Fishing continues to attract people to the ocean and bay waters around Long Key.

The park has walking and canoe trails for the non-angler. These bring the nature-seeker close to the shallow lagoons where birds feed on the varied marine fish and invertebrates.

Along the oceanside are natural sandy beaches, accessible only by boat. In the summer, these narrow beaches are reserved for nesting sea turtles. Because sandy beaches are rare in the Keys, this is one of the few places around where sea turtles can lay their eggs.

Location, Mailing Address and Phone

Park entrance is at MM 67.6 on U.S. 1 oceanside on Long Key. Layton Trail is difficult to find; it's outside the park entrance, a few hundred yards north of MM 68 on U.S. 1 bayside. Look for a green historical marker sign "Long Key Fishing Club" and the small "Layton Trail" sign next to it. Park on the shoulder of the road.

P.O. Box 776, Long Key, FL 33001   (305) 664-4815.

Facilities and Activities

Nature trails, canoeing and canoe rentals, campground, picnicking, swimming, fishing. Admission fee charged at main entrance (no admission fee for Layton Trail). Fees for camping and rentals are additional.

Nature Trails

Golden Orb Trail

This is a one-mile loop trail around a lagoon and beach. Plaques along the way explain the natural history. An observation tower provides a scenic view.

Layton Trail

If you are driving down the Keys and want to take a break to stretch your legs, this is just the place. This short shady loop trail will take about 15 minutes to walk. It goes through a tropical hardwood hammock, rich with native Keys plants, such as wild-lime, Jamaica dogwood, buttonwood, and seven-year-apple. Plaques identify the trees. The trail opens onto the rocky shore of Florida Bay. Not handicapped accessible.

Canoe Trail

The Long Key Lakes Canoe Trail is a 1.3-mile self-guided canoe trail. It takes about an hour to paddle the loop around the mangroves, seagrass patches, and soft corals. You can rent a canoe here or bring your own. The trail is suitable for novices.

Best Time of Year

The nonmosquito season (November to May).

Pets

Allowed on a leash. Not allowed on beaches or in camping areas.

CRANE POINT HAMMOCK
(MUSEUM OF NATURAL
HISTORY OF THE FLORIDA KEYS)

A MAJOR VICTORY FOR CONSERVATION in the Florida Keys came when the Florida Keys Land and Sea Trust acquired the 63.5-acre Crane Point Hammock in Marathon in 1988. This hammock contains probably the last intact virgin thatch palm hammock left in North America. It was a prime site for development on the crowded land-starved island of Key Vaca. The area did not escape development by accident. The Crane family, who bought the property in 1949, were ardent conservationists.

The hammock supports 160 native species of plants, and artifacts of pre-Columbian native people have been found here. The million-dollar museum was completed in 1990, but new sections being built over the next few years promise to add even more value to a visit. Allow about a half day for your tour of the museum and a walk on the nature trail.

The Florida Keys Land and Sea Trust is a private, nonprofit organization that acquires natural areas in the Keys to protect habitats and cultural history.

Location, Mailing Address and Phone

MM 50, U.S. 1, Marathon. Look for a small sign on the bay side, opposite the "K-Mart" store.

Florida Keys Land and Sea Trust, P.O. Box 536, Marathon, FL 33050 (305) 743-9100

Facilities And Activities

Adult and children's museums, artificial lagoon, self-guided nature trail, gift shop. Admission fee charged.

Museum

The main attraction is the new museum housing 20 major exhibits and additional rotating displays of cultural and natural history. In the main building is the "adult" museum, which boasts a 600-square-foot walk-through replica of a coral reef cave. It extends 30 feet above you as you walk through, and you will see mounts of many fish common and not-so-common in the Florida Keys reefs.

Also in the museum are two life-sized wildlife dioramas, one on wading birds and shorebirds, and one on Key deer. The Key deer display features a two-day-old fawn that drowned in a ditch dug years ago for mosquito control. Numerous ditches remain in the Keys, a hazard for deer that drown when they try to cross the ditch and cannot climb the steep sides. Strategically placed near the mother and fawn in the diorama is a mounted bald eagle that cleverly shows how diminutive the deer really are.

Exhibits in the main museum depict the 5000-year human history of the Marathon area. Rare and unusual artifacts of cultural history, some dating back 5000 years, are highlights. Other exhibits include an authentic dugout canoe, a tree snail display, a satellite photo of the Keys, a crocodile skull and mount, and displays about the ship-wrecking business.

This building also houses a small gift shop which vends natural history-oriented jewelry, tee-shirts, hats, and knick-knacks. There is a good selection of local field guides and books on the Florida Keys. The profits go to the Florida Keys Land and Sea Trust for conservation.

As you exit by the rear door of the main building, a walkway passes over an artificial lagoon, where live sharks, snappers, barracudas, parrotfish, and angelfish may be seen swimming around as they might just offshore from the hammock.

The walkway leads to the children's museum, a one-room building created especially for inquisitive children. Here children can handle the objects in the touch tank and study the fish in either of the two 200-gallon saltwater tanks. A terrarium houses a live box turtle, and other tanks have horseshoe crabs and sea urchins. One corner of the room is devoted to a "library," where children can plunk down comfortably on the fluffy pillows and read to themselves or each other from the shelf of children's nature books. The museum is a regular field trip destination for local public school classes.

147

Trails

Behind the main building is the beginning of the nature trail. This is a quarter-mile self-guided loop that runs through tropical Crane Point Hammock. Pick up a printed trail guide at the museum. The guide explains about the ecology of the hammock and some of the native trees you'll see. Many trees along the trail have identification tags. You'll see the Key (or brittle) thatch palm, Florida thatch palm, wild dilly, black ironwood, Jamaica dogwood, and paradise-tree. All the poisonwood trees are labeled, so you'll know not to touch them.

The trail is a narrow dirt path (with the intent of being as undisruptive to the hammock as possible) and is not suitable for wheelchairs. However, handicapped people may ask to go on the dirt service road a short way to see some of the hammock.

The Florida Keys Land and Sea Trust has plans to build a one-mile-long boardwalk through Crane Point Hammock. This will be a star destination for nature lovers who visit the Keys. It will be handicapped accessible.

A recent addition to the museum's facilities is a small amphitheater for natural history programs. Call ahead for the schedule of programs.

Group tours and programs are available if arranged in advance. A possible tour could be a guided walk through the hammock. A program might be on sea life or hammock plants. In other words, the staff is knowledgeable and flexible and will try to work with your group's needs. You must call in advance, preferably at least one week, to arrange a special group program or tour. Fees are dependent on the group size, but includes admission to the museum, a very good deal.

Best Time of Year

Any time of year is fine for the museum. The trail is beautiful year-round, with plenty to see, but it may be buggy and muggy in the summer. October, November, March, and April are good months to see migrating warblers and raptors.

Pets

Not allowed.

BAHIA HONDA STATE PARK

THE SPANISH INFLUENCE in this area is obvious by the name of the park, which means "deep bay." Indeed, the channel at the west end is one of the deepest natural channels in the Florida Keys. The bridge that spans it is correspondingly high, since the deeper the water, the higher the waves. The 635-acre park preserves many plant species of West Indian origin. One of the largest remaining stands of silver palm is found here.

Flagler's railroad passed through Bahia Honda, and remnants of the hurricane-torn tracks still rise above the park. Because of its height above the water, the old bridge is a good scenic observation spot.

This is Florida's southernmost state recreation area. It was changed from recreation area status to state park status in 1991. The park encompasses lagoons, beach dunes, coastal berms, mangroves, submerged marine habitats, and tropical hardwood hammocks. Several rare and unusual plants are found here: satinwood, manchineel, silver palm, key thatch palm, and the endangered small-flowered lily thorn (or spiny catesbaea).

Location, Mailing Address and Phone

MM 36.9, U.S. 1 on Bahia Honda Key; 12 miles south of Marathon.
Route 1, Box 782, Big Pine Key, FL 33043   (305) 872-2353.

Facilities and Activities

Nature trail, birding, campground, swimming, picnicking, boat ramp, marina, dive shop, cabins, fishing, windsurfing. Admission fee charged. Fees for camping, cabins, rentals, and boat trips are extra.

There are three camping areas with 80 sites for trailers and tents. Six cabins can accommodate eight people each; linens and utensils are provided.

The concession runs daily dive trips to the coral reef at Looe Key.

Looe Key is part of the Florida Keys National Marine Sanctuary. Swimming and snorkeling are excellent from the beaches on the ocean and bay sides.

At the marina, charter boats and fishing guides are for hire. There is a boat ramp and overnight docking facilities. The concession store sells marina supplies and limited groceries.

In the autumn, Bahia Honda is a good place to watch for migrating birds. The birds fly south along the chain of keys, resting, feeding, and searching for a way to cross the big water.

Silver Palm Trail

This is a short loop trail, about a 15-minute walk, near the swimming beach on the Atlantic side. A printed trail guide follows the numbered posts, explaining the hammock and dune ecology. The shrubby silver palms are common along the way because they are protected here. Elsewhere, silver palms are stolen from their natural settings to be planted in peoples' yards. The silvery undersides of the fronds are indeed beautiful.

Other plants along the trail, such as bay-cedar and black-torch, are typical of Keys beaches. Sea oats and sea grape, seen along the beach, are state-protected dune stabilizers. Animals include land crabs and white-crowned pigeons in the hammock and wading birds in the lagoon.

Best Time Of Year

For migrating raptors, shorebirds, and warblers, March, April, and September to November. For wintering birds, December to April. For diving and snorkeling, April to November.

Pets

Allowed on a leash; not allowed in campground, swimming areas, concession areas.

NATIONAL KEY DEER REFUGE

IT WAS A CLOSE CALL. The diminutive Key deer (*Odocoileus virginianus clavium*, a sub-species of white-tailed deer) had reached the perilously low population size of about 50 individuals, when protection came in the form of a refuge created specifically for them. The islands had never supported great herds of the deer and human interference had whittled the numbers down by hunting, habitat destruction, automobile collisions, and other hazards. With the establishment of the refuge in 1957 came total protection from hunting, reduced speed limits, and regulations preventing harassment. The population has partially recovered, largely due to the persistent efforts of Jack Watson, the first warden of the refuge. Watson tirelessly and fearlessly pursued poachers and succeeded in getting them convicted. The present population has stabilized at about 250-300 deer.

The small size of these deer can be attributed to island living. Since the islands provide limited food and fresh water, the smaller deer thrive. Key deer bucks weigh about 80 pounds and does average about 64 pounds, the size of large dogs. Other than that, they look like their larger northern cousins.

Since this is a refuge for wildlife (part of the National Wildlife Refuge system), and most of the 7,900 acres is covered by the Gulf of Mexico, you won't find "people" facilities as in a national park. A nature trail and a wildlife observation spot are all that were created for visitors. The deer may be found wandering anywhere on Big Pine or No Name Keys. With patience and careful looking, you will see these beautiful animals.

A special word of caution: *drive very slowly and carefully around Big Pine and No Name Keys to protect the deer*. They are too often killed by cars. Also, *do not feed the deer*. Besides the improper diet they might receive, they learn to associate humans (and thus houses and cars) with food. A sign on U.S. 1 near the refuge keeps the grim tally of the year's deer mortality. Ten to fifteen percent of the population may be killed by cars in a single year. Free-ranging dogs are also deadly. Observe the deer quietly from a distance, and you will be rewarded by seeing more natural behavior.

Location, Mailing Address and Phone

From the north: On U.S. 1, go to first traffic light on Big Pine Key (MM 30.5). This is Key Deer Blvd. intersection. Turn right, but the road forks immediately, so stay to the left and follow the signs. From the south: On U.S. 1, turn left at Key Deer Blvd. (MM 30.5). Stay to the left fork after turning. On Key Deer Blvd., go 1.8 miles to Watson Blvd. and turn left. The Headquarters building is 0.8 miles. To Blue Hole: From the junction of Watson and Key Deer Blvds., go north on Key Deer Blvd. 1.2 miles to sign saying "Blue Hole Observation Pool Entrance." Parking lot is on the left. To Watson Hammock Trail: Go 0.3 miles past Blue Hole (north). Look for small sign saying "Wildlife Trail Entrance." Parking lot is on the left.

Key Deer Refuge, P.O. Box 510, Big Pine Key, FL 33043   (305) 872-2239

Facilities and Activities

Nature trail, wildlife observation area. No admission fee.

The headquarters building, open on weekdays, is where the administrative offices are located. There are no visitor displays, but refuge personnel will be happy to answer your questions. If you arrive after hours, you can obtain a refuge map at the display sign at the far end of the parking lot. The map will show the most likely places to see the deer. Drive around the roads marked on the map in early morning or late afternoon and evening and you'll have a good chance of seeing a deer.

Blue Hole (Observation Area)

Formerly a rock quarry mined for road construction, this gaping hole is now filled with fresh water, a rare commodity in the Keys. The fresh water attracts many terrestrial animals that come to drink, including the deer. Freshwater aquatic animals, uncommon elsewhere on the Keys, may be found here. These include alligators, frogs, soft-shelled turtles, and largemouth bass. There are no trails at the Blue Hole, but it's a good place to photograph (you need only lug your equipment a few yards from your car) or just sit and watch the wildlife parade.

Watson Trail

The trail was named for Jack Watson, the first refuge manager, and is 0.6 mile long. As the name "Big Pine Key" suggests, the island is wooded with slash pines (*Pinus elliotii var. densa*), and so is this trail.

The varietal name refers to the high specific gravity of the wood. Enough light gets through the canopy to allow the understory hardwoods to outcompete the pines. Under natural conditions, that doesn't happen, since wildfires suppress the hardwoods.

Under the pines are saw palmetto, wax myrtle, sawgrass, blackbead, buttonwood, key thatch palm, silver palm, and sweet acacia, to name some species along the trail. From May to October, expect to see white-crowned pigeons flying around. They feed on mast from figs and poisonwoods in Watson's Hammock, which the trail passes near. Also look for old, small ditches cut through the limestone years ago and stocked with mosquitofish for mosquito control. The ditches are treacherous to Key deer fawns that drown while trying to cross them.

The trail is flat and surfaced with a very thin layer of gravel. It is wide enough for a wheelchair, with no obstructions.

Best Time of Year

The deer are visible any time of the year. Early morning and late evening are the best times.

Pets

Allowed on a leash.

DRY TORTUGAS
NATIONAL PARK

FLUNG FAR OUT INTO THE GULF OF MEXICO are the rest of the Florida Keys. Few visitors realize that the Keys don't end at Key West — just the road does. Almost 70 miles farther west, and another world away, is a small cluster of seven coral islands known as the Dry Tortugas. Fort Jefferson, the "Gibraltar of the Gulf," is located on one of these islands.

Ponce de León was credited with discovering the islands for the Old World in 1513. He named them *Las Tortugas* (Spanish for "the turtles") because of the numerous sea turtles he found there. The adjective "dry" was added later to warn mariners that there was no fresh water on the islands. Located strategically in the shipping path between Central America and the United States, the islands became the sanctum of pirates for several centuries. When Florida became part of the United States in 1821, so did the Dry Tortugas.

In 1846, the U.S. Corps of Engineers began to build the fort (named after Thomas Jefferson) on 16-acre Garden Key. Although construction continued for three decades, the fort was never completed. Still, it was the largest seacoast fortress from Maine to Texas at that time, with a perimeter of a half-mile. The 8-foot-thick, 45-foot-high walls contain 16 million hand-made bricks. During the Civil War, Fort Jefferson became a military prison for army deserters. The most famous political prisoner was Dr. Samuel Mudd, accused of conspiring to assassinate President Lincoln. His misfortune was that he set the broken leg of the fugitive John Wilkes Booth. Although sentenced to life imprisonment, he was pardoned after saving the army garrison from a yellow fever epidemic. His predicament is still echoed by the popular phrase "Your name is Mudd!" The Navy took over the fort for a refueling station in 1889. President Franklin D. Roosevelt proclaimed the fort and adjacent islands a national monument (known as Fort Jefferson National Monument) in 1935 for their historic and educational values. In November 1992, the monument achieved national park status in recognition of its exceptional natural resources.

But enough of the human history. Let's talk about birds. Just as the islands are located in the middle of the shipping lanes, so they are also located in the middle of the migration flyways between North and South America. For as long as the lonely coral islands have poked their heads above the water, sea birds and land-dwelling migrants have found a haven on them. Nesting birds start arriving in March, and by April, up to 100,000 terns have eggs on Bush, Hospital, and Long Keys. Most are sooty terns, but brown noddies and roseate terns also nest here. Gulls, other terns, shorebirds, raptors, frigatebirds, boobies, and accidentals from the West Indies can all be found most of the year. In 1832, John James Audubon visited the Tortugas to study the spectacular bird life.

Not to be outdone, the scene underwater is equally spectacular. Excellent snorkeling and scuba diving sites abound. The clear shallow waters are perfect for the growth of coral and associated reef fish. Four endangered species of sea turtles — the hawksbill, green, Atlantic Ridley, and leatherback — have been found here.

Although it's expensive to arrange an overnight camping stay unless you're with a group tour or on your own boat (because the seaplane captain would have to make a separate trip to pick you up), it's worth it. There is so much to see for such a small group of islands. It's also the ideal place to relax — cellular phones and fax machines don't work out here!

Location, Mailing Address and Phone

68 miles west of Key West, in the Gulf of Mexico. Accessible only by private boat, chartered boat, or commercial seaplane. Several private concessions run seaplanes from the Keys and southern Florida cities to Dry Tortugas. Call the Florida Keys and Key West Tourist Bureau, the Florida Board of Tourism, or the Greater Key West Chamber of Commerce (see Other Sources of Information for phone numbers) for the current list of licensed operators. You can also send for the list of charter tour operators by contacting the Superintendent's Office at Everglades National Park.

Boat trips are not recommended unless you're looking for pelagic birds. The water can get uncomfortably rough, causing trips to be canceled often. Boats take about five hours. Seaplanes are much quicker (about 45 minutes), but occasionally it is too rough for seaplanes to land. The standard seaplane trips are half-day or full-day, but overnight trips can be individually negotiated.

The Florida Audubon Society sponsors an excellent guided birding trip to Dry Tortugas every April or early May, coinciding with spring migrations and tern nesting (see Other Sources of Information for how to contact Florida Audubon). Reserve early, for this is a popular trip.

Superintendent, Everglades National Park, P.O. Box 279, Homestead, FL 33030. (The Everglades National Park superintendent oversees Dry Tortugas as well.) For group camping permits: Site Manager, Dry Tortugas National Park P.O. Box 6208, Key West, FL 33041. (305) 242-7700 (same as Everglades National Park; Dry Tortugas has no phone).

Facilities and Activities

Visitor center, self-guided tour, birding, fishing, snorkeling, scuba diving, campground. No admission or camping fee.

Note: Visitors must bring all their own provisions. This includes drinking water and food. No fresh water is available. No lodging is available; overnight stays on land require camping. All garbage must leave with you. The fort, visitor center, and campground are on Garden Key.

Visitor Center

The Visitor Center contains historical exhibits, an interpretive slide program, and books for sale. Ranger-led programs are offered in the winter. Check the Center for the schedule. Ask for the bird checklist here; it's very thorough. Snorkel equipment can be borrowed from the Visitor Center.

The Fort

The half-mile self-guided tour leads you around the historic fort. Ignore the sign that says it takes a half hour for the trip. It's just too fascinating to breeze through that quickly. Interpretive signs guide you inside and outside the brick fortress, through bastions and narrow stairwells, past the ammunition magazine, and even into Mudd's spartan cell. Calcified water percolates through the ceiling in places, creating mini-stalactites and corresponding stalagmites inside the building. The fort was never completed because of the invention of the rifled cannon, which could penetrate even the 8-foot-thick walls. Old and new cisterns can be seen. The old ones cracked from settling, letting in salt water. The original lighthouse stands defunct. From the roof of the fort (accessible by stairs), the view across the water is spectacular.

Entirely surrounding the fort is a brick sea wall constructed as added protection to the fort, much as the coral reefs protect the islands.

Between the fort and the seawall is a moat containing quiet, sheltered water. You can walk on top of the sea wall for its entire length and see into the clear water on both sides. Nonswimmers will be treated to a view of marine life almost as good as a snorkeler's view if the water is calm. Bring a strong flashlight if you're staying at night, and try looking into the moat after dark. The wind often dies down after dusk, making the water calmer. The nocturnal creatures emerge, and wonderful views of active conchs, lobsters, crabs, shrimp, moray eels, urchins, and sea stars can be seen.

Loggerhead Key

About two miles west of Garden Key is the largest of the seven islands. Boaters are permitted to dock at Loggerhead and climb the 180 steps to the top of the functioning lighthouse. It affords a glorious view of the Dry Tortugas. The island was named after the loggerhead turtles that nest on the sandy beaches in the summer. The nests are carefully protected by park rangers.

Birding

Birders from around the country and many other countries come to the Dry Tortugas to see seabirds and migrating land birds. There are 285 species known to occur here. Many are accidentals from far away, appearing briefly after getting blown off course from a cold front or tropical storm. The late winter cold fronts blow flocks of weary migrants onto the islands. The exhausted birds perch listlessly on branches, recovering strength enough to feed. This is when binoculars just get in the way. The metaphor "the trees were dripping with warblers" is appropriate after cold fronts.

From March to October, tens of thousands of sooty terns and brown noddies can be watched from Garden Key. Most nest on Bush and Long Keys, only a few hundred yards from Garden Key. A strong spotting scope will give an impressive view of the nest islands from Garden Key.

In October and November, the north winds bring migrations of raptors (such as merlins, peregrine falcons, sharp-shinned hawks, and broad-wings), warblers, and shorebirds. All are hoping to rest, feed, and store up energy for the remaining marathon flight across the havenless water to Cuba and beyond.

Snorkeling and Swimming

Snorkeling and swimming is exceptional around the outside of the sea wall on Garden Key. Snorkelers will find a rich variety of marine life in a mere three or four feet of water. Colorful fish, lobsters, sea cucumbers, conchs, corals, and so on are all easily visible. Look for loggerhead and hawksbill sea turtles feeding in the seagrasses. Scuba divers must bring their own diving equipment, but snorkeling equipment can be borrowed at the Visitor Center.

Boating and Fishing

Many sailboaters find the Dry Tortugas a great destination from cities on both coasts of Florida. Motor boaters usually "jump off" from Key West. If you bring your own boat to the islands, make sure you have the Dry Tortugas NOAA Chart #11438 to navigate safely around the shallow reefs. No permit is necessary to anchor within the park boundaries. The waters between Key West and the Tortugas can get rough during the winter or during summer thunderstorms, so check the forecast before casting off. No fuel or provisions of any type are available at the islands; you must be completely self-sufficient. There are no overnight slips in the Dry Tortugas. Mooring at the dock on Garden Key is limited to two hours during daylight. Boats must be anchored away from the coral at night. Water skiing and jet skiing are not permitted.

Between March 1 and October 1, nesting and fledging birds have priority over Bush Key, and the island is off-limits to human visitation. Also, because sea turtles nest on East, Middle, Hospital, Long, Bush, and Loggerhead Keys, these islands are closed from sunset to sunrise from May through September.

Fishing is excellent, but even out here a saltwater fishing license is required by all non-Florida residents (must be purchased before your arrival). Florida residents must obtain a license to fish from a boat (not needed for dock fishing). No bait is available other than what you catch. Lobster and conch are protected from harvest and spearfishing is prohibited. Snappers, groupers, grunts, and tarpon are often caught. A fish cleaning table is located at the dock on Garden Key. If you're not a fisherman, bartering for fresh fish is worth a try (steaks are good trade items).

Campground

A more peaceful, picturesque, relaxing setting for camping can't be found in Florida. Your tent is pitched under a palm tree, birds "drip" from the trees, and with a mere two skips you're slipping into the warm coral reef waters. Even better, your office can't reach you.

Camping is permitted only in the designated camping area on Garden Key. Picnic tables, grills, and saltwater toilets are provided. Camping is free, but on a first-come first-served basis, since there are a limited number of sites. Groups of 10 or more must obtain a permit in advance by writing to the Site Manager at Dry Tortugas. All supplies must be packed in and all trash must be packed out. There are no showers.

Best Time of Year

For birding: April to September for nesting terns; spring and autumn for migrants; year-round for sea birds. For snorkeling: the water is warmest and calmest in summer. For fishing: year-round.

Pets

Allowed on leash. Not allowed inside the fort or left unattended.

VI.
SEMI-NATURAL AREAS

PRESTON B. BIRD & MARY HEINLEIN FRUIT & SPICE PARK

THIS 20-ACRE FACILITY in the Redland Historic District of Dade County is a credit to the MetroDade County Parks and Recreation Department. Since 1944, the park has displayed over 500 varieties of tropical and subtropical fruit, herb, spice, and nut trees from all over the world. They thrive in this climate. The park's primary functions are education and agricultural research.

This park is included in this book because it adds a little "spice" to the total enjoyment of exploring tropical Florida. Few of the trees are native, but many of the trees growing here are ones you will see along roadsides in the Homestead area. Many birds are attracted to feed on the variety of fruits ripening year-round. You can see the park in as little as an hour, but allowing two to three hours (including browsing the store) will be better. Considering the proximity to other natural areas, the very reasonable admission fee, and all you can learn, this is a worthwhile side trip.

Location, Mailing Address and Phone

24801 SW 187th Ave., Homestead, on the corner of Redland Rd. and SW 187th Ave.

24801 SW 187th Ave., Homestead, FL 33031   (305) 247-5727

Facilities and Activities

Tours of the groves and gardens, Gourmet & Fruit Store, picnic tables, weekly plant workshops. Admission fee charged for groves; fees charged for programs.

Groves and Gardens

Twice a day on Saturdays and Sundays a guide will lead tours that last about an hour. The guide will gather ripe fruits for you to taste. You may also walk around on your own. You can buy or borrow a guide book that describes area of origin, uses, propagation techniques, flowering season, and so on of the trees found here, as well as recipes and some natural history. It also contains the park's list of the 81 species of birds that have been seen here. You may try any fruit you find on the ground.

Gourmet and Fruit Store

The Gourmet and Fruit Store has a wonderful selection of dried and canned exotic fruits and vegetables from all over the tropics. Herbs and spices, jams and jellies, teas, chips, and many other unusual foods are sold here. Cold natural fruit juices and soft drinks are available. Try something new! Also for sale are books on tropical fruits, gardening, cookbooks, and a few on local natural history. No admission fee is required if you just wish to visit the store.

The store and groves are handicapped accessible; the restrooms are not.

Special Events

A special event draws large crowds each year: the Natural Arts Festival in January. For a nominal admission fee, you will be treated to dozens of exhibits and demonstrations on natural foods, crafts, plants, gardening, and horticulture. Food booths sell tasty exotic foods for lunch. Plants and gifts are for sale.

Local residents may wish to inquire about the park's workshops, classes, and off-site tours on tropical fruit cooking and growing.

Best Time of Year

There is always something in fruit. In summer more things ripen, but heat and mosquitoes can be bad.

Pets

Not allowed.

HURRICANE ANDREW UPDATE

Since this park was directly in the worst part of the storm, it sustained severe damage. Some of the magnificent old trees were destroyed. Workers spent three weeks after the storm propping up windthrown trees. Extensive repairs were made, and the park reopened with full services by the end of 1992.

FAIRCHILD TROPICAL GARDEN

"THE LARGEST TROPICAL BOTANICAL GARDEN in the continental United States." This 83-acre garden, established in 1938, is a horticultural gem that showcases tropical and subtropical native and exotic plants. Fairchild Garden is a nonprofit institution operated for display, education, scientific research, and conservation. Thousands of species and varieties of trees, shrubs, vines, ground covers, orchids, and other epiphytes are established. There are sections emphasizing such plant groups as palms, cycads, bromeliads, and orchids. Explore the special "Everglades Area" and "Mangrove Preserve." Don't miss the "Rare Plant House," a collection of difficult-to-grow plants such as breadfruit, orchids, aroids, and giant tree ferns.

Despite the many exotics planted here, there are many natives, and many species which have become naturalized in South Florida. If you want to learn plant identifications better, this may be a good place to start. Allow about a half day to walk around (more if you're a hard-core botanist).

Location, Mailing Address and Phone

10901 Old Cutler Rd., Coral Gables. Take Kendall Dr. (SW 88th St.) east from Kendall and turn right onto Old Cutler Rd. Fairchild is just south of Matheson Hammock Park.

10901 Old Cutler Rd., Miami, FL 33156   (305) 667-16519

Facilities and Activities

Gardens with labeled woody and herbaceous plants, tram tour, botanically oriented bookstore, educational programs on plants, snack bar. No picnicking or bicycling permitted. Admission fee charged, includes tram tour.

The Bookstore
If you're a nut for plant books, you'll cotton to the bookstore. It has a wonderful assortment of books for sale — mostly botanical, but also tropical cookbooks, gardening, local history, and wildlife. Many plant identification guides and horticultural books are stocked. The bookstore also serves as a small visitor center and includes a palm museum containing exhibits of products made from palm fronds, trunks, and fruits from all over the world. Clothing, mats, jewelry, statues, carvings, hats, and utensils are displayed.

Trails
Fairchild Tropical Garden is well arranged for self-guided tours with the map provided at the admission booth. The trees and plants have identification labels. Several miles of paved and unpaved walkways cover the area, but you can walk anywhere off the roads for closer examination of the plants.

Guided tours are also available. Tram tours leave hourly; guided walking tours are available seasonally. Special group tours can be arranged (call in advance).

Almost all areas (including the bathrooms) are wheelchair accessible. The tram makes it easy for everyone to get around. The bookstore has several wheelchairs available for loan.

The snack bar serves sandwiches and drinks and has outdoor tables under a huge sapodilla tree.

Best Time of Year
There is something flowering every month of the year, particularly in the summer. Winter may be more comfortable weatherwise.

Pets
Not allowed.

 HURRICANE ANDREW UPDATE
The garden was at the outer edge of the northern eye wall. FTG botanists estimated 60-70% of the total collection of trees and plants was damaged or destroyed. Releafing of the remaining trees occurred within weeks. Staff and volunteers replanted hundreds of fallen trees, particularly palms, within weeks of the storm. It may take a year or two to know how successful this effort will be. The garden reopened about six weeks after the hurricane.

MATHESON HAMMOCK PARK

SEMI-NATURAL

WHEN WILLIAM J. MATHESON DONATED 84 ACRES to Dade county in 1930, he stipulated that the hammock be used as a botanical park for the public's benefit, to be preserved in its natural state. The park currently covers 629 acres of land, most of which is left natural.

This MetroDade County park along Biscayne Bay has two sections. One is a fee area with water recreation and the other is a non-fee area for picnicking and walking. The water recreation area is frequently crowded. The trail area is small and is surrounded by suburban development, but if you happen to be in the area (to visit Fairchild Tropical Garden, for example), it's worth a short side trip.

Location, Mailing Address and Phone

9610 Old Cutler Rd., Coral Gables, just north of Fairchild Tropical Garden.

9610 Old Cutler Rd., Miami, FL 33156   (305) 666-6979

Facilities and Activities

At the fee area, there is windsurfing, a boat ramp, a snack bar, wading and swimming beaches, and a large marina. At the non-fee area, there are shaded picnic tables with grills and walking trails. Bathrooms are available in many locations in both areas (all are handicapped accessible). There is a short bicycle path that wends through mangroves.

Trails

The water sports area has little to offer an exploring naturalist. Go instead to the non-fee picnic area where there are a few foot trails for getting off the beaten path. The parking lot near the trails is not marked, so it's easiest to follow these directions: Go north on Old Cutler

Rd. from the Fairchild Tropical Garden parking lot. The first right turn (only a few hundred yards from Fairchild) is the picnic area and parking lot.

In the vicinity of the parking lot (on same side of the road) are the picnic tables. Spot-breasted orioles and hill mynas may be seen here. There are several small ponds surrounded by red mangroves that occasionally harbor alligators and wading birds. Near the boundary fence of Fairchild Gardens is a gate that says "No Dumping." Behind the gate is a short trail that passes black mangroves, sea ox-eye daisies, and the repugnant Australian-pine. It will take about 10 minutes to walk to the end, where it meets a road in the recreation area.

The better trails are on the other side of Old Cutler Rd., where there is a remnant West Indian hardwood hammock. Go directly across the street to a gated-off parking lot with a sign "Nature Trail Matheson Hammock." The trail on the left is a wide and straight old road bed. It passes through some native vegetation, but much of the vegetation is exotic. The most notable of the exotics is the stand of large melaleuca (cajeput) trees near the end of the trail. Because they are beautiful trees, it is difficult to remind ourselves what a menace they are to our native vegetation. The trail opens out to a stand of royal palms and a road at the boundary of the park, signaling it's time to turn around and retrace your steps. Go back to the gated-off parking lot, but this time to the right side. The beginning of the trail is small and obscure. This trail is definitely *not* wide and straight, and is also not marked. In fact, there are so many side trails that it is easy to get confused — don't get lost! Live oaks laden with resurrection ferns and bromeliads will be found here.

Best Time of Year

September, October, March, and April for migrating warblers and small land birds in the hammock.

Pets

Not allowed.

 HURRICANE ANDREW UPDATE

The park was just outside the northern eye wall. It sustained heavy damage from wind and storm surge. The park has reopened, but extensive damage to the hammock will be visible for years.

GREYNOLDS PARK

A SMALL DADE COUNTY PARK within the urban confines of Miami, Greynolds Park has a special claim to fame. The 240-acre park is renowned for the water birds that nest on the mangrove islands in close proximity to the trails. Such species as great egret, great blue heron, tricolored heron, little blue heron, snowy egret, cattle egret, anhinga, and cormorant commonly nest here. This is the most accessible and convenient way for most people to see nesting wading birds.

Of further interest is the history of the scarlet ibis's introduction into the park. In the 1950s, a neighbor living adjacent to the rookery imported scarlet ibis eggs from Trinidad and Surinam to place into the nests of the white ibises already nesting there. He hoped that the scarlet ibises would reside at Greynolds when they grew up and would be visible from his yard. The first batch of eggs failed, and a second batch was imported in the early 1960s. Some chicks survived and later mated with the white ibises. The resulting pink or orange offspring have been seen occasionally around south Florida to the present.

Location, Mailing Address and Phone

17530 West Dixie Highway, North Miami Beach, FL. There is also an entrance on NE 22nd Ave.: from Miami, take I-95 north to SR 860 (Miami Gardens Dr.), then east to NE 22nd Ave. and turn right.

17530 West Dixie Highway, North Miami Beach, FL 33160

(305) 945-3425. For special group tours, call Naturalists' Services at (305) 662-4124.

Facilities and Activities

Nature trails, bird nesting rookery (colony) and roost, biking paths, boat rentals, paddleboats, picnic tables, snack bar, children's

167

playground, golf course. Fee charged on weekends and holidays.

Nature Trails

At the park office, you can pick up a map of the park's roads and trails. The Lakeside Nature Trail circumnavigates the mangrove pond and islands where the wading birds nest and roost. It is narrow and rocky, not handicapped accessible; other trails, however, are accessible.

A guided bird walk is offered by a park naturalist every Thursday at 5:00 PM from October to April and at 6:00 PM from May to July (no August or September walks) to watch the birds come in to roost.

A bird checklist, containing over 130 species, is available from the office. Many introduced parrots and parakeets have naturalized in the Miami area, and this is a good place to see them.

Bird Rookery

From the trail on the edge of the mangrove rookery pond, you can sit and watch the magnificent courtship displays of the wading birds. The great egrets usually start nesting by late February. The other species (such as little blue herons, snowy egrets, white ibises, scarlet ibises, and black-crowned night herons) start soon after and continue through summer until October. The birds gather nesting material, build their nests, and raise their chicks all within view of the trail.

Even when nesting season is over, the herons, egrets, and ibises come to roost in the mangroves at dusk. It is a thrilling site to see hundreds of these colorful, showy birds drifting in to the treetops to spend the night quietly resting. At sunrise, they'll be off again to their favorite feeding sites in nearby marshes.

Best Time of Year

February to August for nesting birds; year-round for roosting birds (evenings).

Pets

Allowed on a leash.

HURRICANE ANDREW UPDATE

Greynolds was at the northern edge, outside of the eye wall, and thus sustained minimal damage. Some of the mangroves that the wading birds use were uprooted or denuded, but most survived. Subsequent nesting seasons should not be hampered. Some kapok trees were blown over and later removed. Other trees were stood back up and hopefully will survive. The park was closed for about a month.

MICCOSUKEE INDIAN VILLAGE

THE TINY RESERVATION set aside for the Miccosukee Tribe is squeezed between Everglades National Park and Big Cypress National Preserve. The Miccosukees are Native Americans whose ancestors, the Creeks, lived in Alabama, Georgia, and northern Florida. Many Miccosukees were killed during the 1600s and 1700s by disease, probably introduced by the Spanish and British. During the Indian Wars of the 1800s, most of the survivors were killed by the colonists or sent to a reservation in Oklahoma.

The remaining few hundred Miccosukees were pushed south and hid in the Everglades in family-sized groups that could escape detection by soldiers. Besides farming small patches of upland on the hammocks, they fished and hunted in the marshes and hammocks. Game animals were plentiful until the newly dug canals of 1906 and 1913 began draining the Everglades. In 1928, the completion of the Tamiami Trail cut the tribe in two, literally and figuratively. Not only did the road bisect their territory, but it also caused many tribal people to be drawn into the encroaching white civilization. Through all the broken treaties, encroachment on their land, and destruction of their hunting grounds, the Miccosukees never surrendered to the American government.

In 1962, the Miccosukees were recognized by the U.S. government as an Indian tribe, separate from the Seminoles. Their reservation is small, only a 500-foot-wide strip of land between Everglades National Park and the Tamiami Trail. Not all of the approximately 450 Miccosukees live on the reservation; some live elsewhere in Florida. The Miccosukee clans maintain their original ways of life as best they can in our modern world. Some still live on tree islands in the Everglades that are not accessible by road.

Unlike the Indians of the Great Plains, who lived in large multi-family villages, the Miccosukees lived in small extended family clans. Each family lived on a separate tree island, and they visited each other by cypress dugout canoes. The village that now is set up for the guided tours originally was a one-family village.

These native people currently make their living through the tourist industry (craft-making, village tours, and airboat tours of the Everglades). They cannot support themselves "off the land" because the reservation is surrounded by land protected by white people's laws. Their alternative would be to go to the city and assimilate into white people's jobs. The tourist industry gives the natives a chance to maintain their ways of life and teach outsiders about their culture.

Although the village is not distinguished as a natural area, the value in visiting it is to learn how these people lived off the land naturally. For example, logging cypress trees is one of their livelihoods. Before felling a cypress, they first determine how high above the waterline on the trunk to cut so the stump will later sprout. The resulting tree will not be good for lumber, but it will replace the one they removed. Since cypress trees normally only regenerate from seed under certain water conditions (which may not occur in an area for many years), this is an important method for maintaining cypress stands. Also, when the Miccosukees cut palmetto fronds for thatched roofs, they leave enough for the tree to stay healthy. Your tour guide will be able to speak on such subjects, so ask questions.

The Indian creed is worth mentioning, since it should apply to all people, including non-Indians. The Miccosukees feel that the land and its resources are sacred gifts to them, and it is their privilege (not their *right*) to use them. Since the trees, animals, rivers, and so on are gifts, they must all be treated with respect. If they abuse these gifts, they will be taken away. Haven't our higher spirits already started doing that?

Allow about a half day to see the village and airboat tour. A good plan would be to combine this with a visit to the Shark Valley section of Everglades National Park for a whole day trip.

Location, Mailing Address and Phone

On Tamiami Trail, 18.5 miles west of Krome Ave. or 0.5 miles west of the Shark Valley entrance to Everglades National Park.

P.O. Box 440021, Tamiami Station, Miami, FL 33144   (305) 223-8388

Facilities And Activities

Village (with museum and gift shop), restaurant, airboat tours. Admission fee charged; fee for airboat tour extra.

Village

The focal point of the reservation is the Indian Village. Guided tours leave every one or two hours from 10:00 AM. For a self-guided tour, ask for the village map and the schedule of alligator shows. The village consists of a family living chickee, a cooking chickee, displays of basketry, a crafts area (bows, arrows, canoes, etc.), a nature walk, a museum, an alligator arena, and a bow-shooting range. Authentic cypress dugout canoes are on display.

"Chickee"is the Miccosukee word for house. A traditional chickee was about 16 feet long and 9 feet wide and was made from cypress logs. It had a platform floor raised about three feet off the ground to keep water out during the wet season, to discourage snakes, and to catch the cooling breezes. The roof was thatched with cabbage palmetto fronds and there were no walls. Today many Miccosukees still live in chickees. The term "chickee" is now widely used in Florida for similar structures that non-natives have, such as backyard pavilions and picnic shelters. Very often it is the expert Miccosukees that are hired to build these backyard chickees, providing them with a source of income.

The museum has displays of cooking utensils, clothing, games, local wildlife, and village life. There is a 10-minute film on Miccosukee history. The paintings by local Miccosukee artist, Stephen Tiger, are fascinating.

The nature walk is a short boardwalk into the Everglades, with a vista across the sawgrass and tree islands on the horizon. Watch for wading birds, limpkins, and rails.

The alligator arena is an outdoor pit that houses some hefty alligators for cultural demonstrations. These demonstrations don't really resemble a traditional method of gator handling, but they do attract a lot of thrill-seeking tourists. There are shows periodically throughout the day.

The gift shop sells Miccosukee and Seminole patchwork clothing, crafts from other Native Americans, local guide books, and Florida souvenirs. You can get Miccosukee and American food at the snack chickee.

After leaving the village, try driving west on the small dead-end road paralleling Tamiami Trail on the south side. This is the original Tamiami Trail and the road that many Miccosukees live on now. It passes the tribal headquarters, school, and health clinic. The men who specialize in making chickees for a living can be seen shaving cypress poles and piling thatch by the roadside.

Airboat Tours

The airboat tours begin across the street (Tamiami Trail). They are 30 minutes long and leave whenever there are enough people. If you choose to take an airboat ride during your visit in South Florida, the Miccosukee tour would be a good choice. The guide will take you to an isolated hammock to see how a family would live the traditional way. A word of caution: the boats are very noisy. You may want to come prepared with inexpensive foam hearing protectors.

For those readers unfamiliar with airboats, a short explanation is offered here. Airboats are shallow, flat-bottomed boats that skim over the surface of the water. Propulsion comes from an airplane propeller mounted on the back of the boat, high above the water. In effect, the propeller pushes the boat through air rather than water, as in a typical motorboat. Airboats are able to cross vast expanses of sawgrass-covered marsh that may have only two inches of water.

The first airboat was designed by Glenn Curtiss in 1920 for gliding over the Everglades. The idea didn't catch on until Johnny Lamb and Russell Howard built a similar boat for frog hunting in 1933. Other "froggers" copied their design. Now the Miccosukees use them regularly; in fact, many depend on them for logging and transportation to their chickees. Airboats are very noisy and disruptive to wildlife, but the alternative forms of transportation are worse (such as swamp buggies and all-terrain-vehicles, which cause serious permanent damage to the ecosystem). Park rangers and wildlife managers in the Everglades use airboats regularly.

Restaurant

The two restaurants near the village are run by Miccosukees and offer both Miccosukee and American meals. Miccosukee specialties include pan-fried bread (regular and pumpkin), frog legs, and catfish.

Best Time of Year

Winter is best for the village. Airboat tours may not be possible during the dry months (January-May). There is a major Indian Arts Festival (annually from December 26 to January 1) that features authentic Indian arts, crafts, dancing, and music from over 40 tribes across North America, including local Miccosukees and Seminoles.

Pets

Allowed in the village, not allowed on the airboats.

HURRICANE ANDREW UPDATE

Damage to the village was repaired quickly and the village reopened shortly after the storm. It was on the northern edge of the storm, with moderately strong winds.

NAPLES NATURE CENTER

SEMI-NATURAL

IN THE HEART OF NAPLES lies a quiet refreshing break from city life. The Naples Nature Center, located on a 13.5-acre sanctuary, is owned and operated by The Conservancy, Inc., a private nonprofit conservation organization active in the Naples area (see BRIGGS NATURE CENTER for background on The Conservancy). The Naples Nature Center was completed in 1981 and has since been serving Collier County with educational programs. The Conservancy's extensive schedule of quality programs is enhanced by the dedication of several hundred well-trained volunteers.

The Nature Center Complex contains a natural science museum, auditorium, nature store, wildlife rehabilitation center, classrooms, and nature trails. Altogether, it is one of the best examples in south Florida of a complete environmental education and conservation center. Because their programs encompass all ecosystems of south Florida, The Conservancy encourages people to visit the Nature Center before exploring natural areas such as the ones described in this book. Then they will have a good understanding of all they are seeing.

Location, Mailing Address and Phone

On 14th Ave. North off Goodlette Rd. in Naples. From the south: from the intersection of SR 29 and Tamiami Trail, go west on Tamiami Trail about 23 miles to SR 851 (Goodlette Rd.). Turn right and go north on Goodlette about 2 miles. Turn right onto 14th Ave. North and go short distance to end of street. From the north: Get onto SR 851 either from SR 886 (Golden Gate Parkway) or Tamiami Trail. Go south on Goodlette to 14th Ave. North. Turn left and go short distance to end.

1450 Merrihue Dr., Naples, FL 33942   (813) 262-0304

Facilities and Activities

Natural Science Museum, nature trails, boat tours, wildlife rehabilitation center and aviary, nature store, and environmental education programs. Admission fee charged for the museum.

Around the Nature Center complex are special conservation plantings. A xeriscape demonstration plot shows what plants to add to your garden that don't require watering. A screened-in butterfly garden has both the plants that attract butterflies and the live butterflies that feed on them. The aviary, which houses injured birds, can be seen from the outside. There is much to see and do in the small area of the Nature Center. School groups and children's summer camps are Nature Center specialties. Call ahead for a schedule of tours and programs.

Natural Science Museum

This 5,000-square foot interactive museum, opened in 1986, has been hosting thousands of visitors a month. Just about every aspect of south Florida natural history is represented in the exhibits: hydrology, habitats, wildlife, early Indians, and so on. Exhibits include a life-sized diorama of part of a cypress swamp and its bird life, a rare shell collection, and a 2,300-gallon marine aquarium. The live serpentarium houses virtually every species of snake found locally. You will want to spend at least an hour looking around.

Trails

Three self-guided interpretive trails radiate from the Nature Center complex. All three are short (about 10 minutes). The wide, wood-chipped trails are carefully maintained. The numbered markers correspond to the guide booklet available at the Nature Store. Characteristic of everything The Conservancy does, the booklet is thorough and excellently prepared.

The Hammock Trail goes through a typical hardwood hammock. Bromeliads and ferns are abundant in the live oaks. The Arboretum Trail displays a variety of native plants, including those suitable for xeriscaping. The Peninsula Trail takes you to the edge of a tidal lagoon, where you may see an alligator or a manatee.

Boat Tours

The Conservancy offers complimentary boat tours from the Nature Center every morning. They are on a first-come basis and the boat seats five to six people. The trip lasts 45 minutes and cruises through a tidal lagoon to the Gordon River. Mangroves line the water. There is even a mangrove planting along the way, the result of a mitigation agreement by a developer who destroyed mangroves and was required to replace them. Mangroves are protected by state law; for every one destroyed, five must be planted. Wading birds, like yellow-crowned night herons, can be viewed along the way. It's hard to believe you're still in the middle of Naples when you take this tour.

Nature Store

If you're looking to buy nature-related items, this store has an exceptional selection. Get those birthday lists ready! Among the thousands of items for sale are jewelry, tee-shirts, nature art prints, children's educational toys, and bird feeders. There is an excellent selection of field guides, children's books, hard-to-find regional books, and other natural history books.

Best Time of Year

Year-round. Although naturalist programs are reduced in the summer, there are still boat tours and other programs. The museum, trails, and gardens are worth a visit any time.

Pets

Not allowed.

VII.
ADDITIONAL INFORMATION

WILDLIFE CHECKLISTS

The following checklists are intended to include all the known native and some of the more common, naturalized vertebrates (except fish) found in south Florida. Species of unknown status, accidentals, or those numbering only a few individuals may not be included. Obscure subspecies, particularly in the Florida Keys, may be excluded.

Population status is given in relative terms as follows:

abundant — likely to be seen in the right habitat, population dense

common — often seen in the right habitat, population numerous

uncommon — infrequently seen, population low

rare — not likely to be seen, population very small or endangered

Geographic areas may be defined as follows:

Mainland — Florida mainland, excluding the Florida Keys

Keys — the developed islands of the Florida Keys

Everglades — the freshwater marsh system from Lake Okeechobee to Florida Bay

+known breeder in southern Florida (bird checklist only)

* exotic species (breeds locally)

BIRD CHECKLIST

The following list of 323 bird species includes some which have occurred rarely in the south Florida region but which may be expected to occur in the future. At least 75 other naturally occurring species reported in the region are less likely to be found in the future and have been omitted. More than 100 exotic species having uncertain reproductive success in southern Florida have been omitted. Readers who desire detailed information should refer to FLORIDA BIRD SPECIES: AN ANNOTATED LIST by William B. Robertson, Jr., and Glen E. Woolfenden (published in 1992 by the Florida Ornithological Society; for ordering information write to: Glen Woolfenden, Editor of Special Publications, Archbold Biological Station, Venus, Florida 33960). Another excellent resource is FLORIDA'S BIRDS: A HANDBOOK AND REFERENCE, by Herbert W. Kale and David S. Maehr, available through Pineapple Press, Inc., P.O. Drawer 16008, Sarasota, Florida 34239. The following list has been compiled predominantly by William B. Robertson, Jr. and P. William Smith.

Loons and Grebes

- ☐ **Common loon** (*Gavia immer*) — variably common migrant and winter visitor; ocean and bays
- ☐ **+Pied-billed grebe** (*Podilymbus podiceps*) — common migrant and winter visitor, some resident; fresh water
- ☐ **Horned grebe** (*Podiceps auritus*) — uncommon winter visitor; bays

Shearwaters and Storm-petrels

- ☐ **Cory's shearwater** (*Calonectris diomedea*) — uncommon summer and fall migrant; pelagic
- ☐ **Greater shearwater** (*Puffinus gravis*) — uncommon late spring and summer migrant; pelagic
- ☐ **Sooty shearwater** (*Puffinus griseus*) — rare, chiefly spring migrant; pelagic
- ☐ **Audubon's shearwater** (*Puffinus lherminieri*) — fairly common; pelagic
- ☐ **Wilson's storm-petrel** (*Oceanites oceanicus*) — uncommon late spring and summer migrant; pelagic

Pelicans and Allies

- ☐ **White-tailed tropicbird** (*Phaethon lepturus*) — rare, chiefly spring and summer visitor; Dry Tortugas and pelagic
- ☐ **+Masked booby** (*Sula dactylatra*) — uncommon resident at Dry Tortugas, rare elsewhere; pelagic
- ☐ **Brown booby** (*Sula leucogaster*) — uncommon visitor; pelagic and Dry Tortugas
- ☐ **Red-footed booby** (*Sula sula*) — rare spring and summer visitor; Dry Tortugas
- ☐ **Northern gannet** (*Morus bassanus*) — common migrant and winter visitor; chiefly pelagic

☐ **American white pelican** (*Pelecanus erythrorhynchos*) — common in winter, some in summer; bays, rare in Keys

☐ **+Brown pelican** (*Pelecanus occidentalis*) — abundant resident; coasts and bays

Cormorants and Anhingas

☐ **+Double-crested cormorant** (*Phalacrocorax auritus*) — abundant resident; coasts, bays, and deeper inland waters

☐ **+Anhinga** (*Anhinga anhinga*) — common resident; fresh water, mainland

Frigatebird

☐ **+Magnificent frigatebird** (*Fregata magnificens*) — variably common resident, breeds Dry Tortugas; coast and bays

Herons, Egrets, and Other Waders

☐ **American bittern** (*Botaurus lentiginosus*) — fairly rare migrant and winter visitor; fresh water marshes

☐ **+Least bittern** (*Ixobrychus exilis*) — uncommon resident; fresh water marshes

☐ **+Great blue heron** (*Ardea herodias*) — common resident; shallow fresh and salt water

☐ **+"Great white heron"** (*Ardea "occidentalis"*) — locally common resident; usually shallow salt water, mainly Florida Bay and Keys

☐ **+Great egret** (*Casmerodius albus*) — common resident; shallow fresh and salt water

☐ **+Snowy egret** (*Egretta thula*) — common resident; shallow fresh and salt water

☐ **+Little blue heron** (*Egretta caerulea*) — common resident; shallow fresh and salt water

☐ **+Tricolored heron** (*Egretta tricolor*) — common resident; shallow fresh and salt water

☐ **+Reddish egret** (*Egretta rufescens*) — uncommon resident; shallow salt water, mainly Keys and Florida Bay

☐ **+Cattle egret** (*Bubulcus ibis*) — abundant resident, less common in winter; agricultural fields and roadsides

☐ **+Green-backed heron** (*Butorides striatus*) — fairly common resident; shaded shallow fresh and salt water shorelines

☐ **+Black-crowned night-heron** (*Nycticorax nycticorax*) — fairly common resident; shallow fresh and salt water, scarce in Keys

☐ **+Yellow-crowned night-heron** (*Nyctanassa violacea*) — common resident (less common in east); shallow salt and fresh water

☐ **+White ibis** (*Eudocimus albus*) — common resident; shallow fresh and salt water, agricultural fields and lawns

☐ ***Scarlet ibis** (*Eudocimus ruber*) — occasional escapees or hybrids from

BIRD CHECKLIST

past introduction; shallow fresh and salt water

☐ **+Glossy ibis** (*Plegadis falcinellus*) — uncommon resident; shallow fresh water, mainland

☐ **+Roseate spoonbill** (*Ajaia ajaja*) — locally common resident; shallow salt water, Florida Bay and Ten Thousand Islands

☐ **+Wood stork** (*Mycteria americana*) — common resident; fresh water margins and swamps, mainland

☐ **Greater flamingo** (*Phoenicopterus ruber*) — rare visitor or escapee (mainly fall and winter); bays (particularly northern Florida Bay)

Ducks

☐ **Fulvous whistling-duck** (*Dendrocygna bicolor*) — rare visitor; fresh water marshes; breeds L. Okeechobee area

☐ ***Muscovy duck** (*Cairina moschata*) — locally common resident; urban ponds

☐ **+Wood duck** (*Aix sponsa*) — rare resident; wooded swamps

☐ **Green-winged teal** (*Anas crecca*) — variably uncommon winter visitor; ponds and bays

☐ **+Mottled duck** (*Anas fulvigula*) — uncommon resident; ponds and marshes, chiefly mainland

☐ ***Mallard** (*Anas platyrhynchos*) — fairly common resident; urban ponds

☐ **White-cheeked pintail** (*Anas bahamensis*) — rare winter and spring visitor, also some escapees; mangrove ponds

☐ **Northern pintail** (*Anas acuta*) — variably uncommon migrant and winter visitor; ponds and bays

☐ **Blue-winged teal** (*Anas discors*) — common migrant and winter visitor, some summer; ponds and bays

☐ **Northern shoveler** (*Anas clypeata*) — variably uncommon migrant and winter visitor; ponds and bays

☐ **Gadwall** (*Anas strepera*) — rare migrant and winter visitor; ponds and bays

☐ **American wigeon** (*Anas americana*) — fairly common migrant and winter visitor; ponds and bays

☐ **Ring-necked duck** (*Aythya collaris*) — fairly common migrant and winter visitor; mainly ponds

☐ **Lesser scaup** (*Aythya affinis*) — variably uncommon migrant and winter visitor; mainly bays, rare in east

☐ **Black scoter** (*Melanitta nigra*) — rare to uncommon migrant and winter visitor; ocean and bays

☐ **Hooded merganser** (*Lophodytes cucullatus*) — fairly rare migrant and winter visitor; ponds

☐ **Red-breasted merganser** (*Mergus serrator*) — common migrant and winter visitor, some summer; ocean and bays

☐ **Ruddy duck** (*Oxyura jamaicensis*) — variably uncommon migrant and winter visitor; ponds and bays

Hawks, Falcons, Kites, and Other Raptors

☐ **+Black vulture** (*Coragyps atratus*) — locally common resident; mainland

☐ **+Turkey vulture** (*Cathartes aura*) — abundant winter visitor, fewer resident; mainland and Keys

☐ **+Osprey** (*Pandion haliaetus*) — common resident; bays, canals, and ponds

☐ **+American swallow-tailed kite** (*Elanoides forficatus*) — common spring and summer visiting breeder; wet and dry woodlands

☐ **+Black-shouldered kite** (*Elanus caeruleus*) — rare resident; former sawgrass prairies that have dried out, mainland

☐ **+Snail kite** (*Rostrhamus sociabilis*) — variably uncommon resident; freshwater marshes

☐ **Mississippi kite** (*Ictinia mississippiensis*) — rare migrant

☐ **+Bald eagle** (*Haliaeetus leucocephalus*) — fairly common resident; mainly bays

☐ **Northern harrier** (*Circus cyaneus*) — common migrant and winter visitor; agricultural fields and marshes

☐ **Sharp-shinned hawk** (*Accipiter striatus*) — common migrant, uncommon winter visitor

☐ **Cooper's hawk** (*Accipiter cooperii*) — fairly rare migrant and winter visitor

☐ **+Red-shouldered hawk** (*Buteo lineatus*) — common resident; woodlands and edges

☐ **Broad-winged hawk** (*Buteo platypterus*) — common migrant and variably uncommon winter visitor

☐ **+Short-tailed hawk** (*Buteo brachyurus*) — uncommon fall and winter visitor, rare in spring and summer; woodlands, usually near creeks

☐ **Swainson's hawk** (*Buteo swainsoni*) — variably uncommon migrant and rare winter visitor

☐ **+Red-tailed hawk** (*Buteo jamaicensis*) — uncommon migrant and winter visitor, rare in summer

☐ **+American kestrel** (*Falco sparverius*) — common migrant and winter visitor (throughout), also former or rare breeder (northern mainland); fields and edges

☐ **Merlin** (*Falco columbarius*) — fairly common migrant and uncommon winter visitor

☐ **Peregrine falcon** (*Falco peregrinus*) — fairly common migrant and uncommon winter visitor

Turkeys and Quails

☐ **+Wild turkey** (*Meleagris gallopavo*) — rare resident; undisturbed woodlands, mainland (except extreme southern)

☐ **+Northern bobwhite** (*Colinus virginianus*) — uncommon resident; mainly old fields, groves, and pine woods, mainland

Rails, Limpkins, and Cranes

☐ **Black rail** (*Laterallus jamaicensis*) — variably rare migrant and possible resident; extensive damp marshes

☐ **+Clapper rail** (*Rallus longirostris*) — uncommon resident; mangroves and salt marshes

☐ **+King rail** (*Rallus elegans*) — fairly common resident; fresh water marshes

☐ **Virginia rail** (*Rallus limicola*) — rare winter visitor; fresh water marshes

☐ **Sora** (*Porzana carolina*) — common migrant and uncommon winter visitor; fresh water marshes and concealed margins

☐ **+Purple gallinule** (*Porphyrula martinica*) — variably uncommon migrant and local resident; fresh water marshes

☐ **+Common moorhen** (*Gallinula chloropus*) — common resident; fresh water ponds and marshes

☐ **+American coot** (*Fulica americana*) — variably common migrant and winter visitor, uncommon in summer; bays, ponds, and marshes

☐ **+Limpkin** (*Aramus guarauna*) — locally uncommon resident; fresh water swamps and marshes, chiefly northern mainland

☐ **+Sandhill crane** (*Grus canadensis*) — uncommon resident; prairies, chiefly northern mainland

Plovers, Sandpipers, and Other Shorebirds

☐ **Black-bellied plover** (*Pluvialis squatarola*) — common migrant and winter visitor, some summer; coastal and interior shallow water and fields

☐ **Lesser golden-plover** (*Pluvialis dominica*) — rare migrant, chiefly fall; usually interior fields

☐ **+Snowy plover** (*Charadrius alexandrinus*) — rare winter visitor (Gulf coast and Keys), also former or rare breeder (Gulf coast); undisturbed sandy beaches

☐ **+Wilson's plover** (*Charadrius wilsonia*) — locally common resident; spoil banks, especially Florida Bay and Keys

☐ **Semipalmated plover** (*Charadrius semipalmatus*) — common migrant and winter visitor; coastal flats, sometimes inland

☐ **Piping plover** (*Charadrius melodus*) — uncommon migrant and winter visitor; salt water banks and pond edges, mainly Florida Bay and Keys

☐ **+Killdeer** (*Charadrius vociferus*) — common resident; fields and fresh water margins, chiefly mainland

☐ **American oystercatcher** (*Haematopus palliatus*) — rare visitor (mostly winter); salt water flats, chiefly Gulf coast

☐ **+Black-necked stilt** (*Himantopus mexicanus*) — common resident, except uncommon and local in winter; mainly fresh water ponds and margins

☐ **American avocet** (*Recurvirostra americana*) — rare migrant and winter visitor; usually salt water ponds and flats

☐ **Greater yellowlegs** (*Tringa melanoleuca*) — common migrant, less common winter visitor; flats and margins

☐ **Lesser yellowlegs** (*Tringa flavipes*) — common migrant, less common winter visitor; flats and margins

☐ **Solitary sandpiper** (*Tringa solitaria*) — uncommon migrant, rare winter visitor; fresh water margins

☐ **+Willet** (*Catoptrophorus semipalmatus*) — common migrant and winter visitor, less common in summer; chiefly salt marshes and flats

☐ **Spotted sandpiper** (*Actitis macularia*) — fairly common migrant and winter visitor; margins, usually fresh water

☐ **Upland sandpiper** (*Bartramia longicauda*) — uncommon migrant; chiefly fields

☐ **Whimbrel** (*Numenius phaeopus*) — uncommon migrant and winter visitor; salt water flats

☐ **Long-billed curlew** (*Numenius americanus*) — rare winter visitor; salt water flats, chiefly Gulf coast

☐ **Marbled godwit** (*Limosa fedoa*) — abundant migrant and winter visitor; salt water flats, mainly Gulf coast and Florida Bay

☐ **Ruddy turnstone** (*Arenaria interpres*) — common migrant and winter visitor; beaches and rocky areas

☐ **Red knot** (*Calidris canutus*) — locally common migrant and winter visitor; salt ponds and flats, mainly Gulf coast

☐ **Sanderling** (*Calidris alba*) — common migrant and winter visitor; beaches

☐ **Semipalmated sandpiper** (*Calidris pusilla*) — common migrant, rare in winter; flats and margins

☐ **Western sandpiper** (*Calidris mauri*) — abundant migrant and winter visitor; flats and margins, chiefly salt water

☐ **Least sandpiper** (*Calidris minutilla*) — common migrant and winter visitor; flats and margins, chiefly fresh water

☐ **White-rumped sandpiper** (*Calidris fuscicollis*) — uncommon (especially in spring) migrant; beaches, flats, and margins

☐ **Baird's sandpiper** (*Calidris bairdii*) — rare migrant; usually fields and fresh water margins

☐ **Pectoral sandpiper** (*Calidris melanotos*) — common migrant; fields, flats, and margins (usually fresh water)

☐ **Purple sandpiper** (*Calidris maritima*) — rare winter visitor; rock jetties

☐ **Dunlin** (*Calidris alpina*) — abundant migrant and winter visitor; flats and margins (usually salt water)

☐ **Stilt sandpiper** (*Calidris himantopus*) — uncommon migrant, usually rare in winter; flats and shallow ponds (often fresh water)

☐ **Buff-breasted sandpiper** (*Tryngites subruficollis*) — rare migrant, chiefly fall; usually interior fields

☐ **Short-billed dowitcher** (*Limnodromus griseus*) — abundant migrant and winter visitor; chiefly flats and shallow salt ponds

☐ **Long-billed dowitcher** (*Limnodromus scolopaceus*) — variably common migrant and winter visitor; usually shallow fresh water ponds

☐ **Common snipe** (*Gallinago gallinago*) — fairly common migrant, less common in winter; fresh water margins, chiefly mainland

☐ **+American woodcock** (*Scolopax minor*) — uncommon winter visitor, rarely breeds; old fields, mainland

☐ **Wilson's phalarope** (*Phalaropus tricolor*) — rare migrant; fresh water margins

☐ **Red-necked phalarope** (*Phalaropus lobatus*) — rare migrant or winter visitor; usually pelagic, sometimes ashore

☐ **Red phalarope** (*Phalaropus fulicaria*) — rare migrant, may winter; usually pelagic, rarely ashore

Gulls and Terns

☐ **Pomarine jaeger** (*Stercorarius pomarinus*) — fairly common migrant, less common in winter; usually pelagic

☐ **Parasitic jaeger** (*Stercorarius parasiticus*) — fairly common migrant, some may winter; usually pelagic, sometimes coastal

☐ **+Laughing gull** (*Larus atricilla*) — abundant resident; chiefly coasts and bays, sometimes inland

☐ **Bonaparte's gull** (*Larus philadelphia*) — variably uncommon migrant and winter visitor; usually coasts and bays

☐ **Ring-billed gull** (*Larus delawarensis*) — abundant migrant and winter visitor, some summer; coasts, bays, and inland ponds and fields

☐ **Herring gull** (*Larus argentatus*) — uncommon winter visitor; coasts, bays, and ponds

☐ **Lesser black-backed gull** (*Larus fuscus*) — rare winter visitor; coasts, bays, and ponds

☐ **Glaucous gull** (*Larus hyperboreus*) — rare winter visitor; coasts, bays, and ponds

☐ **Great black-backed gull** (*Larus marinus*) — rare winter visitor; coasts, bays, and ponds

☐ **+Gull-billed tern** (*Sterna nilotica*) — local and uncommon resident and uncertain breeder; salt marshes and flats, chiefly mainland

☐ **Caspian tern** (*Sterna caspia*) — common migrant and winter visitor, some summer; coasts and bays, less common in east

☐ **Royal tern** (*Sterna maxima*) — abundant migrant and winter visitor, many summer; coasts and bays

☐ **Sandwich tern** (*Sterna sandvicensis*) — fairly common migrant and winter visitor, some summer; coasts and bays, less common in east

☐ **+Roseate tern** (*Sterna dougallii*) — variably common late spring and summer breeding visitor, rare at other seasons; coastal, chiefly lower Keys and Dry Tortugas

☐ **Common tern** (*Sterna hirundo*) — fairly common migrant, rare in winter; coasts and bays, less common in east

☐ **Arctic tern** (*Sterna paradisaea*) — rare migrant (stops over during transcontinental migrations); coastal

- [ ] **Forster's tern** (*Sterna forsteri*) — common migrant and winter visitor, some summer; bays and ponds
- [ ] +**Least tern** (*Sterna antillarum*) — fairly common spring and summer visitor; bays, ponds, and urban rooftops
- [ ] +**Bridled tern** (*Sterna anaethetus*) — uncommon, probably resident, rare breeder; offshore, lower Keys
- [ ] +**Sooty tern** (*Sterna fuscata*) — abundant spring and summer visitor and breeder, common offshore except absent in late fall and winter; Dry Tortugas, pelagic when not breeding
- [ ] **Black tern** (*Chlidonias niger*) — locally common migrant, chiefly summer and fall; fresh water ponds and offshore
- [ ] +**Brown noddy** (*Anous stolidus*) — common spring and summer visitor and breeder, uncommon offshore except absent in late fall and winter; Dry Tortugas, pelagic
- [ ] **Black noddy** (*Anous minutus*) — rare spring visitor; Dry Tortugas
- [ ] +**Black skimmer** (*Rynchops nigra*) — locally common resident; flats, spoil islands

Doves and Pigeons

- [ ] *****Rock dove** (*Columba livia*) — common resident; urban areas
- [ ] +**White-crowned pigeon** (*Columba leucocephala*) — common resident, fewer in winter; tropical hardwood hammocks and mangroves, Keys and extreme southern mainland
- [ ] *****Eurasian collared-dove** (*Streptopelia decaocto*) — locally abundant resident; southern suburban areas, including Keys
- [ ] +**White-winged dove** (*Zenaida asiatica*) — locally common resident; groves and suburban areas
- [ ] +**Mourning dove** (*Zenaida macroura*) — common resident; open areas
- [ ] +**Common ground-dove** (*Columbina passerina*) — uncommon resident; fields

Parakeets

- [ ] *****Monk parakeet** (*Myiopsitta monachus*) — locally common resident; suburban areas
- [ ] *****Canary-winged parakeet** (*Brotogeris versicolurus*) — uncommon resident; Coconut Grove area of Miami

Cuckoos, Anis

- [ ] **Black-billed cuckoo** (*Coccyzus erythropthalmus*) — rare migrant; woodlands
- [ ] +**Yellow-billed cuckoo** (*Coccyzus americanus*) — common migrant and uncommon summer visitor and breeder; woodlands
- [ ] +**Mangrove cuckoo** (*Coccyzus minor*) — uncommon resident, seldom seen in fall and winter; tropical hammocks and mangroves, Keys and

southern mainland

☐ **+Smooth-billed ani** (*Crotophaga ani*) — local and decreasing resident; brushy areas

Owls

☐ **+Barn owl** (*Tyto alba*) — uncommon permanent resident; chiefly mainland

☐ **+Eastern screech-owl** (*Otus asio*) — common resident; suburbs and woodlands, mainland and upper Keys

☐ **+Great horned owl** (*Bubo virginianus*) — uncommon resident; chiefly pine woodlands, mainland

☐ **+Burrowing owl** (*Speotyto cunicularia*) — locally common resident; airports, campuses, and other open grassy areas

☐ **+Barred owl** (*Strix varia*) — common resident; mesic woodlands, mainland

☐ **Short-eared owl** (*Asio flammeus*) — rare winter and spring visitor; chiefly Keys, Dry Tortugas; also grassy marshes and fields on mainland

Goatsuckers

☐ **Lesser nighthawk** (*Chordeiles acutipennis*) — rare spring migrant; chiefly Dry Tortugas

☐ **+Common nighthawk** (*Chordeiles minor*) — common migrant and summer breeding visitor; open areas and urban rooftops, chiefly mainland and upper keys

☐ **+Antillean nighthawk** (*Chordeiles gundlachii*) — uncommon spring and summer breeding visitor; open areas and urban rooftops, chiefly lower Keys

☐ **+Chuck-will's-widow** (*Caprimulgus carolinensis*) — common migrant and uncommon winter visitor throughout, fairly common summer breeder; woodlands, mainland and upper Keys

☐ **Whip-poor-will** (*Caprimulgus vociferus*) — common fall and winter visitor; woodlands, chiefly mainland

Swifts

☐ **+Chimney swift** (*Chaetura pelagica*) — fairly common migrant throughout and uncommon summer breeder on suburban mainland

Hummingbirds

☐ **+Ruby-throated hummingbird** (*Archilochus colubris*) — common migrant and winter visitor throughout, rare breeding visitor on northern mainland; around flowering plants

☐ **Rufous hummingbird** (*Selasphorus rufus*) — rare migrant and winter visitor; around flowering plants

Kingfishers

☐ **Belted kingfisher** (*Ceryle alcyon*) — common visitor from late summer through early spring; canals and ponds

Woodpeckers

- [ ] **+Red-headed woodpecker** (*Melanerpes erythrocephalus*) — rare migrant throughout, resident in pine-oak woodlands, northern mainland
- [ ] **+Red-bellied woodpecker** (*Melanerpes carolinus*) — common resident; suburban and wooded areas
- [ ] **Yellow-bellied sapsucker** (*Sphyrapicus varius*) — fairly common migrant and uncommon winter visitor; suburban and wooded areas
- [ ] **+Downy woodpecker** (*Picoides pubescens*) — fairly common resident; suburban and wooded areas, mainland
- [ ] **+Hairy woodpecker** (*Picoides villosus*) — rare resident; pine woodlands, mainland
- [ ] **+Red-cockaded woodpecker** (*Picoides borealis*) — rare resident; pine woodlands, northern mainland
- [ ] **+Northern flicker** (*Colaptes auratus*) — fairly common resident; suburban and wooded areas
- [ ] **+Pileated woodpecker** (*Dryocopus pileatus*) — uncommon resident; suburban and wooded areas, chiefly mainland

Flycatchers

- [ ] **Olive-sided flycatcher** (*Contopus borealis*) — rare migrant, chiefly fall
- [ ] **Eastern wood-pewee** (*Contopus virens*) — uncommon migrant, chiefly fall
- [ ] **Yellow-bellied flycatcher** (*Empidonax flaviventris*) — rare migrant, chiefly fall
- [ ] **Acadian flycatcher** (*Empidonax virescens*) — rare migrant, chiefly fall
- [ ] **Willow flycatcher** (*Empidonax traillii*) — rare migrant, chiefly fall
- [ ] **Least flycatcher** (*Empidonax minimus*) — uncommon migrant and winter visitor; second growth, edges
- [ ] **Eastern phoebe** (*Sayornis phoebe*) — common fall and winter visitor; suburban and wooded areas, chiefly mainland
- [ ] **+Great crested flycatcher** (*Myiarchus crinitus*) — common migrant and resident; suburban and wooded areas
- [ ] **Brown-crested flycatcher** (*Myiarchus tyrannulus*) — rare winter visitor; woodlands
- [ ] **La Sagra's flycatcher** (*Myiarchus sagrae*) — rare winter and spring visitor; coastal hammocks
- [ ] **Western kingbird** (*Tyrannus verticalis*) — locally uncommon migrant and winter visitor; open areas, fruiting trees
- [ ] **+Eastern kingbird** (*Tyrannus tyrannus*) — uncommon spring migrant and summer breeder, very common late summer migrant; woodland edges, only breeds on mainland
- [ ] **+Gray kingbird** (*Tyrannus dominicensis*) — uncommon migrant and summer breeder (local away from Keys); suburban and wooded areas

BIRD CHECKLIST

☐ **Scissor-tailed flycatcher** (*Tyrannus forficatus*) — locally uncommon migrant and winter visitor; open areas, around fruiting trees

☐ **Fork-tailed flycatcher** (*Tyrannus savana*) — rare visitor, chiefly summer; open areas, around fruiting trees

Swallows

☐ **+Purple martin** (*Progne subis*) — common winter and spring breeder, spring and fall migrant; open areas, only nests in man-made nesting structures on mainland

☐ **Tree swallow** (*Tachycineta bicolor*) — variably abundant visitor, late fall through early spring; marshy and open areas

☐ **Bahama swallow** (*Tachycineta cyaneoviridis*) — rare spring and summer migrant

☐ **+Northern rough-winged swallow** (*Stelgidopteryx serripennis*) — uncommon migrant throughout in open areas, rare summer breeder in holes near water on mainland

☐ **Bank swallow** (*Riparia riparia*) — uncommon spring, common late summer and fall migrant; open areas

☐ **Cliff swallow** (*Hirundo pyrrhonota*) — rare spring, uncommon late summer and fall migrant; open areas

☐ **+Cave swallow** (*Hirundo fulva*) — rare migrant throughout in open areas, locally uncommon breeder under highway bridges near water in southeast Miami area

☐ **+Barn swallow** (*Hirundo rustica*) — abundant migrant throughout in open areas, rare breeder under highway bridges in Keys

Jays and Crows

☐ **+Blue jay** (*Cyanocitta cristata*) — common resident; suburban and wooded areas, mainland and upper Keys

☐ **+American crow** (*Corvus brachyrhynchos*) — common resident; wilder wooded areas, chiefly mainland

☐ **+Fish crow** (*Corvus ossifragus*) — common resident; suburban areas, chiefly mainland

Titmice, Nuthatches, and Bulbuls

☐ **+Tufted titmouse** (*Parus bicolor*) — uncommon resident; chiefly cypress woodlands, northern mainland

☐ **+Brown-headed nuthatch** (*Sitta pusilla*) — locally rare resident; pine woodlands, northern mainland

☐ ***Red-whiskered bulbul** (*Pycnonotus jocosus*) — uncommon resident; suburbs, Kendall area

Wrens

☐ **+Carolina wren** (*Thryothorus ludovicianus*) — common resident; woodlands, mainland and upper Keys

☐ **House wren** (*Troglodytes aedon*) — common migrant and winter visitor; suburban and brushy areas

☐ **Sedge wren** (*Cistothorus platensis*) — variably uncommon winter and spring visitor; damp grassy marshes, mainland

☐ **Marsh wren** (*Cistothorus palustris*) — variably uncommon winter and spring visitor; reedy marshes, mainland

Kinglets and Gnatcatchers

☐ **Ruby-crowned kinglet** (*Regulus calendula*) — uncommon winter visitor; woodlands, chiefly mainland

☐ **+Blue-gray gnatcatcher** (*Polioptila caerulea*) — common migrant and winter visitor throughout in suburbs and wooded areas, local breeder in wooded areas on northern mainland

Bluebirds and Thrushes

☐ **+Eastern bluebird** (*Sialia sialis*) — local, uncommon resident; pine-oak woodland edges, northern mainland

☐ **Veery** (*Catharus fuscescens*) — variably uncommon migrant

☐ **Gray-cheeked thrush** (*Catharus minimus*) — variably uncommon migrant

☐ **Swainson's thrush** (*Catharus ustulatus*) — variably uncommon migrant

☐ **Hermit thrush** (*Catharus guttatus*) — variably rare winter visitor; woodlands, chiefly mainland

☐ **Wood thrush** (*Hylocichla mustelina*) — variably uncommon migrant, rare in winter

☐ **American robin** (*Turdus migratorius*) — variably abundant winter visitor;suburban and wooded areas, chiefly mainland and upper Keys

☐ **Gray catbird** (*Dumetella carolinensis*) — abundant migrant and common winter visitor; brushy areas

Mockingbirds and Thrashers

☐ **+Northern mockingbird** (*Mimus polyglottos*) — abundant resident; suburban and open wooded areas

☐ **Bahama mockingbird** (*Mimus gundlachii*) — rare spring and summer visitor; coastal woodlands and brush

☐ **+Brown thrasher** (*Toxostoma rufum*) — uncommon resident; brushy wooded areas, chiefly mainland and upper Keys (has nested to Key West)

Pipits

☐ **American pipit** (*Anthus rubescens*) — variably rare winter visitor; fields

Waxwings

☐ **Cedar waxwing** (*Bombycilla cedrorum*) — variably uncommon winter and spring visitor; in fruiting trees

Shrikes

☐ +**Loggerhead shrike** (*Lanius ludovicianus*) — uncommon resident; open areas with brush, mainland

Starlings and Mynas

☐ *****European starling** (*Sturnus vulgaris*) — common resident; suburbs

☐ *****Common myna** (*Acridotheres tristis*) — locally uncommon resident; chiefly shopping centers, mainland

☐ *****Hill myna** (*Gracula religiosa*) — locally uncommon resident; suburban areas with trees, chiefly Coconut Grove area

Vireos

☐ +**White-eyed vireo** (*Vireo griseus*) — common migrant and somewhat local resident; brushy woodlands

☐ **Thick-billed vireo** (*Vireo crassirostris*) — rare migrant and winter visitor; brushy coastal woodlands

☐ **Bell's vireo** (*Vireo bellii*) — rare migrant and winter visitor; brushy woodlands

☐ **Solitary vireo** (*Vireo solitarius*) — uncommon migrant and winter visitor; woodlands

☐ **Yellow-throated vireo** (*Vireo flavifrons*) — uncommon migrant and rare winter visitor; woodlands

☐ **Warbling vireo** (*Vireo gilvus*) — rare migrant, chiefly fall

☐ **Philadelphia vireo** (*Vireo philadelphicus*) — rare migrant, chiefly fall

☐ +**Red-eyed vireo** (*Vireo olivaceus*) — common migrant throughout, local summer breeding visitor in mesic woodlands on northern mainland

☐ +**Black-whiskered vireo** (*Vireo altiloquus*) — common summer breeding visitor; tropical woodlands, chiefly Keys and coastal mainland

Warblers

☐ **Blue-winged warbler** (*Vermivora pinus*) — variably uncommon migrant and rare winter visitor; woodlands

☐ **Golden-winged warbler** (*Vermivora chrysoptera*) — rare migrant

☐ **Tennessee warbler** (*Vermivora peregrina*) — uncommon migrant, chiefly fall

☐ **Orange-crowned warbler** (*Vermivora celata*) — fairly common winter visitor; brushy woodlands

☐ **Nashville warbler** (*Vermivora ruficapilla*) — variably uncommon migrant and rare winter visitor; brushy woodlands

☐ +**Northern parula** (*Parula americana*) — common migrant and uncommon winter visitor throughout, local summer breeder in mesic woodlands on northern mainland

☐ +**Yellow warbler** (*Dendroica petechia*) — uncommon resident (mangroves, chiefly Keys) and uncommon migrant elsewhere

☐ **Chestnut-sided warbler** (*Dendroica pensylvanica*) — variably uncommon

migrant
- [ ] **Magnolia warbler** (*Dendroica magnolia*) — variably common migrant and rare winter visitor; woodlands
- [ ] **Cape May warbler** (*Dendroica tigrina*) — common migrant and locally uncommon winter visitor; in flowering and fruiting trees
- [ ] **Black-throated blue warbler** (*Dendroica caerulescens*) — common migrant and rare winter visitor; woodlands
- [ ] **Yellow-rumped warbler** (*Dendroica coronata*) — variably abundant winter visitor; brushy and wooded areas
- [ ] **Black-throated gray warbler** (*Dendroica nigrescens*) — rare migrant and winter visitor
- [ ] **Black-throated green warbler** (*Dendroica virens*) — variably uncommon migrant and winter visitor; woodlands
- [ ] **Blackburnian warbler** (*Dendroica fusca*) — variably uncommon migrant
- [ ] **Yellow-throated warbler** (*Dendroica dominica*) — common migrant and winter visitor; woodlands and palms
- [ ] **+Pine warbler** (*Dendroica pinus*) — common resident; pine woodlands, mainland (also rare migrant elsewhere)
- [ ] **+Prairie warbler** (*Dendroica discolor*) — common resident in mangroves, abundant migrant and uncommon winter visitor in brushy woodlands
- [ ] **Palm warbler** (*Dendroica palmarum*) — abundant migrant and winter visitor; brushy areas and lawns
- [ ] **Bay-breasted warbler** (*Dendroica castanea*) — variably uncommon migrant
- [ ] **Blackpoll warbler** (*Dendroica striata*) — variably common spring migrant and variably rare fall migrant
- [ ] **Cerulean warbler** (*Dendroica cerulea*) — rare migrant
- [ ] **Black-and-white warbler** (*Mniotilta varia*) — common migrant and fairly common winter visitor; woodlands
- [ ] **American redstart** (*Setophaga ruticilla*) — common migrant and fairly rare winter visitor; woodlands
- [ ] **+Prothonotary warbler** (*Protonotaria citrea*) — fairly common migrant and rare winter visitor throughout, local breeding visitor in cypress swamps, northern mainland
- [ ] **Worm-eating warbler** (*Helmitheros vermivorus*) — common migrant and fairly rare winter visitor; brushy woodlands
- [ ] **Swainson's warbler** (*Limnothlypis swainsonii*) — uncommon migrant; usually in woods on damp leaf litter
- [ ] **Ovenbird** (*Seiurus aurocapillus*) — common migrant and uncommon winter visitor; woodlands
- [ ] **Northern waterthrush** (*Seiurus noveboracensis*) — common migrant and uncommon winter visitor; damp margins, often in mangroves
- [ ] **Louisiana waterthrush** (*Seiurus motacilla*) — uncommon migrant and fairly rare winter visitor; slightly damp margins, usually fresh water

- ☐ **Kentucky warbler** (*Oporornis formosus*) — rare migrant
- ☐ **Connecticut warbler** (*Oporornis agilis*) — uncommon spring and fairly rare fall migrant; brushy leaf litter
- ☐ **Mourning warbler** (*Oporornis philadelphia*) — rare migrant, chiefly fall; brushy areas
- ☐ **+Common yellowthroat** (*Geothlypis trichas*) — common migrant and winter visitor throughout, fairly common resident in swampy brush on mainland
- ☐ **Hooded warbler** (*Wilsonia citrina*) — uncommon migrant and rare winter visitor; woodlands
- ☐ **Wilson's warbler** (*Wilsonia pusilla*) — variably uncommon migrant and rare winter visitor; brushy areas
- ☐ **Canada warbler** (*Wilsonia canadensis*) — variably uncommon migrant
- ☐ **Yellow-breasted chat** (*Icteria virens*) — variably uncommon migrant and rare winter visitor; brushy areas

Bananaquits and Tanagers

- ☐ **Bananaquit** (*Coereba flaveola*) — rare visitor, chiefly winter; flowering trees usually near coast
- ☐ **Stripe-headed tanager** (*Spindalis zena*) — rare winter and spring visitor; fruiting trees
- ☐ **+Summer tanager** (*Piranga rubra*) — uncommon migrant and rare winter visitor throughout; local breeding visitor in pine-oak woodlands on northern mainland
- ☐ **Scarlet tanager** (*Piranga olivacea*) — variably uncommon migrant
- ☐ **Western tanager** (*Piranga ludoviciana*) — rare winter visitor; fruiting trees

Cardinals, Grosbeaks, and Buntings

- ☐ **+Northern cardinal** (*Cardinalis cardinalis*) — common resident (rare near Key West); suburban and wooded areas
- ☐ **Rose-breasted grosbeak** (*Pheucticus ludovicianus*) — variably uncommon migrant and rare winter visitor; woodlands
- ☐ **Blue grosbeak** (*Guiraca caerulea*) — variably uncommon migrant and rare winter visitor; brushy areas
- ☐ **Indigo bunting** (*Passerina cyanea*) — common migrant and uncommon winter visitor; brushy areas
- ☐ **Painted bunting** (*Passerina ciris*) — common migrant and winter visitor; brushy areas
- ☐ **Dickcissel** (*Spiza americana*) — variably uncommon migrant and rare winter visitor; brushy areas

Towhees and Sparrows

- ☐ **+Rufous-sided towhee** (*Pipilo erythrophthalmus*) — common resident; chiefly pine woodlands, mainland
- ☐ **Chipping sparrow** (*Spizella passerina*) — variably uncommon migrant and winter visitor; brushy areas and lawns

☐ **Clay-colored sparrow** (*Spizella pallida*) — variably rare migrant and winter visitor; brushy areas

☐ **Field sparrow** (*Spizella pusilla*) — rare migrant and winter visitor; brushy areas, mainland

☐ **Vesper sparrow** (*Pooecetes gramineus*) — rare migrant and winter visitor; fallow fields with brush, mainland

☐ **Lark sparrow** (*Chondestes grammacus*) — variably rare migrant and winter visitor; brushy areas

☐ **Savannah sparrow** (*Passerculus sandwichensis*) — common migrant and winter visitor; open areas, chiefly mainland

☐ **Grasshopper sparrow** (*Ammodramus savannarum*) — uncommon migrant and winter visitor; fallow fields with brush, chiefly mainland

☐ **Sharp-tailed sparrow** (*Ammodramus caudacutus*) — uncommon winter visitor; salt marsh prairie

☐ **+Seaside sparrow** (*Ammodramus maritimus*) — fairly common resident; fresh-to-brackish sloughs, mostly Everglades

☐ **Lincoln's sparrow** (*Melospiza lincolnii*) — rare winter visitor; brushy areas

☐ **Swamp sparrow** (*Melospiza georgiana*) — variably uncommon migrant and winter visitor; swampy areas, chiefly mainland

☐ **White-throated sparrow** (*Zonotrichia albicollis*) — rare migrant and winter visitor; brushy areas

☐ **White-crowned sparrow** (*Zonotrichia leucophrys*) — locally uncommon winter and spring visitor; brushy areas

☐ **Bobolink** (*Dolichonyx oryzivorus*) — common migrant; fields and agricultural areas

Blackbirds and Orioles

☐ **+Red-winged blackbird** (*Agelaius phoeniceus*) — common resident; brushy fields and swamps

☐ **+Eastern meadowlark** (*Sturnella magna*) — common resident; fields, mainland

☐ **Yellow-headed blackbird** (*Xanthocephalus xanthocephalus*) — rare migrant and winter visitor; fields and swamps

☐ **+Boat-tailed grackle** (*Quiscalus major*) — abundant resident; swamps and fields, mainland

☐ **+Common grackle** (*Quiscalus quiscula*) — common resident; suburbs and fields, absent from Keys in winter

☐ **+Shiny cowbird** (*Molothrus bonariensis*) — variably uncommon spring migrant, chiefly Keys and Gulf coast; local resident throughout

☐ **Bronzed cowbird** (*Molothrus aeneus*) — variably rare winter visitor; mainland

☐ **+Brown-headed cowbird** (*Molothrus ater*) — common migrant and winter visitor, some breed; fields and edges, chiefly mainland

☐ **Orchard oriole** (*Icterus spurius*) — variably common migrant (rarer to the east); wooded areas

☐ ***Spot-breasted oriole** (*Icterus pectoralis*) — uncommon resident; suburbs with fruiting trees, Miami area

☐ **Northern oriole** (*Icterus galbula*) — common migrant, fairly rare winter visitor; wooded areas

Finches

☐ **Pine siskin** (*Carduelis pinus*) — variably rare winter and spring visitor; wooded edges

☐ **American goldfinch** (*Carduelis tristis*) — variably uncommon winter and spring visitor; wooded edges

Old World Sparrows

☐ ***House sparrow** (*Passer domesticus*) — common resident; urban areas, local in Keys

MAMMAL CHECKLIST

☐ **Opossum** (*Didelphis virginiana pigra*) — abundant; most habitats on mainland and Keys

☐ **Short-tailed shrew** (*Blarina brevicauda peninsulae*) — uncommon; mainland

☐ **Least shrew** (*Cryptotis parva floridana*) — common; mainland

☐ **Eastern mole** (*Scalopus aquaticus porteri*) — common; mainland

☐ **Eastern pipistrelle** (*Pipistrellus subflavus floridanus*) — uncommon; trees and crevices (in rocks, structures) on mainland and Keys

☐ **Big brown bat** (*Eptesicus fuscus osceola*) — rare; buildings and trees, range unconfirmed

☐ **Seminole bat** (*Nycteris seminola*) — rare; trees and Spanish moss, possibly south to Miami, not southwestern Florida or Keys

☐ **Northern yellow bat** (*Nycteris intermedia floridana*) — uncommon; trees around Big Cypress and Atlantic coastal ridge south to Miami

☐ **Evening bat** (*Nycticeius humeralis subtropicalis*) — common; trees and buildings on mainland

☐ **Brazilian free-tailed bat** (*Tadarida brasiliensis cynocephala*) — common; buildings, trees, and crevices (in rocks, structures) near coasts

☐ **Florida mastiff bat** (*Eumops glaucinus floridanus*) — rare; buildings and trees in South Miami (the most restricted range of any Florida mammal)

☐ **Nine-banded armadillo** (*Dasypus novemcinctus mexicanus*) — introduced? uncommon; drier areas of mainland

☐ **Marsh rabbit** (*Sylvilagus palustris paludicola)* — common; most habitats (prefers marshes) on mainland; *S. p. hefneri*: rare on Lower Keys

☐ **Eastern cottontail** (*Sylvilagus floridanus floridanus* and *S. f. paulsoni*) — uncommon; in pinelands and hammocks on mainland

☐ **Gray squirrel** (*Sciurus carolinensis extimus*) — common; hammocks on mainland and Keys

☐ **Mangrove fox squirrel** (*Sciurus niger avicennia*) — uncommon; mangroves, cypress, and pinelands on western mainland; extirpated elsewhere

☐ ***Red-bellied squirrel** (*Sciurus aureogaster*) — found only on Elliott Key and a few nearby keys

☐ **Southern flying squirrel** (*Glaucomys volans querceti*) — uncommon; pinelands on mainland

☐ **Marsh rice rat** (*Oryzomys palustris coloratus*) — common; fresh and salt water marshes on mainland

☐ **Oldfield mouse** (*Peromyscus polionotus niveiventris*) — rare (extirpated?); beaches on mainland and Keys

☐ **Cotton mouse** (*Peromyscus gossypinus allapaticola* and *P. g. telmaphilus*) — common; hammocks on mainland and upper Keys

☐ **Florida mouse** (*Peromyscus floridanus*) — uncommon; along coastal uplands on mainland to Dade County

☐ **Hispid cotton rat** (*Sigmodon hispidus exsputus, S. h. floridanus* and *S. h. spadicipygus*) — abundant; ubiquitous, mainland and Keys

☐ **Key Largo woodrat** (*Neotoma floridana smalli*) — rare (almost extirpated); hardwood hammocks on Key Largo

☐ **Round-tailed muskrat** (*Neofiber alleni struix*) — uncommon; marshes and sloughs on mainland

☐ ***Black (Roof) rat** (*Rattus rattus*) — common; near development on mainland and Keys

☐ ***Norway rat** (*Rattus norvegicus*) — common; near development on mainland and Keys

☐ ***House mouse** (*Mus musculus*) — common; near development on mainland and Keys

☐ **Atlantic bottle-nosed dolphin** (*Tursiops truncatus*) — common; shallow waters and estuaries of Atlantic Ocean, Gulf of Mexico, and Florida Bay

☐ **Gray fox** (*Urocyon cinereoargenteus floridanus*) — common; particularly eastern mainland near development

☐ ***Red fox** (*Vulpes vulpes*) - status unknown; local in interior mainland

☐ **Black bear** (*Ursus americanus floridanus*) — rare; uplands on mainland (mostly Big Cypress region)

☐ **Raccoon** (*Procyon lotor auspicatus, P. l. elucus, P. l. incautus, P. l. inesperatus, P. l. marinus*) — abundant; all habitats on mainland and Keys

☐ **Long-tailed weasel** (*Mustela frenata peninsulae*) — rare; occurs in Big Cypress region

☐ **Mink** (*Mustela vison evergladensis* and *M. v. lutensis*) — rare; freshwater wetlands on mainland

☐ **Spotted skunk** (*Spilogale putorius ambarvalis*) — uncommon; palmetto scrub and hammocks on mainland

☐ **Striped skunk** (*Mephitis mephitis elongata*) — uncommon; uplands on mainland

☐ **River otter** (*Lutra canadensis lataxina*) — common; freshwater wetlands on mainland

☐ **Panther** (*Felis concolor coryi*) — rare (almost extirpated); pinelands, cypresses, hammocks; rarely seen south of Tamiami Trail

☐ **Bobcat** (*Lynx rufus floridanus*) — common; mainland, rarely to Key Largo

- ❏ **White-tailed deer** (*Odocoileus virginianus seminolus* and *O. v. clavium*) *O. v. seminolus* — common on mainland; *O. v. clavium* locally common only around Big Pine Key area
- ❏ **West Indian manatee** (*Trichecus manatus latirostris*) — locally common in shallow marine and estuary waters around mainland and Keys
- ❏ ***Feral pig** (*Sus scrofa*) — common; many habitats in interior of mainland; nuisance

REPTILE CHECKLIST

Crocodilians

☐ **American crocodile** (*Crocodylus acutus*) — rare; coastal mangroves on mainland and Keys

☐ **American alligator** (*Alligator mississippiensis*) — abundant; freshwater wetlands on mainland (occasionally on coasts) and fresh water on a few lower Keys

☐ ***Spectacled caiman** (*Caiman crocodilus*) — rare; fresh water in Miami area

Turtles

☐ **Florida snapping turtle** (*Chelydra serpentina osceola*) — common; fresh water on mainland

☐ **Striped mud turtle** (*Kinosternon baurii*) — common; freshwater wetlands on mainland and Keys

☐ **Florida mud turtle** (*Kinosternon subrubrum steindachneri*) — common; freshwater wetlands and salt marshes on mainland and Keys

☐ **Common musk turtle** or **stinkpot** (*Sternotherus odoratus*) — common; fresh water on mainland

☐ **Florida box turtle** (*Terrapene carolina bauri*) — common; pinelands and hammocks on mainland and some Keys (not middle Keys)

☐ **Diamondback terrapin** (*Malaclemys terrapin tequesta, M. t. rhizophorarum, and M. t. macrospilota*) — uncommon; mangroves and saltmarshes on coastal mainland and Keys

☐ **Peninsula cooter** (*Pseudemys floridana peninsularis*) — abundant; fresh water on mainland, except extreme southwest

☐ **Florida redbelly turtle** (*Pseudemys nelsoni*) — abundant; mostly freshwater wetlands, also mangrove borders on mainland

☐ ***Red-eared slider** (*Trachemys scripta elegans*) — established in canals in Dade County

☐ **Florida chicken turtle** (*Deirochelys reticularia chrysea*) — uncommon; freshwater marshes and ponds on mainland

☐ **Gopher tortoise** (*Gopherus polyphemus*) — uncommon and rapidly declining; pinelands and scrub of Atlantic coastal ridge, Long Pine Key (few), Middle Cape Sable, Big Cypress, and Naples

☐ **Atlantic leatherback turtle** (*Dermochelys coriacea*) — rare; marine waters

☐ **Green turtle** (*Chelonia mydas*) — rare; marine waters

☐ **Atlantic hawksbill turtle** (*Eretmochelys imbricata imbricata*) — rare; marine waters

☐ **Loggerhead turtle** (*Caretta caretta*) uncommon in summer; marine waters near Cape Sable and other sandy beaches, and Florida Keys

☐ **Atlantic Ridley turtle** (*Lepidochelys kempii*) — rare; marine waters

☐ **Florida softshell turtle** (*Apalone ferox*) — common; freshwater marshes on mainland (introduced to Big Pine Key)

Lizards

☐ ***Tokay gecko** (*Gekko gekko*) — locally established near development; Miami area

☐ ***Mediterranean gecko** (*Hemidactylus turcicus turcicus*) — locally established; near development on Atlantic coast of mainland and upper and lower Keys

☐ ***Indopacific gecko** (*Hemidactylus garnotii*) — locally common, nocturnal; near development on mainland and upper Keys

☐ ***Ashy gecko** (*Sphaerodactylus elegans elegans*) — locally established, nocturnal; lower Keys and Miami area

☐ **Florida reef gecko** (*Sphaerodactylus notatus*) — common; pinelands and hammocks on southeast mainland and Keys

☐ ***Ocellated gecko** (*Sphaerodactylus argus argus*) — locally established; lower Keys

☐ ***Yellowhead gecko** (*Gonatodes albogularis fuscus*) — locally established; around Miami and lower Keys

☐ **Green anole** (*Anolis carolinensis*) — common; many habitats on mainland and Keys

☐ ***Knight anole** (*Anolis equestris*) — locally common; near development on southeast mainland and upper Keys

☐ ***Brown anole** (*Anolis sagrei*) — abundant and increasing; many habitats on mainland and Keys

☐ ***Jamaican giant anole** (*Anolis garmani*) — locally established; around Miami

☐ ***Puerto Rican crested anole** (*Anolis cristatellus cristatellus*) — locally established; around Miami

☐ ***Largehead anole** (*Anolis cybotes cybotes*) — locally established; around Miami

☐ ***Bark anole** (*Anolis distichus*) — locally common; Miami area only

☐ ***Brown basilisk** (*Basiliscus vittatus*) — locally established; around Miami

☐ ***Common iguana** (*Iguana iguana*) — uncommon; around Miami

☐ ***Spinytail iguana** (*Ctenosaura pectinata*) — locally established; South Miami near Biscayne Bay

☐ **Florida scrub lizard** (*Sceloporus woodi*) — rare; pinelands and scrub along coasts north from Miami and Marco

- [ ] ***Northern curlytail lizard** (*Leiocephalus carinatus armouri*) — locally established; around Miami
- [ ] ***Red-sided curlytail lizard** (*Leiocephalus schreibersii schreibersii*) — locally established; around Miami
- [ ] **Six-lined racerunner** (*Cnemidophorus sexlineatus*) — locally common; uplands on mainland and Keys
- [ ] ***Giant ameiva** (*Ameiva ameiva*) — locally established; around Miami
- [ ] ***Rainbow whiptail** (*Cnemidophorus lemniscatus*) — locally established; around Miami
- [ ] **Ground skink** (*Scincella lateralis*) — common; hammocks and pinelands on mainland (except Everglades and Keys)
- [ ] **Southeastern five-lined skink** (*Eumeces inexpectatus*) — common; often seen on trails on mainland and Keys
- [ ] **Florida Keys mole skink** (*Eumeces egregius egregius*) — rare, secretive; found under debris near shore on Keys and Dry Tortugas
- [ ] **Peninsula mole skink** (*Eumeces egregius onocrepis*) — uncommon; sandy scrub on mainland except Everglades
- [ ] **Eastern glass lizard** (*Ophisaurus ventralis*) — uncommon; pinelands and hammocks on mainland
- [ ] **Slender glass lizard** (*Ophisaurus attenuatus*) — uncommon; dry grasslands or woods on mainland except Everglades
- [ ] **Island glass lizard** (*Ophisaurus compressus*) — common; marshes and pinelands on eastern mainland

Snakes

- [ ] ***Brahminy blind snake** (*Ramphotyphlops braminus*) — worm-like burrower, locally common; east coast south to Homestead, also upper and lower Keys
- [ ] **Florida green water snake** (*Nerodia floridana*) — common; fresh or brackish marshes on mainland
- [ ] **Brown water snake** (*Nerodia taxispilota*) — common; clear, quiet waters on mainland
- [ ] **Florida water snake** (*Nerodia fasciata pictiventris*) — common; marshes and canals on mainland
- [ ] **Mangrove salt marsh snake** (*Nerodia clarkii compressicauda*) — common; mangrove swamps and salt marshes on coastal mainland and Keys
- [ ] **South Florida swamp snake** (*Seminatrix pygaea cyclas*) — common; freshwater wetlands on mainland
- [ ] **Florida brown snake** (*Storeria dekayi victa*) — common; pinelands, hammocks, and freshwater marshes on mainland and lower Keys

☐ **Eastern garter snake** (*Thamnophis sirtalis sirtalis*) — common; many habitats on mainland

☐ **Peninsula ribbon snake** (*Thamnophis sauritus sackenii*) — common; many habitats on mainland and lower Keys

☐ **Striped crayfish snake** (*Regina alleni*) — locally common; very aquatic, fresh water on mainland

☐ **Eastern hognose snake** (*Heterodon platyrhinos*) — rare; sandy areas of mainland

☐ **Southern ringneck snake** (*Diadophis punctatus punctatus* and *D. p. acricus*) — common; woodlands on mainland to upper Keys (*punctatus*), pinelands and hammocks on lower Keys (*acricus*, uncommon)

☐ **Eastern mud snake** (*Farancia abacura abacura*) — locally common; freshwater marshes, ponds, and canals on mainland

☐ **Southern black racer** (*Coluber constrictor priapus*) — abundant; many habitats on lower Keys

☐ **Everglades racer** (*Coluber constrictor paludicola*) — abundant; many habitats on mainland and upper Keys

☐ **Eastern coachwhip** (*Masticophis flagellum flagellum*) — locally common; many habitats on mainland

☐ **Rough green snake** (*Opheodrys aestivus*) — abundant; many habitats on mainland and Keys

☐ **Eastern indigo snake** (*Drymarchon corais couperi*) — rare; primarily dry areas on mainland and lower Keys

☐ **Corn snake or red rat snake** (*Elaphe guttata guttata*) — abundant; mostly around development on mainland and Keys

☐ **Everglades rat snake** (*Elaphe obsoleta rossalleni*) — locally common; freshwater marshes, hammocks, and pinelands in Everglades

☐ **Yellow rat snake** (*Elaphe obsoleta quadrivitatta*) — uncommon; many habitats on mainland (except Everglades) and upper Keys

☐ **Florida kingsnake** (*Lampropeltis getula florida*) — uncommon; freshwater marshes, hammocks, and pinelands on mainland

☐ **Scarlet kingsnake** (*Lampropeltis triangulum*) — rare; pinelands and hammocks on mainland and Keys (except middle Keys)

☐ **Florida scarlet snake** (*Cemophora c. coccinea*) — rare; pinelands and hammocks on mainland

☐ **Rim rock crowned snake** (*Tantilla oolitica*) — rare, secretive; limestone areas along Atlantic coast of mainland to upper Keys

☐ **Eastern coral snake** (*Micrurus fulvius*) — locally common; pinelands and hammocks on mainland and Key Largo; venomous

☐ **Florida cottonmouth or water moccasin** (*Agkistrodon piscivorus* *conanti*) — common; freshwater marshes and mangroves on mainland and Keys (except lower Keys); venomous

☐ **Dusky pygmy rattlesnake** (*Sistrurus miliarius*) — common; pinelands and freshwater marshes on mainland; venomous

☐ **Eastern diamondback rattlesnake** (*Crotalus adamanteus*) — locally common; many habitats on mainland and Keys (including Florida Bay); venomous

AMPHIBIAN CHECKLIST

Salamanders

☐ **Two-toed amphiuma** (*Amphiuma means*) — common; freshwater marshes and sloughs on mainland

☐ **Greater siren** (*Siren lacertina*) — common; freshwater marshes, sloughs, and ponds on mainland

☐ **Everglades dwarf siren** (*Pseudobranchus striatus belli*) — common; freshwater marshes, sloughs, and ponds on mainland

☐ **Peninsula newt** (*Notophthalmus viridescens piaropicola*) — abundant; freshwater marshes and ponds on mainland

Toads and Frogs

☐ **Eastern spadefoot toad** (*Scaphiophus holbrookii holbrookii*) — uncommon, secretive; sandy, dry areas on Atlantic coastal ridge and upper and lower Keys

☐ **Southern toad** (*Bufo terrestris*) — abundant (uncommon in Everglades); hammocks, pinelands, and freshwater marshes on mainland and lower Keys

☐ **Oak toad** (*Bufo quercicus*) — common; hammocks, pinelands, and freshwater marshes on mainland and Keys (except lower Keys)

☐ ***Giant toad** (*Bufo marinus*) — common; breeds in fresh or brackish water around Miami area and Keys

☐ ***Greenhouse frog** (*Eleutherodactylus planirostris*) — may be immigrant; under leaf litter on mainland and Keys

☐ ***Puerto Rican coqui** (*Eleutherodactylus coqui*) — local, uncommon; Miami area

☐ **Florida cricket frog** (*Acris gryllus dorsalis*) — common; freshwater marshes on mainland

☐ **Green treefrog** (*Hyla cinerea*) — abundant; hammocks, pinelands, and freshwater marshes on mainland and Keys

☐ **Barking treefrog** (*Hyla gratiosa*) — uncommon; mainland except Dade and Monroe counties

☐ **Pine woods treefrog** (*Hyla femoralis*) — common; often around artificial lights on mainland

☐ **Squirrel treefrog** (*Hyla squirella*) — abundant; all habitats with fresh water on mainland and Keys

☐ **Cuban treefrog** (*Osteopilus septentrionalis*) — immigrant, locally abundant; often found around buildings on Atlantic coastal ridge, Keys, and Naples area

☐ **Florida chorus frog** (*Pseudacris nigrita verrucosa*) — common; freshwater swamps and marshes on mainland

☐ **Little grass frog** (*Pseudacris ocularis*) — abundant; freshwater swamps and marshes on mainland

☐ **Eastern narrowmouth toad** (*Gastrophryne carolinensis*) — common, but a secretive burrower; under leaf litter in hammocks on mainland and Keys

☐ **Pig frog** (*Rana grylio*) — abundant, commercially exploited; all fresh water habitats on mainland

☐ **Southern leopard frog** (*Rana utricularia*) — abundant; all fresh water habitats on mainland and lower Keys

☐ **Florida gopher frog** (*Rana capito aesopus*) — uncommon; found in gopher tortoise burrows on mainland

SCIENTIFIC NAMES OF PLANTS

This is a list of the scientific names of the plants mentioned in the text. All the plants are found in south Florida. However, it is not intended to be a complete list of plants found in the region covered by this book. There are too many to list comfortably.

TREES AND WOODY PLANTS

*exotic

Gymnosperms:

CYCADACEAE Cycad family
coontie (*Zamia pumila*)

PINACEAE Pine family
slash pine (*Pinus elliottii var. densa*)

TAXODIACEAE Redwood family
bald-cypress (*Taxodium distichum*)
pond-cypress (*Taxodium ascendens* or *T. distichum var. nutans*)

Angiosperms:

ANACARDIACEAE Cashew family
Brazilian pepper (*Schinus terebinthifolius*)*
poison-ivy (*Toxicodendron radicans*)
poisonwood (*Metopium toxiferum*)

ANNONACEAE Custard-apple family
pond-apple (*Annona glabra*)

ARECACEAE Palm family

cabbage palm (*Sabal palmetto*)
coconut palm (*Cocos nucifera*)*
Florida (or Jamaica) thatch palm (*Thrinax radiata*)
Key (or brittle) thatch palm (*Thrinax morrisii*)
paurotis palm (*Acoelorrhaphe wrightii*)
royal palm (*Roystonea elata*)
saw palmetto (*Serenoa repens*)
silver palm (*Coccothrinax argentata*)

AVICENNIACEAE Black mangrove family
black mangrove (*Avicennia germinans*)

BURSERACEAE Torchwood family
gumbo-limbo (*Bursera simaruba*)

CASUARINACEAE Beefwood family
Australian-pine (*Casuarina litorea* and *C. glauca*)*

CHRYSOBALANACEAE Coco-plum family
coco-plum (*Chrysobalanus icaco*)

COMBRETACEAE Combretum family
buttonwood (*Conocarpus erectus*)
white mangrove (*Laguncularia racemosa*)

EUPHORBIACEAE Spurge family
manchineel (*Hippomane mancinella)*

FABACEAE Pea family
blackbead (*Pithecellobium guadalupense*)
catclaw (*Pithecellobium unguis-cati*)
coral bean (*Erythrina herbacea*)
Jamaica dogwood (*Piscidia piscipula*)
necklace pod (*Sophora tomentosa*)
sweet acacia (*Acacia farnesiana*)
wild-tamarind (*Lysiloma latisiliquum*)

FAGACEAE Beech family
live oak (*Quercus virginiana*)

LAURACEAE Laurel family
lancewood (*Ocotea coriacea*, formerly *Nectandra coriacea*)
redbay (*Persea borbonia*)

MAGNOLIACEAE Magnolia family
sweet bay (*Magnolia virginiana*)

MELASTOMATACEAE Melastoma family
tetrazygia (*Tetrazygia bicolor*)

MELIACEAE Mahogany family
mahogany (*Swietenia mahagoni*)

MORACEAE Mulberry family
fig (*Ficus* spp.)
strangler fig (*Ficus aurea*)

MYRICACEAE Bayberry family
wax myrtle (*Myrica cerifera*)

MYRSINACEAE Myrsine family
myrsine (*Myrsine floridana*)

MYRTACEAE Myrtle family
melaleuca, cajeput (*Melaleuca quinquenervia*)*
white stopper (*Eugenia axillaris*)

POLYGONACEAE Buckwheat family
pigeon-plum (*Coccoloba diversifolia*)
sea grape (*Coccoloba uvifera*)

RHAMNACEAE Buckthorn family
black ironwood (*Krugiodendron ferreum*)

RHIZOPHORACEAE Mangrove family
red mangrove (*Rhizophora mangle*)

ROSACEAE Rose family
West-Indian cherry (*Prunus myrtifolia*)

RUBIACEAE Madder family
black-torch (*Erithalis fruticosa*)
firebush (*Hamelia patens*)
rough velvetseed (*Guettarda scabra*)
indigo-berry (*Randia aculeata*)
seven-year-apple (*Casasia clusiifolia*)
wild coffee (*Psychotria nervosa*)

RUTACEAE Citrus family

satinwood (*Zanthoxylum flavum*)
torchwood (*Amyris elemifera*)
wild-lime (*Zanthoxylum fagara*)

SALICACEAE Willow family
coastal plain willow (*Salix caroliniana*)

SAPINDACEAE Soapberry family
varnish-leaf (*Dodonaea viscosa*)

SAPOTACEAE Sapodilla family
mastic (*Mastichodendron foetidissimum*)
saffron-plum (*Bumelia celastrina*)
sapodilla (*Manilkara zapota*)
satinleaf (*Chrysophyllum oliviforme*)
willow bustic (*Dipholis salicifolia*)
wild dilly (*Manilkara bahamensis*)

SIMAROUBACEAE Quassia family
paradise-tree (*Simarouba glauca*)

SOLANACEAE Nightshade family
canker-berry (*Solanum bahamense*)

SURIANACEAE Bay-cedar family
bay-cedar (*Suriana maritima*)

ZYGOPHYLLACEAE Caltrop family
lignum vitae (*Guaiacum sanctum*)

OTHER PLANTS

AGAVACEAE Agave family
Spanish bayonet (*Yucca aloifolia*)

AIZOACEAE Carpetweed family
sea purslane (*Sesuvium portulacastrum*)

ASTERACEAE Aster family
sea ox-eye daisy (*Borrichia frutescens*)

BATACEAE Saltwort family
saltwort (*Batis maritima*)

BROMELIACEAE air plant family
twisted air plant (*Tillandsia flexuosa*)

CACTACEAE Cactus family
prickly-pear (*Opuntia* spp.)

CHENOPODIACEAE
glasswort (*Salicornia virginica*)

CONVOLVULACEAE Morning glory family
pineland jacquemontia (*Jacquemontia curtissii*)

CYPERACEAE Sedge family
sawgrass (*Cladium jamaicensis*)
spike rush (*Eleocharis cellulosa*)

EUPHORBIACEAE Spurge family
pineland croton (*Croton linearis*)

LENTIBULARIACEAE Bladderwort family
bladderwort (*Utricularia* spp.)

POACEAE Grass family
  Florida gamagrass (*Tripsacum floridanum*)
  muhly grass (*Muhlenberghia filipes*)

POLYPODIACEAE Polypodium family
  golden polypody (*Phlebodium aureum*)
  resurrection fern (*Polypodium polypodioides*)
  shoestring fern (*Vittaria lineata*)
  strap fern (*Campyloneurum* spp.)

PONTEDERIACEAE Pickerel-weed family
  pickerel-weed (*Pontederia cordata*)

ORCHIDACEAE Orchid family
  butterfly orchid (*Encyclia tampensis*)
  cowhorn orchid (*Cyrtopodium punctatum*)
  worm-vine orchid (*Vanilla barellata*)

RUBIACEAE Madder family
  small-flowered lily thorn (*Catesbaea parviflora*)

TYPHACEAE Cattail family
  cattail (*Typha* spp.)

VERBENACEAE Verbena family
  beauty berry (*Callicarpa americana*)

SUGGESTED READING

Asterisk denotes sources used in preparation of this book.

Ashton, Ray E., Jr., and Patricia Sawyer Ashton. 1981. Handbook of Reptiles and Amphibians of Florida. Part One: The Snakes. Miami: Windward Publishing. 176pp.

Ashton, Ray E., Jr., and Patricia Sawyer Ashton. 1985. Handbook of Reptiles and Amphibians of Florida. Part Two: Lizards, Turtles, and Crocodilians. Miami: Windward Publishing. 191pp.

Ashton, Ray E., Jr., and Patricia Sawyer Ashton. 1988. Handbook of Reptiles and Amphibians of Florida. Part Three: The Amphibians. Miami: Windward Publishing. 191pp.

Bell, C. Ritchie and Bryan J. Taylor. 1982. Florida Wild Flowers and Roadside Plants. Chapel Hill, NC: Laurel Hill Press. 308pp.

Brookfield, Charles M. and Oliver Griswold. 1985. They All Called It Tropical. Miami: Historical Association of Southern Florida. 77pp.*

Carmichael, Pete and Winston Williams. Florida's Fabulous Reptiles and Amphibians. Tampa, FL: World Publications. 120pp.

Carter, Elizabeth F. 1987. A Guide to the Trails of Florida. Birmingham, AL: Menasha Ridge Press. 129pp.

Cox, W. Eugene. 1989. Everglades: The Continuing Story. Las Vegas, NV: K.C. Publications. 48pp.

De Golia, Jack. 1978. Everglades: The Story Behind the Scenery. Las Vegas, NV: K.C. Publications. 64pp.

Douglas, Marjory Stoneman. 1988 (rev.). The Everglades: River of Grass. Sarasota, FL: Pineapple Press. 448pp.

FNPMA. 1991. Motorist's Guide to Everglades National Park. Homestead, FL: Florida National Parks and Monuments Association.

FNPMA. 1991. An Activity Guide for Teachers: Everglades National Park (grades 4-6). Homestead, FL: National Parks and Monuments Association.

Gato, Jeanette. 1991. The Monroe County Environmental story. Big Pine Key, FL: Seacamp Association. 368pp.

George, Jean Craighead. 1988. Everglades Wildguide. Homestead, FL: U.S. Dept. of Interior, NPS. Natural History Series, Everglades National Park. 103pp.

Gerberg, Eugene J. and Ross H. Arnett. 1989. Florida Butterflies. Baltimore, MD: Natural Science Publications. 90pp.*

Greenberg, Idaz and Jerry Greenberg. 1977. Guide to Corals and Fishes of Florida, the Bahamas, and the Caribbean. Miami: Seahawk Press. 65pp. Paperback and waterproof editions.

Hoffmeister, John Edward. 1982. Land from the Sea, the Geologic Story of South Florida. Coral Gables, FL: University of Miami Press. 143pp.*

Holt, Harold R. 1990. A Birder's Guide to Florida. Distr. by ABA Sales, P.O. Box 6599, Colorado Springs, CO 80934. 164pp.

Kale, Herbert W., II, and David S. Maehr. 1990. Florida's Birds. Sarasota, FL: Pineapple Press. 288pp.*

Kalma, Dennis. 1988. Boat and Canoe Camping in the Everglades Back-country and Ten Thousand Islands Region. Miami: Florida Flair Books. 64pp.

Kaplan, Eugene H. 1988. A Field Guide to Southeastern and Caribbean Seashores. Boston: Houghton Mifflin. 425 pp.*

Landrum, L. Wayne. 1990. Biscayne, the Story Behind the Scenery. Las Vegas, NV: K.C. Publications. 48pp.

Laughlin, Maureen H., John C. Ogden, William B. Roberston, Jr., Ken Russell, and Roy Wood. 1991. Everglades National Park Bird Checklist. Homestead, FL: Florida National Parks and Monuments Association. 20pp.*

Lazell, James D., Jr. 1989. Wildlife of the Florida Keys. Washington, DC: Island Press. 254pp.*

McIver, Stuart. 1989. True Tales of the Everglades. Miami: Florida Flair Books. 64pp.*

Morton, Julia F. 1982. Wild Plants for Survival in South Florida. Miami: Fairchild Tropical Garden. 80pp.

Neill, Wilfred T. 1956. Florida's Seminole Indians. St. Petersburg, FL: Great Outdoors Publishing Co. 128pp.

Robertson, William B., Jr. 1989 (rev.). Everglades - The Park Story. Homestead, FL: Florida National Parks and Monuments Association. 63pp.*

Stevenson, George B. 1969. Trees of the Everglades National Park and the Florida Keys. Miami: Banyan Books. 32pp.*

Stone, Calvin. 1979. Forty Years in the Everglades. Tabor City, NC: W. Horace Carter, Atlantic Publishing Co. 224pp.

Tebeau, Charleton W. 1968. Man in the Everglades. Coral Gables, FL: University of Miami Press. 192pp.*

Tomlinson, P.B. 1980. The Biology of Trees Native to Tropical Florida. Allston, MA: Harvard University Printing Office. 480pp.*

Toops, Connie M. 1988. The Alligator: Monarch of the Marsh. Homestead, FL: Florida National Parks and Monuments Assn. 58pp.

Toops, Connie M. 1989. Everglades. Stillwater, MN: Voyager Press. 96pp.

Toops, Connie and Willard E. Dilley. 1986. Birds of South Florida. Conway, AR: Conway Printing Co. 150pp.

Truesdell, William G. 1985. A Guide to the Wilderness Waterway of Everglades National Park. Coral Gables, FL: University of Miami Press, 64pp.

Voss, Gilbert L. 1988. Coral Reefs of Florida. Sarasota, FL: Pineapple Press. 80pp.*

Will, Lawrence E. 1984. A Dredgeman of Cape Sable. Belle Glade, FL: The Glades Historical Society. 158pp.*

Additional Sources Used in Preparation of This Book (Technical or not readily available)

Artman, L.P., Jr. 1974. The Overseas Railroad. [no publisher listed]. 14pp.

Clarke, Mary Helm. 1949. South Florida Treasure Trails. Tallahassee, FL: Kay Publishing Co. 103pp.

Craighead, Frank C. 1963. Orchids and Other Airplants of the Everglades National Park. Coral Gables, FL: University of Miami Press. 127pp.

SUGGESTED READING

Downs, Dorothy. 1982. Miccosukee Arts and Crafts. Miami: Miccosukee Indian Tribe of Florida. 21pp.

Duever, Michael J., John E. Carlson, John F. Meeder, Linda C. Duever, Lance H. Gunderson, Lawrence A. Riopelle, Taylor R. Alexander, Ronald L. Myers, and Daniel P. Spangler. 1986. The Big Cypress National Preserve. Research Report No. 8 of the National Audubon Society, New York. 444pp. (Originally 1979, Resource inventory and analysis of the Big Cypress National Preserve, Univ. of Florida, Gainesville. 455pp.

Everglades Natural History. March 1953 (Vol. 1, No. 1) - June 1955 (Vol. 3, No. 2). Everglades Natural History Association.

Gleason, Patrick J. (ed.) 1974. Environments of South Florida: Past and Present. Memoir 2: Miami Geological Society. Miami: Miami Geological Society. 452pp.

Griswold, Oliver. 1965. The Florida Keys and the Coral Reef. Miami: The Graywood Press. 143pp.

McGeachy, Beth. 1955. Handbook of Florida Palms. St. Petersburg, FL: Geat Outdoors Publishing Co. 62pp.

Meyers, Ronald L. and John J. Ewel (eds.). 1990. 2nd pr 91. Ecosystems of Florida. Orlando, FL: University of Central Florida Press. 763pp.

MMWR. 1989. Seizures temporally associated with DEET insect repellent — New York and Connecticut. Morbidity and Mortality Weekly R. 38(39):678-680.

NOAA. 1982. Monthly normals of temperature, precipitation, and heating and cooling degree days 1951-1980, Florida. National Climatic Center, Asheville, NC. September 1982.

NOAA. 1984. Climatography of the United States No. 20. Climatic summaries for selected sites, 1951-80. National Climatic Data Center, Asheville, NC.

Parks, Pat. 1968. The Railroad that Died at Sea. Brattleboro, VT: The Stephen Greene Press. 44pp.

Stevenson, Henry M. 1976. Vertebrates of Florida (Identification and Distribution). Gainesville, FL: University Presses of Florida. 607pp.

OTHER SOURCES
OF INFORMATION

FLORIDA - GENERAL

DeLorme Mapping Company
P.O. Box 298
Freeport, ME 04032
(207) 865-4171
*publishes "Florida Atlas & Gazet-
teer" (detailed road maps with
guide to outdoor recreation)*

Florida Association of Canoe
Liveries & Outfitters
Box 1764
Arcadia, FL 33821
free list of canoe outfitters

Florida Audubon Society
460 Hwy. 436, Suite 200
Casselberry, FL 32707
(407) 260-8300

Florida Board of Tourism
(904) 487-1462

Florida Department of Natural
Resources
Division of Recreation and Parks
3900 Commonwealth Blvd.
Tallahassee, FL 32399-3000
(904) 488-9872
information on state parks

Florida Game and Fresh Water Fish Comm.
620 S. Meridian Street
Tallahassee, FL 32399-1600
*(904) 488-4674 general information
(904) 488-1960 for Florida freshwater
fishing handbook*

Florida Trail Association, Inc.
P.O. Box 13708
Gainesville, FL 32604
(800) 343-1882

Florida Wildlife Federation
2545 Blairstone Pines Drive
P.O. Box 6870
Tallahassee, FL 32314-6870
(904) 656-7113

FLORIDA - SOUTH

Anhinga Audubon Society
P.O. Box 1138
Homestead, FL 33090-1138

Florida National Parks and
Monuments Association
P.O. Box 279, Homestead, FL 33030
(305) 247-1216

Friends of the Everglades
101 Westward Drive, Suite #2
Miami Springs, FL 33166

Greater Homestead-Florida City
Chamber of Commerce
43 North Krome Ave.
Homestead, FL 33030
(305) 247-2332

Miami Space Transit Planetarium
3280 S. Miami Avenue
Miami, FL
*(305) 854-4242 general information
(305) 854-2222 Cosmic Hotline
recording for locally visible events*

OTHER SOURCES OF INFORMATION

National Weather Service in Miami
(305) 661-5065 24-hour local weather
recording

Sierra Club - Miami Group
P.O. Box 43-0741
S. Miami, FL 33243-0741

Tropical Audubon Society
5530 Sunset Drive
South Miami, FL 33143
(305) 666-5111 general information
(305) 667-PEEP Birding Hotline
recording for local Miami area
sitings

Tropical Everglades Visitor
Association
160 U.S. 1
Florida City, FL 33034
(305) 245-9180

FLORIDA - THE KEYS

Dolphin Research Center
P.O. Box 2875
Marathon Shores, FL 33052
(305) 289-0002
nonprofit dolphin research/education
center; dolphin rides

Dolphins Plus
P.O. Box 2728
Key Largo, FL 33037
(305) 451-1993
nonprofit marine mammal
research/education center;
dolphin rides

Florida Keys Audubon Society
c/o The Audubon House
205 Whitehead Street
Key West, FL 33040
(305) 294-2116

Florida Keys and Key West
Tourist Bureau
1-800-LAST-KEY

Greater Key West Chamber of
Commerce
402 Wall Street
Key West, FL 33040
(305) 294-2587

Key Largo National Marine Sanctuary
P.O. Box 1083
Key Largo, FL 33037
(305) 451-1202

Looe Key National Marine Sanctuary
Rt. 1, Box 782
Big Pine Key, FL 33043
(305) 872-4039

National Audubon Society
Research Department
115 Indian Mound Trail
Tavernier, FL 33070
(305) 852-5092
"Birding in the Florida Keys"
publication

The Nature Conservancy
Florida Keys Office
P.O. Box 4958
Key West, FL 33041
(305) 296-3880

The Wilderness Society
Florida Keys Office
8065 Overseas Highway
Marathon, FL 33050
(305) 289-1010

GLOSSARY

aquifer an underground porous rock formation containing water, especially one that supplies water for wells or springs.

bayhead a tree island in the freshwater marsh that may be submerged during the wet season; so named because it usually contains redbay or sweet bay trees.

brackish water that contains some salt and may vary considerably in salinity; usually found where a river meets the ocean.

bromeliad (pronounced "bro-me'-lee-ad") airplant; a plant from the pineapple family that is an epiphyte. Examples: Spanish moss, ball-moss, needle-leaved airplant, banded wildpine.

coastal prairie areas along the mangrove belt lacking trees and having predominantly succulent-type salt-tolerant plants, such as glasswort and saltwort.

conch (pronounced "conk") a large marine snail common in the shallow waters of south Florida; prized for its food value and decorative shell.

coral a colony of invertebrates bound together by a limestone skeleton that forms the "backbone" of the reef off of south Florida.

cumulonimbus thunderhead; a tall, unstable cloud formation that imparts lightning and rain, common in south Florida in the wet season.

Dade County pine the local name for the variety of slash pine (*Pinus elliotti var. densa*) that grows in Dade County; historically very popular for building construction because of its resistance to insect damage and rot.

endangered species a species of plant or animal that has been declared (by a state or federal agency) in danger of becoming extinct if not protected.

endemic originating in a particular locality; indigenous.

epiphyte a plant growing upon or attached to another plant or non-living structure but is not parasitic. Florida has numerous epiphytic bromeliads, orchids, and ferns.

estuary a shallow wetland formed where a river meets an inlet of the sea; among the most productive habitats in the world.

GLOSSARY

exotic any species of plant or animal that was introduced (intentionally or unintentionally) by humans to an area it did not previously inhabit. Exotic species are undesirable in natural environments because they may outcompete or deplete native species. Examples are melaleuca, Brazilian pepper, domestic cat, common pigeon.

hammock a large tree island; an elevated, well-drained tract of land slightly higher than the surrounding wetlands where hardwood trees grow naturally.

hurricane a cyclone in the Atlantic Ocean having wind speeds of 74 mph or greater.

hydroperiod the length of time in any given year that an area of wetland is inundated by water.

key a small, low-lying island; occasionally used to mean a hammock.

liana a climbing plant or vine.

marl mud composed primarily of calcium carbonate, formed chiefly in short-hydroperiod freshwater wetlands; may become solidified.

muck organic soil that accumulates under wet conditions; the plant remains are too decomposed to be identified.

native species plants or animals indigenous to an area.

old growth a forest that has never been logged.

peat organic soil that accumulates under wet conditions and has great water storage capacity; the plant remains can still be identified.

periphyton an assemblage of small plant organisms (mostly algae) attached to surfaces under water or floating; may form a spongy mat insulating the ground from total dehydration during the dry season; vital to the Everglades freshwater marshes.

pineland an area elevated on a ridge, dry most of the year and periodically swept by fires, allowing the establishment of pine trees; also called pine flatwoods.

pneumatophore pencil-like appendage rising from the root of a black mangrove tree; functions as respiratory organ at low tide.

prop root stilt-like root that supports the trunk of a red mangrove tree.

propagule a seed that begins to germinate while still on the tree.

prescribed burn an intentionally set fire on an undeveloped area, planned and controlled by fire ecologists to maintain a healthy habitat.

slough (pronounced "slew") a channel of slow-moving water, slightly deeper than the surrounding freshwater marsh.

solution hole a depression in limestone rock formed by the dissolving action of acidic water, which is created by rainwater mixing with decomposing vegetation.

strand a forest in a slough.

willow head a small cluster of willow trees in a slough; usually has a gator hole associated with it, and the water under the willows is often deeper than the surrounding slough to support the water-loving willows year-round.

xeriscape a landscape or garden with plants that require little water to thrive; especially useful in desert regions and in south Florida where water must be conserved.

ACKNOWLEDGMENTS

Numerous people contributed their knowledge and expertise for the benefit of this book. I would like to thank the following people for their help: Paul Allen, John Andrew, Oron (Sonny) Bass, John Curnett, Robert Ducham, Charles DuToit, Michael Duever, Michael Eng, Ted Fleming, Richard Haley, Roger Hammer, Wallace Hibbard, Archie Jones, Jay Robinson, Jr., James Sanders, Camille Sewell, Alexander (Sandy) Sprunt, Janet Tachi, Stephen Tiger, and Pat Wells.

I am especially indebted to John Ogden of Everglades National Park for numerous helpful suggestions on the text and continuous encouragement. Also, I thank Bill Robertson and Bill and Sue Smith for tackling the mountainous task of creating a south Florida bird list.

As always, I'm grateful to my family, whose moral support never waivers, no matter how wild my schemes may be. I also wish to acknowledge Pineapple Press for their patience and concern for me while I dug myself out of Hurricane Andrew's wake.

INDEX

Page numbers in bold refer to illustrations. CP refers to the color plates between pages 96 and 97. Checklists and glossary are not indexed.